Culture and Revolution

BORDER HISPANISMS

Jon Beasley-Murray, Alberto Moreiras, and Gareth Williams, series editors

Culture and Revolution

VIOLENCE, MEMORY, AND THE MAKING OF MODERN MEXICO

Horacio Legrás

University of Texas Press *Austin*

Printed in the United States of America
First edition, 2017

♾ The paper used in this book meets the minimum requirements of ANSI/NISO Z39.48-1992 (R1997) (Permanence of Paper).

LIBRARY OF CONGRESS CATALOGING-IN-PUBLICATION DATA
Names: Legrás, Horacio, author.
Title: Culture and revolution : violence, memory, and the making of modern Mexico / Horacio Legrás.
Other titles: Border Hispanisms.
Description: First edition. | Austin : University of Texas Press, 2017. | Series: Border Hispanisms | Includes bibliographical references and index.
Identifiers: LCCN 2016018051
ISBN 978-1-4773-1074-8 (cloth : alk. paper)
ISBN 978-1-4773-1075-5 (pbk. : alk. paper)
ISBN 978-1-4773-1172-1 (library e-book)
ISBN 978-1-4773-1173-8 (nonlibrary e-book)
Subjects: LCSH: Mexico—History—Revolution, 1910–1920—Influence. | Mexico—History—1910–1946. | Mexico—Social conditions. | Mexico—Politics and government—1910–1946. | Collective memory—Mexico—History—20th century. | Mexico—Civilization.
Classification: LCC F1234 .L49 2017 | DDC 972.08/2—dc23
LC record available at https://lccn.loc.gov/2016018051

doi:10.7560/310748

Contents

Acknowledgments

It took a long time to bring this book to completion. Alberto Moreiras first directed my attention to the Mexican Revolution, and more particularly to that admirable repository of revolutionary imagination that is Martín Luis Guzmán's *The Eagle and the Serpent,* when I was a graduate student at Duke University. It is not only for this that he goes first in my list of acknowledgments. Sharing one's work with other people is a healthy habit that I, unfortunately, lack. Over the almost ten years that I used to compose this book, only my wife, Adriana Johnson, was forcefully "invited" to read every single page of its many iterations. I did not teach the contents of the book but still learned a good deal from my graduate students both at Georgetown University and at the University of California-Irvine. My efforts to grapple with the subject of the Mexican Revolution benefited enormously from a series of invitations to specialized conferences or to academic talks. I thank the following colleagues for the opportunity they gave me to present my work on Mexico at their institutions: John Kraniauskas at Birkbeck College-London, Lucas Izquierdo at University of Richmond, Irina Feldman and Roberto Pareja at Middlebury College, Jacobo Sefami at UCI, Hector Hoyos and Ximena Briceño at Stanford University, Victoria Garret at West Virginia University, Ignacio Sánchez Prado and Mabel Moraña at Washington University in St. Louis, Karen Benezra at Columbia University, Maarten van Delden at UCLA, Oswaldo Zavala at CUNY, and Ryan Long at the University of Maryland. Sara Castro-Klaren invited me to write on Mexican muralism for Blackwell's *A Companion to Latin American Literature and Culture.* Adela Pineda Franco and Viviane Mahieux—who was simply a name at the time but is now a dear colleague at UCI—included part of my reading of Vasconcelos in an issue they edited for the *Revista de Crítica Literaria Latinoamericana.* These sections are, although transformed, the only two portions of the book that have been previously published.

Over the years I have been lucky enough to forge long-standing friendships, even if I am bad at e-mails and even worse on the phone. Some long-running conversations with these friends inform the content of these pages: Gareth Williams, Juan Poblete, Idelber Avelar, Claudia Soria, Alejandro Manara, Jon Beasley Murray, Kate Jenckes, Cristina Moreiras, Teresa Vilarós, Freya Schiwy, Marta Hernández Salván, Sergio Villalobos, Alessandro Fornazzari, Jorge Marturano, Andrea Henderson, Patrick Dove, Brett Levinson, Fernando Rosenberg, Gabriela Copertari, Eduardo González, Michael Szaley, Luis Avilés, John Smith, Santiago Morales Rivera, Nahum Chandler, Erin Graff, Jane Newman, and Ivette Hernández Torres. I am sure that this list is incomplete. I apologize to those overlooked by the ingratitude of my memory.

At different stages of this project I received institutional support from Duke University, Georgetown University, University of California–Irvine, the Universidad Nacional Autónoma de México, the Fototeca Nacional in Pachuca, Mexico, the Museo de Historia de la Revolución, the Getty Institute in Los Angeles, and the Colegio de México. A special thanks to my editor at the University of Texas Press, Kerry Webb, who rescued the project when it was necessary. The University of California–Irvine is a marvelous place to work and has sustained this project in a myriad of intangible but effective ways.

This book is dedicated to my wife, Adriana Johnson, and to my children, Anaís, Diego, and Patricio.

Culture and Revolution

CHAPTER ONE

1921

The being we are is first of all inheritance.

JACQUES DERRIDA, *SPECTERS OF MARX*

Vasconcelos . . . called Mexico's artists, poets, writers, all the talented people, from wherever they might be, and said: "Here. Do it." "Do what?" "Do whatever you think should be done."

ANITA BRENNER, *IDOLS BEHIND ALTARS*

THIS IS A BOOK ABOUT THE CULTURE OF THE MEXIcan Revolution. More precisely, it is about the first two decades of postrevolutionary rule, when the revolutionary events were still fresh in the memories of its participants and the universe of enigmas brought into existence by the revolution had not yet settled into a definitive, reproducible form. Historically speaking, the 1920s and 1930s were quite distinct from one another. The 1920s were still politically unstable, and the state found itself competing with artistic and cultural discourses in the establishment of a social canon able to guide the entry of Mexico into modernity. By the early 1930s, however, the institutionalization of the revolution had acquired a new pace. State power consolidated rapidly and its policies extended throughout Mexican territory through the educational apparatus.

HOW CULTURE INVENTED A NATION FOR THE MEXICAN REVOLUTION

Historians and cultural analysts agree that the revolution created modern Mexico and that very little in the way of a nation existed before Francisco Madero's call to arms. This act of creation is itself intriguing. What mechanisms could connect two realms as different as culture and revolution? These orders cannot be bridged by causality alone. Yet the revolution pressed against the immediate aftermath and demanded the realization of some of its most recalcitrant features. It would be more proper to say that revolutions are inherited. As Derrida notes, we are, to begin with, inheritance. But Anita Brenner observes that a disconcerting dimension of freedom marks this inheritance. Thus, asking how Mexico inherited its revolution is tantamount to asking, How was modern Mexico imagined into existence?

We possess a formidable amount of information to answer this question. Few periods in the history of Latin America have received as much attention as revolutionary Mexico. The number of sources and specialized studies on the revolutionary period exceeds the ability of any researcher to master. Furthermore, as the idea that formerly irrelevant areas of existence are in fact relevant increasingly dominates academic approaches to the revolution, an exorbitant expansion of the archive ensues. Who can assert that one realm of this map of textual allusions and confusions is more important for the sedimentation of a postrevolutionary ideology than any other? Nobody can doubt the importance of political histories of the revolution, but what about agrarian histories, regional histories, labor histories? Among the so-called elite discourses, should we grant preeminence to literature or ethnography, to painting or poetry, to the avant-garde of the 1920s or to the folklorists of the same period, to education policies or to social changes more loosely rooted in "civil society," to studies of everydayness or to studies of the intellectual conformation of national elites, to cinema or photography, to popular heroes and their afterlives in popular culture or to the enshrinement of political figures into a national pantheon? The previously overlooked or subsumed popular voices of the revolution are also finding their way into the archive of revolutionary memory. The study of grassroots participation in the revolt has grown in recent years; volume 5 of *Historia de la vida cotidiana en México* (coordinated by Aurelio de los Reyes) delves into the fragmentary, chaotic, and multilayered experience of the revolution. A magnificent series edited by Guillermo Bonfil Batalla, *Mi pueblo durante la Revolución,* brings together popular memories of the revolt in three volumes. Likewise, a number of films have recently been restored and edited, and new versions of old classics have been made available. If we take into account the vast panoply of international observers and bystanders, what names can we consider within the orbit of revolutionary phenomena? There are very good reasons to argue that Sergei Eisenstein and the enigmatic B. Traven, John Reed and Antonin Artaud, Tina Modotti and André Breton, Anita Brenner and Leon Trotsky, Paul Strand and Frank Tannenbaum, Michael Lowry and Luis Buñuel have all left imprints on the history of the revolution and perhaps altered, if only imperceptibly, its path.

This intense academic interest in the revolutionary period gave rise to a peculiar predicament that art historian Leonard Folgarait summarizes as follows: "The causes, origins, and early development of the Mexican Revolution of 1910 are less clearly known today than ever before, an ironic result of the tremendous proliferation of highly sophisticated scholarship on this subject of the last twenty or so years."[1] The archive is so vast that it precludes comprehension. How can we reach the uniqueness of the revolutionary past if everything we discover about it adds another layer of meaning that removes us from its center?

However, the proliferation of names and references that characterize our experience of the revolutionary archive evokes and convokes the plasticity of the historical time under scrutiny. In the revolution, works, people and ideas are not contained by firm and established identities. Rather they enter into unexpected conjunctions and borrowings. Emiliano Zapata never posed for Diego Rivera's murals. The picture of Zapata published by Agustín Casasola in *Historia gráfica de la Revolución mexicana* and taken, according to a now-disputed version of events, by Hugo Brehme, served as a model for Rivera's painting. There is no documented collaboration between Brehme and Rivera, but in those cases in which collaboration is documented, the path taken by cultural production is no less tortuous. One of Rivera's self-portraits at the Secretaría de Educación Pública (SEP) murals is, as a matter of fact, the reproduction of a photo that Edward Weston took of Rivera in 1924. The examples are easily multiplied, and they extend across poetry, film production, labor organization, and political apparatuses.

A mood, a way of behaving and understanding the world—which I call textuality—authorized these borrowings. Evoking a well-known distinction drafted by Roland Barthes, we can say that Porfirismo lived in the realm of the work, and the dictator himself acted as transcendental signifier to be respected and imitated. The revolution, on the other hand, introduced a regime of social and ideological signification in which the most disparaged elements could share a stage.[2] Understanding society as a text gives the element of contiguity precedence over previous forms of relationship based on hierarchies, policed distributions of bodies, and old forms of social and cultural subordination. The photos that show us a lawyer, an army general, and a peasant with a bandaged head sharing the same table suggests this contiguity. Under the sway of textuality, social groupings that were unthinkable in a previous period become the norm in the new one. The surge of textuality as a modeling force upon culture has far-reaching consequences. Whole areas of Mexican life that were invisible or idealized before the revolution—including indigenous people, laboring women, homosexuals, children, peasants—acquired rights of visibility. Of course, inequality, bigotry, homophobia, and patriarchy persisted in postrevolutionary Mexico, as they do everywhere and at all times. But the revolution shocked the legitimacy of the discourses propagating social alienation.

Mexican culture inherited this textuality and exhibited it with baroque passion any time the heritage of the revolution was at stake. John Mraz evokes this dazzling and frantic spectacle of a past that never allows us to establish our distance from it:

> Historical photographs are everywhere in Mexico. Huge banners with the faces of Francisco I. Madero, Pancho Villa, and Emiliano Zapata hover over political rallies. Restaurant walls are flavored by sepia-toned reproductions of soldiers embracing their sweethearts in train stations. Bureaucrats in government offices labor under the gaze of legendary heroes. Hotel and bank lobbies are decorated with pictures of cavalrymen under wide-brimmed sombreros who ride their steeds through cornfields, while the unfailing *soldaderas* walk alongside. Markets of folk art have the inevitable stall dedicated to vendors of washed-out, overexposed copies, often from the Casasola Bazar, as well as other forms of visual history: postcards, calendars, posters, T-shirts, jackets, coffee mugs, ashtrays, and other bric-a-brac. Illustrated magazines and newspapers reproduce classic images constantly, as do the multitude of illustrated *historias gráficas* celebrating Mexico's revolutionary past.[3]

The appearance of Rivera's murals on the covers of so many books about the history of the revolution betrays the centrality of the textuality of revolutionary Mexico. The murals at the SEP can be read horizontally and vertically, from panel to panel, from the top of the stairs, or from the patio; and sometimes the composition sends the viewer outside the painting, to look into the depth of his or her own existential position for a meaning the mural does not grant. Jean Charlot identifies this textuality as the most distinctive mark of Mexican popular culture even before the revolution:

> Art was everywhere: devotees bribed saints with ex-votos, lovers melted the hearts of their beloveds with portraits, artisans and merchants hired the painter to beautify their shops with murals and thus increase business. Sculpture existed for specialized aims—dark pieces, idols of secret worship, semblances used for black magic; innocent pieces, those marvelous toys worth a few cents, beautiful as

> Han Thom figures. The output was so varied as to be unclassifiable, so cheap as to be despised, so close to all, so thrust under everyone's eyes as to become invisible.[4]

The wealth of information contained in the revolutionary archive carries with it its own risks. This archive seems now a sublime object beyond control or description. The archival sublime has bred an entire scholarship—be it literary, historical, or sociological in nature—that treasures the endless accumulation of anecdotes and small details. Cultural critics and historians approach this sublime object with the spirit of the collector. How do we introduce analysis into such a tightly compacted body of texts and references? Moreover, how do we do it while respecting the textuality of the revolution, which is, after all, the real historical event? This book thus attempts a difficult balancing act. It endeavors to honor the textuality of the revolution while at once seeking to propose an analytic of this textuality. Briefly stated, I argue that the complexity of the revolutionary text can be schematized around five notions: extension, depth, life, fantasy, and synchronicity. Following this chapter, I devote one chapter to each of these notions, which represent general forms for organizing experience and making sense of the present. And each of them inherits, as I hope to show, some unique feature of that still mostly unexplored territory that is the revolution itself.

Extension refers to the fact that the revolution uncovered Mexico as a totality that all Mexicans could claim. The Mexican Revolution took the regional as its starting point, then spilled over onto a territory that was only half-imagined. The process of imagining that totality occupied intellectuals and cultural producers throughout the 1920s. While the revolution uncovered the total extension of Mexico, the act of imagining the nation was mostly a Mexico City affair. In a way, we assist here in the fatal sublation of a material revolution into the ideality of the political. Every feature that during the revolution represented a variety of people and regions began to coalesce into a single representation. However, the diversity that lies at its origin persisted. Chapter 2, "Extension," documents this unfinished dialectic.

The second modality, *depth*, probes a question that has plagued Mexicans since the early eighteenth century: How natural or obvious is Mexicans' belonging to the land? As in every Latin American country, justifying the post- or even neocolonial nature of the rapport between inhabitants and territory is an uneasy task. People do not belong naturally to any particular region. People are rather naturalized, and this process of naturalization coincides with the creation of a people. The state is the instrument that declares that there is a land and there are a people, but it can never do so without the assistance of myriad social and cultural discourses. The revolution promoted two predominant ethnic identifications as the means of this naturalization, one centered on the creole population, the other on the rediscovered Indian. Hence, chapter 3, "Depth," sets in dialogue two traditions that are seldom considered together: the painstaking construction of an *indigenista* discourse in Mexico and the establishment of Hispanism under the tutelage of Alfonso Reyes. This dual organization perpetuates the colonial division between Indians and creoles. A middle way or a middle passage between both positions was necessary. In a coda to the chapter, I argue that such mediation was performed by architecture, and more specifically, by the "resolution" of the polemic that pitted colonialists and functionalists against each other in the first years of postrevolutionary rule.

Chapter 4, "Life," was originally titled "Freedom." Although conceptually correct, the old title had two disadvantages. It might have invited an identification of freedom with washed-out liberal categories rather than associating it with the notion of becoming a subject that is at the center of the chapter. Additionally, the actors of the time themselves grasped the open-ended nature of historical subjectivity in terms of life, not freedom. If in normal times bourgeois ideology requires a careful planning of life, the revolution opened an aperture to desires that endangered the seamless reproduction of the social. The chapter explores individual experience following the revolution's destruction of many certainties and the consequent opening up of a space of ideological and subjective possibilities. One way to map these differences is through the conceptual opposition between subject and individual. A person cannot choose to be a subject rather than an individual. We are always subjects in the sense that our narratives of personal containment (or individuality) are convenient fictions allowing us to blend in a universe of imposed social norms. When José Vasconcelos thought of himself as an individual, he conceived of himself as a free agent (and as a lawyer!) firmly in charge of his fate. But his memoirs show that his life only makes sense in terms of subjectivity, in terms of a life marked by tensions and contradictions. In a revolution, I argue in chapter 4, the necessary social dimension of our being is more difficult to ignore, its constant exposition to the vicissitudes of the textual organization of reality more difficult to repress.

Fantasy, the subject of chapter 5, is to some extent a master notion in the book. I use the word in a psychoanalytic intonation. Sigmund Freud, who incorporated the term into psychoanalytic theory, conceived of fantasies as an adaptive mechanism. Human beings cannot live in an average world of facts. Reality is too brutal to bear. This unbearable brutality of meaningless facts shines through the account that Salvador Novo provides of the immediate revolutionary past in *La estatua de sal*: "I don't even know if now, at a distance of several years, it would be possible for me to sketch the true image, the true impression of that nightmare which, despite the revolutionary protestations of my generation, was the senseless brutality of the revolution."[5] Novo, who writes at the high tide of avant-garde experiments with nonmeaning, demands the meaningful redemption of existence. It is from this desolation that a fantasy takes its cue. This is why Slavoj Žižek insists that subjects do not preexist their fantasies, but rather come into being through, and with the aid of, fantasies. In this sense, the Slovenian author continues, the function of the fantasy is similar to that of Kantian "transcendental schematism."[6] Fantasies mediate between a human world and a reality that would be utterly unrecognizable. Unlike the Freudian traumatic event from childhood that the fantasy "remembers" and reorganizes, the Lacanian fantasy that Žižek seeks to illustrate is conceived in relationship to the trauma per se—that is, to the Real as that aspect of life that escapes symbolization or persists in its intractability. The instantiation of a human world requires the production of fantasies, and in this sense their function is positive. But a fantasy is to a large extent a lie. Thus fantasies need to be traversed. The traversing of a fantasy, however, cannot develop a more "correct" relationship to the Real. The Real cannot be "translated" without loss, just as a revolution cannot be inscribed without betrayal. The traversing is directed to unveiling the structuring function of lack as the ultimate truth of historical subjectivity.[7] As the reader will have the chance to confirm, the chapter "Fantasy" can be read independently of this theoretical rumination. The chapter retells how different groups elaborated different fantasies of the revolutionary subject. My main interest, however, lies with the creation of an overarching social fantasy—a task achieved, I argue, in the work of Diego Rivera.

In the last chapter I discuss the notion of *synchronicity* in the contexts of photography and film. The emergence into visibility of different groups of people whose lifestyles seem separated by centuries marked the Mexican Revolution. Synchronicity names above all the technical desire to present a diversity of figures and motives under a unified representation. After photography, film inherited the task of producing a unified portrait of what was, plainly enough, many Mexicos.

Although I discuss each of the five notions through different cultural practices, each of these modalities reappears in almost all the representative examples of the others. The question of synchronicity takes its inspiration from the problems created by the uncovering of extension as the actual form of existence of the nation. While I use Rivera's murals to discuss fantasy, they also reflect concern with depth, and while I use the 1921 celebrations to illustrate the creation of a sense of Mexican popular culture, the strategies mobilized by those celebrations rest on the assumption of life as an instance of self-design or on the uncovering of depth as the truth of the Mexican people.

The fantasy of a contained subjectivity dominates early Mexican film, where the cohesiveness of (post)revolutionary life is the recurring question that stresses postrevolutionary cinema to the limits of verisimilitude.

Extension, depth, life, fantasy, and synchronicity are not intended as transcendental determinations of the revolutionary experience. Their main role is to trace paths that may allow us to crisscross a revolutionary landscape that has become crowded and chaotic. Other headings can surely be imagined. The ones I propose allow us to speak of the revolution with the same textual, overdetermined, and interconnected style that characterized the revolutionary moment and its utopian aftermath.

CONTINGENCY AND DESIGN

That a reality is textually organized does not just mean that anything can appear alongside anything else. It also implies that, in this horizon, all identity is articulatory in nature. Of course, any identity is always an articulation of disparaged motives. But this knowledge is often repressed (or naturalized) in times of social calm. To illustrate how serendipitous these articulations could be, I offer a story.

In 1921 interim Mexican president Adolfo de la Huerta recruited José Vasconcelos for the reorganization of the national university. When a few months later the elected president Álvaro Obregón took office, Vasconcelos convinced him of the need to relaunch the ministry of education and took the post of secretary of public education himself. Vasconcelos also interested Obregón in a project called the "Renaissance of Mexican Culture," for which he had recalled Diego Rivera from Europe. He assigned Rivera, a Cubist painter trained in the classical style and an admirer of the Renaissance fresco, to paint public murals on several prominent state buildings. When Rivera arrived in Mexico in 1921, he was mostly ignorant of deep Mexico. Yet he began a process of reeducation, believing that a national art had to represent national subjects. To Vasconcelos's utter dismay, he populated his murals with revolutionary heroes who were little more than "criminals" in the eyes of the SEP. While Vasconcelos was no elitist, and he respected the ways of popular culture, he would have preferred the popular classes to be the objects of a state pedagogy rather than to serve as models for the reeducation of Mexico's elite. But Rivera had become, in the years since his return to Mexico at Vasconcelos's behest, one of the most learned intellectuals on pre-Columbian lore. His painting *The Courtyard of Labor* at the SEP in 1928 and the murals at the Cortés Palace at Cuernavaca in 1930 reflected his special sensibility towards the complexity of the revolutionary process. Long before the postrevolutionary state fully rehabilitated Zapata, Rivera had elevated Zapata to the status of national hero. Along with Zapata, the anonymous peasant and his family, the industrious Indian, and the industrial worker entered the official representation of the Mexican culture/state apparatus. Rivera's mural *The History of Mexico* in the stairwell of the National Palace included Marx and Lenin as guiding figures for the people. A few years earlier, he had illustrated the first wave of revised textbooks, like *Fermín*, for the rural schools of postrevolutionary Mexico. These textbooks reflect a collaboration between an elite group of writers, painters, and anthropologists and myriad local intellectuals and fervently mobilized schoolteachers.[8] Neither Obregón nor Vasconcelos could have foreseen (and likely did not desire) a socially committed emphasis in the educational campaign and social policies they launched. The story encapsulates the complex relationship that art and culture wove with the process of state formation in postrevolutionary Mexico. If properly interrogated, it also yields the vertigo of its theoretical implications.

The most important of these implications concerns the relationship between cultural creators and the rebuilding of state authority. Artists and intellectuals did not so much "reflect" or "rationalize" an order of the world, but sought to shape it. All through the 1920s, Mexicans treated the reconstruction of Mexico as their joint responsibility, not just the task of the government. In a country that was, in the words of Alan Knight, "less a nation than a geographical expression,"[9] culture was one of the few sites in which the common of the community could be enacted. Hence the tremendous importance of cultural mediation in the period. A bemused Edward Weston recounts that taking a stroll through Mexico City in the company of Dr. Atl meant stopping repeatedly to greet people from all classes and conditions eager to win the eclectic painter's notice.[10] Writers, poets, and painters were celebrities of sorts in the 1920s in Mexico, and newspapers like *El Universal* treated them as authoritative voices, polling them on a variety of subjects and polling the readers of the newspaper about the merits of these artists. The fragile postrevolutionary state itself was deeply invested in foregrounding cultural production. Manuel Gamio, one of the intellectuals most consistently aligned with the project of state formation, had as early as 1916 already spelled out the strategic value of culture for a project of nation formation. In *Forjando patria* he wrote, "Sociologists unconcerned with hearts came to the conclusion that art alone could be trusted to perform certain urgent social tasks, even before the artists themselves had realized it clearly."[11] If Gamio insisted on promoting the role of emotions as the centerpiece of national reconstruction, he was less sure about what artistic form could fulfill that role, an uncertainty everyone else shared. Despite the pronouncements of historical memory, no particular art form or group of artists was mainly responsible for the operation of rationalizing a national space through aesthetic creation. Indeed, a veritable explosion of different cultural languages marked postrevolutionary Mexico.

Only recently have historians begun to address cultural production as a central question in postrevolutionary Mexico. Delving into the buoyant atmosphere of the 1920s, Thomas Benjamin identifies the genius of Mexican artists and intellectuals: to seize the present even before political leaders themselves could adjust to the new situation. When the gun smoke cleared, the state did not need to make any heavy investment in promoting a historical justification of the revolt, because the "*voceros de la Revolución* were already on the job."[12] A curious effect of this intervention was that "the plethora of writings by the revolution's scribblers" became more significant than the pronouncements of the state.[13] Scribblers, artists, and intellectuals created a nonexistent entity Benjamin finds suspicious: "Their talking, singing, drawing, painting, and writing invented la Revolución: a name transformed into what appeared to be a natural and self-evident part of reality and history."[14] Although it is clear what Benjamin means, the assertion seems to beg the question of an objective or nonideological labeling of social processes. He seems to suggest that the revolution created by the scribblers is a sort of fantasy superimposed on a reality. Yet qua ideality, "la Revolución," is no more ideal than the "nation" or, for that matter, "reality" or "history." In addition, people involved in the revolt talked about revolution well before the emergence of the revolutionary scribblers, and their idea of revolution guided (or misled) them well before the scribblers assigned to this notion its definitive and idealized meaning.[15] In fact, the notion Benjamin found suspicious is precisely what makes it relevant to this discussion.

Other Latin American countries have witnessed the supplementary function of intellectuals in the construction of a new state order, but without Mexico's intensity.[16] A comparison of the Mexican case with James Scott's classical account of state and intellectual collaboration in *Seeing Like a State* shows what distinguishes the Mexican case from all the rest. Scott argues that the emergence of modern forms of governmentality is tied to a conceptual simplification of the spaces the state aspires to administer. The state organizes the world along hierarchical and smooth lines that facilitate its own intervention, an intervention always based on regularities, averages, and spatial and dimensional simplifications. The tools of this simplification—maps, cadastral registers, last names, passports—not only probe a reality, they build a reality suitable for the intervention of different agencies. According to Scott, four elements make this gaze possible: a powerful or authoritarian state, the technical ability to actually implement state plans of manipulation, a social-intellectual base imbued with an ideology of modernization who act as purveyors of the project (Scott refers to them as "high-modernists"), and, finally, a weakened or even prostrate society. As Scott summarizes the situation, "The legibility of a society provides the capacity for large-scale social engineering, high-modernist ideology provides the desire, the authoritarian state provides the determination to act on that desire, and the incapacitated civil society provides the leveled social terrain on which to build."[17] He continues to say that these conditions often obtain after wars, massive economic crises, or revolutions. The term "high-modernist" describes intellectuals and artists like Manuel Gamio, José Vasconcelos, Moisés Sáenz, Frida Kahlo, Diego Rivera, Gerardo Murillo, Manuel Gómez Morín, and Tina Modotti. The differences begin to emerge around the two other conditions named by Scott: an authoritarian state and a prostrated society. In postrevolutionary Mexico the state was weak and the populace highly mobilized, which explains why, despite its authoritarian inclinations, the state was unable to establish an uncontested social and political agenda. Even when the postrevolutionary state aspired to reduce a diverse geography to a manageable territory, it encountered instrumental limits to this desire. All through the 1920s and 1930s the state was forced use anthropology, art, and narrative to facilitate its own insertion in Mexico's still tumultuous countryside. The use of these disciplines and discourses did not have—could not have—the same effects as did the direct utilization of well-proven tools for streamlining reality (census, mapping, a strong centralized bureaucracy) in other locations. Even using these instruments had less effect than the state expected. To an important extent, the postrevolutionary state did not see like a state because it did not see with its own eyes. Instead, it borrowed the eyes of painters like Francisco Goitia in the excavation of Teotihuacán or the eyes of a Rivera in the dissemination of its own credo through popular and rural education. This need to enroll practices and discourses that could not be completely subjected to state control was an ongoing characteristic of state formation in Mexico throughout the twentieth century.[18]

CULTURE AND DISCONTINUOUS HISTORY

The tortuous path of state-culture relationships in Mexico explains in part the equally tortuous path of its historical interpretation. In his tirade against the fantasy-making activity of the intellectuals, Thomas Benjamin fails to acknowledge that some of the most important scribblers involved in the creation of the revolutionary myth were indeed historians. Authors like Ernest Gruening (*Mexico and Its Heritage*) or Frank Tannenbaum (*The Mex-*

ican Agrarian Revolution) lie at the origin of a view of the revolution that posterior historiography would describe as distorted and romantic. Revisionists accused these early historians of disavowing the creation of an all-powerful, exploitative capitalist state under revolutionary tutelage. For the revisionists, instead of introducing radical change in Mexican history, the revolution swapped one ruling class for another while retaining the basic features that have characterized capitalist domination in the region. Eventually revisionists themselves were subject to evaluation and criticism, especially around the question of their overvaluation of the state and their undervaluation of popular agency.[19] By the 1980s a wave of social historians sought to reposition the role of popular agency, contending that the powerful state of the revisionists was not even a reality on paper.[20] Alan Knight is conclusive: the Mexican Revolution is "one of these rare occasions in which the action of the masses influenced the course of history."[21]

Given that the Mexican Revolution presents us with the uncontestable importance of the masses and the equally pervasive importance of cultural mediation, up to what point can we say that culture, as the commons of community, functions as one of the vehicles of popular influence over the process of state formation? Mary Kay Vaughan has proposed that the educational campaigns initiated by the SEP constituted a bidirectional system of influences by which the state reached remote locations while letting contact between schoolteachers and distinct geographical, cultural, and political realities influence its policies.[22] Can one make a similar argument in the case of a Rivera, whose artistic practice deeply transformed the knowledge of Mexico's indigenous lore?

But the question itself is misguided. Culture can have political meaning and effects, but it cannot itself be a form of action without ceasing at that very moment to be culture. The paradox of committed art is that its conditions of possibility, rooted in disinterest, are absolutely heterogeneous with its political intentionality. The logical operator that presides over culture is "all," while the one that presides over politics is "some." Of course, the creation of a feeling of all (be it all Mexicans, or all indigenous people) was tremendously important for the emerging postrevolutionary state. However, I believe that the negative rather than positive aspects of cultural mediation granted cultural forms their prestige in the postrevolutionary period. Culture explains the temporally asymptotic nature of revolutionary agency vis-à-vis the forms of political codification of power better than any other discourse, because it itself was a figure of the asymptotic. It reveals the popular pressure upon the formal apparatus of representation because of its inability to properly represent its other, and hence, its reliance on mechanisms of delay and defraction that both reflected and deeply altered the distance between points of origination and points of articulation.[23] The basic discontinuity that presides over the mechanisms of artistic creation made art more attuned to a form of popular demand that was itself necessarily marked by discontinuity in its manifestations. Let us consider, for example, a photograph.

The photograph in question was taken on 6 December 1914, on the occasion of the occupation of Mexico's National Palace by the combined forces of Pancho Villa's Division of the North and Zapata's Liberation Army of the South. Legend tells us that Villa and Zapata had been touring the National Palace for some time when they came across the presidential chair. Villa insisted that Zapata should sit in it, but he refused. In the rapture of the moment, Villa sat himself in the chair and invited Zapata to pose with him. A doubtful version of the story has none other than Agustín Casasola taking the snapshot.[24] Villa's expression is mischievous and yet uneasy; certainly he believed that his pose struck a chord at the very intersection between the comical and the tragic. Zapata—who had a penchant for being photographed—appears uncomfortable, as if he can barely contain his anxiety.[25] How could it be otherwise? The photo is a consummate fantasy. There is no need to read it in any particular way or attempt to interpret it. It says what it shows. But what it shows is the impossible. Both Villa and Zapata had already stated the incommensurability between their own personae and the logic of state power in their meeting at Xochimilco in 1912.

> Villa: I do not need public positions because I do not know how to deal with them. . . .
>
> Zapata: That is why I warn all the friends that they should be careful, or otherwise, the machete will fall on them. . . . We have limited ourselves to prodding them, taking care of them, taking care, taking care, on one side, on the other, to keep then in the pasture.[26]

At the height of their military power, at the very moment of revolutionary triumph, both Villa and Zapata realized that the state machinery was too complex to be run by anybody but experts. Besides, neither desired to control the state. They recognized the difference between fighting a revolution and running a state, and while the fight continued it did not take the form of a bid for national power in Zapata's case; and in the case of Villa increasingly resembled a personal quarrel with Venustiano Carranza.

But if the photo and the story of the joyful occupation of the National Palace hold a key to understanding the conformation of postrevolutionary culture, this is not because both leaders renounced public or political positions. The unrealized scene of power illustrates not only the defeat of the peasant armies but also the origin of the postrevolutionary state, or more precisely of this state's dire need for cultural mediation. After all, contrary to the legend, Villa and Zapata were not touring the palace. They did not stumble upon the presidential chair. They staged the photo and then called the photographers—who would not have dared to photograph either man without his permission—to immortalize the charade. This means that Villa, Zapata, and their troops were not the objects of this photo but its subject. They controlled the irony and hid what they wanted to, enabling any taking of a political position to pass through their nonpresentation.[27]

Villa and Zapata were the incarnation of a roaming passion the revolution had triggered. From that experience, culture inherited the task of finding a subjective space for the revolutionary popular contingents, a space that would not be—as in the photo in the presidential chair—an impossible mimicry of dominant class values and standards. After all, as Gareth Williams cunningly notes, the presidential chair itself is the third main character, a reminder of the unbroken chain of sovereign demands.[28] Virtually any intellectual worthy of that distinction knew of the nature and proportions of this historical challenge. The reconstitution of the prestige and functionality of the sociopolitical bond proved to be the colossal task waiting for the cultural engineers of postrevolutionary Mexico. Artists and intellectuals would channel incredible levels of energy and subtlety into this goal. Throughout the twentieth century cultural managers persevered in this task. The Museo Nacional de Historia in Mexico City exemplifies these qualities by displaying the presidential chair in which Zapata refused to sit within the section of the museum devoted to the agrarian leader from Morelos.

UNDER THE CLOAK OF THE OBVIOUS

All the different cultural and artistic expressions that I survey in this book worked under a common assumption: that they were representative of a national sensibility and marked a foray into the creation of a truly integrative national culture. However, nationalism is not primordial. Nationalism became a successful common language because the dominant imaginary of the social was already textual in nature. Identified with the state, nationalism sought to overcome textuality and to replace it with its own identitarian operations. But soon it became evident that nationalism could not dismiss textuality without throwing itself into irrelevance. As a result, a symptomatic and hybrid term came into existence: "revolutionary nationalism."

By consigning all cultural production to the realm of nationalism, the culture of the postrevolutionary period became the site of a deceptive transparency. Throughout the twentieth century a subtle manipulation made the cult of the revolution indistinguishable from the cult of the patria, thereby authorizing all kinds of useful paradigmatic substitutions.[29] However, official nationalism never went uncontested in the history of postrevolutionary Mexico, although most opposing discourses employed some other form of nationalism.[30] The meaning and function of revolutionary nationalism present an extremely complex problem that scholars have not adequately resolved, in spite of extensive analysis.[31] Nationalism is a presupposition of my analysis; the summary treatment of the concept below provides preliminary indications of its significance.

Alan Knight has underscored how national feelings are a consequence of rather than antecedents to the revolutionary fight.[32] This does not mean that the prerevolutionary landscape had no vestige of nationalism. In fact the ideological cocktail of the politicized middle classes at the turn of the twentieth century depended on nationalism. But Porfirian Mexico lacked the proper bureaucratic-disciplinary apparatuses to inscribe this feeling within the thickness of the real. This in part reflects the sheer heterogeneity that characterizes Mexico's social and cultural makeup. In the 1920s nationalism appeared with the force of an irrefutable demand. Daniel Cosío Villegas describes a marvelous nationalist explosion "that covered the whole country" in the 1920s as "nationalism without a trace of xenophobia. It was not against something, but rather pro-Mexico."[33] For the always lucid Cosío Villegas, nationalism was a form of mapping. By covering the whole country, it allowed Mexico as a nation, and in this sense it was already an index of the revitalization of the question of sovereignty the revolutionary movement itself would imply. But Cosío Villegas errs when he says that "the Revolution . . . demanded nationalism."[34] Culture did not provide the revolution with a nation because the revolution wanted one, but simply because the revolution revealed itself as an almost pure wanting.[35] So the question becomes, Why was the nation the meaning that best satisfied that demand? Héctor Aguilar Camín and Lorenzo Meyer attempted to explain nationalism as a "virtue of isolation."[36] Economically in disarray, with all international credit sources closed and unrecognized in the United States or Europe, Mexico could only look to itself as a source of renovation. Yet European, U.S., and Latin American political and cultural figures gave Mexico enormous international attention. Further, whatever isolation Mexico suffered may have made nationalism necessary, but it did not make it appealing. I propose a three-part alternate explanation for the importance of nationalism as the general political language of the period.

First, nationalism was above all a heuristic device, a rule that guided practice rather than a discourse added to a practice. As a heuristic tool, nationalism was a first attempt at organizing a world shocked to its core by the revolution.

The predominance of the language of nationalism can be traced, I believe, to the nature of the revolt itself. The revolution resulted from multitudinous, multiethnic, and multiclassist contingents mobilized around many competing ideologies. As an idiom, nationalism could accommodate the most variegated meanings: agrarianism and justice, intellectual enlightenment and redress of grievances, cosmopolitanism and erotic freedom. No other language had such reach, and reach was necessary. No other language had such a level of generality, either. Nationalism spoke to the criminal turned revolutionary and to the cloistered young woman turned adventurous rural schoolteacher, to the Indian who had lost all points of communal and traditional references and to the laborer recently initiated in the rituals of the working class. In a world in which so many identities had been set loose and others irremediably lost, nationalism provided a language charged with future.

Second, by introducing an identity rooted in tradition, nationalism could assign meaning to a chaotic present. Writing in the 1950s, art historian Alicia Azuela notes that a dominant nationalist discourse treated postrevolutionary culture as the culminating point of "Mexicanness."[37] The outlines of this development were laid out in the 1920s. However, the culture emerging in the 1920s that identified itself as a recuperation of national traditions was an act of invention, even if the materials used for that invention came indeed from the past. Postrevolutionary Mexico was not just the Mexico of Gamio and Teotihuacán, Vasconcelos and the national stadium, the Zapatistas and their Guadalupan credo, the Campobello sisters and the ballet folklorico, or Rivera and the redemption of the indigenous races. It was also a nation—and especially a city—revolutionized by new technologies such as film, radio, electricity, telephones, air travel, and everything that came with them, from flappers to sportsmen.

Third, through revolutionary nationalism, which included the demonization of the Porfirista period, the state could promote an image of the revolution as a national struggle of liberation rather than a factitious, almost uncontrolled form of class struggle. The history of Zapatism suggests how this active forgetting unfolds. After being vilified and attacked militarily by the Constitutionalists with a murderous rage they had not applied even to the worst expressions of the ancien régime, Zapatismo was partially integrated into a national postrevolutionary alliance in Obregón's government. Nationalist integration was an invitation to forget that the mass executions of women and children in Zapatista villages was, above all, an expression of class hatred, a general response of illustrated revolutionary Mexico to the unbearable mobilization of the underdogs.

The structure of this nationalism, and perhaps of all nationalism, is symptomatic in the sense that it expresses simultaneously the strictures of state power and the force of popular aspirations. Hence the curious fact that in 1950 Octavio Paz complained about the dangers of nationalism in a letter to Alfonso Reyes. Nationalism, Paz observed, can only end up "in aggression with the strong or in narcissism with the miserable—like us."[38] True, the seed of a narcissistic tendency in nationalist discourse was readable early on, as attested by the infamous discussion on virile literature that emerged in 1925. Yet cultural heterogeneity would remain for the rest of the century and up to this day the major force opposing the identitarian claims of national ideologies in Mexico.[39] Mexican nationalism only achieved its dominant position because it is never truly or completely identitarian and because of its complex articulation within the realm of politics. So, although Thomas Benjamin is right to point that "what made la Revolución so affective and effective, powerful and enduring was its seamless integration into Mexico's 'religion of the patria,'" this integration of political and cultural nations worked precisely because it was not absolutely seamless. It worked insofar as it was able to tap into a vast universe of unrepresented and disenfranchised figures that gave the expression "Mexican people" its unique density.

THE REVOLUTION IS (THE) REVOLUTION

Given that our modernity was born of revolutions, we know surprisingly little about them. The predicament reemerges here and there in the specialized bibliography. James Scott believes that a methodological barrier has obscured revolution from the historical gaze, because that gaze is typically state-centric.[40] Alan Knight, on the other hand, calls for the abandonment of the word *revolution*, calling it "a catchall, useful for general conversation but fatal to detailed analysis."[41] The historian becomes uneasy with a concept that occupies the borderland between the empirical and the transcendental. So deep is this problem, that "*la revolución es la revolución*," the famous formula attributed to Luis Cabrera, stands even today as the most synthetic and apt definition of the Mexican process.[42]

The problematic nature of the historical continuity between revolution and its aftermath complicates any talk of inheritance in this case. On the one hand, revolutions by their nature create progeny; on the other hand, they also resist attempts of inscription. Revolutions, Gilles Deleuze and Félix Guattari once wrote, are unable "to survive their own victory."[43] This impossibility is not merely conceptual but, ultimately, practical. The revolution's various languages and intentions are untranslatable by right. Of the numerous promises and possibilities that comprise a revolutionary movement, only a few will come to fruition, leaving a sour taste of unfulfilled expectations in the mouths of historical commentators. In realizing only one possibility, or a limited set of them, a revolution is always and by definition a betrayed revolution.[44] In this order of things, the Mexican Revolution was not different from any other revolution. Like its French counterpart, it was, in the words of François Furet, "a pledge that no event could fully redeem."[45] In a recent work, Enrique Florescano wonders why, if the Mexican Revolution is the decisive historical fact of modern Mexico, its only renderings come from art and literature and not from history or sociology.[46] The reason is perhaps that revolutions are not positive historical facts, even if they are more "real" than these facts. Eric Hobsbawn uses a telling metaphor to underline the limited effect of subjective calculation in revolutionary events: "Revolutions are themselves, in some sense, natural phenomena."[47] Enrique Krauze, for his part, uses a similar metaphor to describe the naturalization of the revolution in Mexican history: "For the common people of Mexico, the revolution was . . . a cataclysm of cosmic proportions and terrestrial origins, an eruption beyond the limits of history."[48] In what sense is the revolution beyond history? In the same sense that the pure potentiality of the social is beyond sovereignty. All revolutions are betrayed insofar as they all expose into the world of actual choices the ontological ground of reality as a system of possibilities. The question then arises: How do we cross from the realm of mere possibilities to that of actual choices? I already suggested that the notion of fantasy may provide an answer to this question. Could not the tried and true notion of ideology do the trick? To some extent, all fantasies become ideology. The contrast between fantasy and ideology is, however, instructive. Ideologies, we often hear, are always overdetermined; yet it should always be possible to trace an ideology's form back to the conditions of its emergence. In the case of fantasy, however, severing rather than asserting the connection best explains the relationship of a cultural form to its cause.[49] Ideological analysis often laments what reality is. Leftist critics, for instance, lament that the Mexican Revolution is not a true revolution since a socialist takeover of the capitalist form of production did not occur. Such criticism runs the risk of simply condemning the existent instead of engaging in its analysis. Fantasy, however, allows us to think about what comes into representation without eliciting the passions of the censor. Seen from the perspective of fantasy, cultural and aesthetic productions still maintain an inextricable link to the event that lies at their origin, but they do not depend on the a priori political or ideological meaning of that event (a meaning that in the case of revolutions is often lacking) for the constitution of their own meaning.

A final vicissitude in our relationship to the Mexican Revolution pertains to our own relationship to this object. Enrique Florescano made for Mexico the same argument that François Furet made for the French Revolution—namely, that we are unable to stand outside its shadow. Florescano writes,

> The Mexican Revolution is not just the series of events that took place between 1910 and 1917 or between 1910 and 1920 or even between 1910 and 1940. It is also the total sum of projections, symbols, memories, images and myths that its actors, interpreters and heirs forged and keep forging around that event.[50]

The revolution solicits all these voices and accretes them with a power of submission that cannot be ignored or rejected. It builds a center that keeps all events subjected to its orbit. The distance of one body or another to the center in this equation is always the same. The same distance separates a revolutionary militant like José Vasconcelos and a self-proclaimed apolitical intellectual like Alfonso Reyes from the gravitational pulse of the revolution. This orbital model suggests that by and large no metacritical approaches to a revolution exist. If sometimes theoretical references are more insinuated than deployed in the pages of this book, it is in recognition of this necessarily immanent relationship that the revolution seems to demand.

A MEXICAN ORDER OF THINGS

Traditional views of revolution tell us that revolutionaries act in the name of certain ideas and that well-established social groups must take them up if they are to transform society. But in Mexico, where the popular and motley nature of the revolt marked its development from the beginning, no revolutionary faction was able to impress its will upon the historical process. The all-encompassing social mobilization inaugurated by the revolt, as well as the lack of unified and cohesive political elites, prevented this transformation. At a critical point in *The Mexican Revolution,* Alan Knight asks why Porfirio Díaz called for a truce as soon as the revolutionaries assaulted and took over a couple of towns and wonders why Madero, in agreeing to that truce, agreed also to the politically onerous terms of those who were supposedly surrendering to him. He argues that both men feared the level of popular mobilization the revolutionary call had achieved. This overflowing of popular participation would continue to be a trademark of the revolution, even after 1913 when the revolutionary forces would coalesce around three more or less distinctive revolutionary groups. Even throughout the 1920s and 1930s, when forces from Sonora effectively won internal revolutionary conflicts, the victors found it extremely difficult to manage the social, political, and cultural dynamism the revolution had unleashed.[51] Florescano describes the social dynamic inaugurated by the revolt as one in which "society rebels against the state, creating through the revolution a vacuum of power that will be slowly, progressively invaded by the same society."[52] So slowly invaded, we might add, that in 1920 the murals on which the hopes and desires of the masses would be inscribed were still a blank page. In this way, culture and nation, both substantial entities, stand opposed to a void. It was the function of the void to elicit an entity able to satiate its own vacuums through the expediency of cultural intervention.

The images this act of invention mobilized have inhabited Mexico for decades and even centuries. Porfirismo even used many of them to cast its own version of a national culture. What really matters, though, is the specific form of articulation of a set of recognizable national stereotypes in relation to the political and existential conditions of a people. Any historical articulation provides bountiful metaphors, but not all these metaphors become the ones we live by. Only after the revolution were many traditional images articulated in such a way that Mexicans could perceive cultural identification as grounds for the acquisition of social and political enfranchisement. The novelty of the already known was the mood of the day. This triggered the awe of a reporter from *El Universal,* in charge of covering the 1921 Exposition of Popular Arts: "I know these objects. I have seen them so many times before. Yet they elicit in me a profound emotion, as if this were the first time I look at them."[53] The witnesses of the time considered the simultaneous novelty and unoriginality of the nationalist wave an elemental datum of their everyday experience. The character of the invention of modern Mexico was for them more blatant and the efficiency of the nationalist imagery even more enigmatic. They could not completely analyze the paradoxical emergence of an already naturalized newness, because, as the reporter remarks, this included, primarily, a dimension of affect characteristic of the collusion of art and social management. The criticism of this act of invention would come much later, when the panoply of nationalist images that different artistic media promoted coalesced into a pop form of national culture. And even then, the massive production of stereotypes would leave an indelible mark on the development of Mexican culture. Stereotypes remained effective, at least in vast areas of the Mexican imaginary, because they kept open the connection with the realms of rights and citizenship while simultaneously pointing toward a potential reconciliation between the state and what Gareth Williams calls "the immanent life of society."[54]

Did all these different trends really coalesce, as the title of this chapter suggests, around the year 1921? The date is arbitrary. The stories told and analyzed in this book both predate and survive the year 1921. But 1921 was meaningful in its own way. It was the year of Rivera's return to Mexico and the year that, in Moscow, Sergei Eisenstein staged Jack London's "The Mexican." It was the year that Zapatismo found its way into a new national revolutionary coalition and the year that Manuel Gamio finished his epochal study of the valley of Teotihuacán. It was the year of the death of Ramón López Velarde and the year when Manuel Maples Arce published the inaugural manifesto of Estridentismo. It was the year Casasola's *Historia gráfica de la Revolución* saw the light and the year of the first radio transmission in Mexico City. It was the year that Vasconcelos began his frantic construction of the Mexican soul and the year when, to his despair, the serape and the mariachi were the guests of honor at the centennial celebration in Chapultepec. It was the year the cypress was chosen as Mexico's national tree and the year that for the first time an Indian could be pretty in Mexico. But above all, 1921 was the year in which, for Mexicans, the conviction began to dawn that the revolution was an act from which they could not return.

CHAPTER TWO

Extension

HÉCTOR AGUILAR CAMÍN AND LORENZO MEYER'S *In the Shadow of the Mexican Revolution* describes the revolution in a snapshot:

> In the tranquil line of the Porfirian towns, massive groups of vagrant Mexicans suddenly arise. The revolutionary armies occupy all the visual sphere. On top of their crowded trains, in large cavalry columns or small infantry groups, they come and go from towns and cities, occupy the Porfirian houses, blow up trains, collect cattle and harvests, move around the country. They kill and are killed. They are a landscape that takes up arms, full of vigor and misery, unruliness and destructive power. Thousands of men leave their homes and their towns, to which otherwise they would have been tied, and learn by themselves what they have only heard before, that the country to which they belong is a vast geographical and human entity and that they can travel throughout the country and make it their own.[1]

Novels, movies, and memories about the period endlessly recount the story: the familiar iconography of trains packed with combatants, *soldaderas* jumping from wagons, unending military campaigns, thirsty soldiers on the verge of exhaustion sleeping in frost-covered fields, generals on their horses roaming about in far-flung territories. Entire communities—often indigenous communities—were relocated from one corner of the country to the other: from Sonora to Yucatán, the Yaquis; from Quintana Roo to Chihuahua, the Maya. Displacement affects above all the most vulnerable members of society: the starving young boy who enlists and comes back one day to pillage his own pueblo; the abandoned woman who decides to pack her few belongings and take to the always dangerous roads. These movements produce a new dimension of spatiality that fascinates the forces stirred up by the revolt.

Such displacements seem to represent the logic of war itself. But when war ended, the frantic need to see it all firsthand endured. In August 1915 Pancho Villa retreated to the north under the pressure of the Constitutionalist army led by Álvaro Obregón, leaving the road open for Venustiano Carranza's return to Mexico City. Instead of proceeding to the capital, however, Carranza embarked on a six-month tour (or detour) through several states. Although he conceived of Mexico as a sum of hierarchies and labels, Carranza felt the need for a direct experience of the territory he was finally going to govern. The idea of starting with region and experience began to exert an irresistible attraction upon Mexican leaders.

The practice of visiting removed corners of Mexico persisted and deepened in the 1920s. After assuming his position at the SEP in 1921, Vasconcelos journeyed through Jalisco and Colima with the goal of inspecting educational facilities. That same year he visited Guerrero, Morelos, and Yucatán to persuade state officials to adopt his national plan of education.[2] These trips dramatically altered the minister's views about the actual needs of the Mexican people. If the Vasconcelos who started the literacy campaign was convinced of the superiority of Western culture over the simplicity and even barbarism of the countryside, the one who journeyed to Puebla on horseback in 1923 would talk of the need to penetrate the mentality of rural folks, "not only to influence them more efficiently, but also to uncover the portion of truth that, beyond any doubt, is preserved in the traditions of the indigenous people."[3]

Direct knowledge of the variegated texture of the Mexican landscape seemed to be a prerequisite even for artistic creation. During this trip to the Yucatán, Vasconcelos enlisted several poets, painters, and intellectuals to be cultural ambassadors. One of them, Diego Rivera, was invited with the express goal of helping him overcome his Europeanism.[4] Some years later, Rivera and Adolfo Best Maugard exposed Sergei Eisenstein to different landscapes before the Russian director set to work on his unfinished *¡Qué viva México!* The same nomadic impulse also infected Tina Modotti and Edward Weston, hired by the Universidad Nacional Autónoma de México (UNAM) in 1926 to embark on a long journey through rural Mexico in order to obtain photographic material for Anita Brenner's *Idols behind Altars*. The new passion for the real transformed the mechanical gaze and deeply affected the technologies of seeing:

> High angles, immobile cameras, and long shots of indigenous peoples performing and workers parading before a Europeanized oligarchy,

> gave place to shots of swirling masses in motion on their own behalf. From their position of privileged superiority, often literally as well as figuratively in the days of the dictators, cameramen descended into the street; from the sheltered urban spaces of the bourgeoisie, they fanned out into the contested countryside.[5]

In the postrevolutionary period, a great variety of social, scientific, and artistic discourses visit and describe, sound out and measure, invoke and probe that "landscape that takes up arms." As Rick López notes, Mexican postrevolutionary leaders themselves were convinced that past efforts to remake society had failed because they had ignored key features of Mexican reality, trying instead to impose artificial, European-derived schemes of social organization.[6] In his always meticulous language, Alfonso Reyes repeatedly referred to the Porfiriato as a fiction. Although a picture of Mexico as subjected to the caprices of the dictator is greatly exaggerated, it does capture the limitations of a style of government that thrived on the art of negating the experiential existence of a national totality. In contrast to this dismissive attitude towards deep Mexico, the revolution uncovered and mobilized an unsuspected multiplicity, "a vast human mosaic . . . a differential totality able to admit the most scandalous extremes of wealth and poverty. It was not in any way that unity preached by the Porfirist elites."[7]

This need for firsthand knowledge of the country complicates Benedict Anderson's famous formula of the nation as an imagined community. The revolutionary act of imagining Mexico seems not to be grounded in an act of imagination at all but rather in the physical appropriation of the territory that implied a direct experience of its enormous dimensions and complex makeup. Land and territory figure as the quintessential object of revolutionary practice. This is not so much because the Mexican Revolution was an agrarian revolution, but because it could only measure its strength in direct confrontation with the territorial strictures that were both the origin and dispositive of Porfirian subjection. We know quite well that revolutionary practices over land were not guided by enlightened principles.[8] Instead, they expressed themselves in a variety of forms, each of them molded by the peculiarities of the encounter between power and popular mobilization. The revolution drew its tactics from a direct encounter with geographical space. Insofar as revolutionary practice took land as its point of inflection and constitution, the history of that land—a history written in all the forms of ownership, surveillance, juridical claims, and traditions—wove itself into the net of revolutionary actions. Above and beyond all the anecdotes of pillaged houses and pianos equitably divided up among their usurpers with an ax, the articulation of revolutionary sovereignty depended on a mapping of grievances that was in principle consubstantial to the history of power and yet heterogeneous to its narrativization as history. The revolutionaries could not blindly impose their will upon reality, but they were able to elicit the contours of their desire from their resistance to that reality.[9] Revolution meant many things in different locations, but always and as a rule it meant some ideal of justice where the specific content of that justice was deduced from the nature of the grievances that preceded the revolutionary movement. The unity of consciousness was often negatively provided by the very discourses and networks of power under assault. The revolution translated this complex memory of layered and overlapping allegiances into politics and rendered synchronous a history of diachronic differences that could, for the first time, claim to be on equal footing in the calculation of the national totality.

The behavior of the revolutionary contingents was as varied as their origin and makeup. Property could be spared out of tradition, respect, or *compadrazgo*. But it could be also confiscated or destroyed. John Womack's *Zapata and the Mexican Revolution* contains, as in a catalogue, a summary of all these possibilities. One element remains constant through all these variations. The world could not be spared. This drive to touch, accept, or appropriate it all is a central component of what I call "revolutionary sovereignty." With this expression, I refer to the simple fact that revolutionaries acted under the assumption that insofar as their actions were revolutionary actions, they had the right to encroach on all dimensions of social, political, and moral life. The principle of revolutionary sovereignty establishes that there is no outside to the revolution. No safe haven can be invoked except the one that lies beyond the political boundaries of Mexico itself. Revolutionary sovereignty is the true schooling of the revolt: the reflective process through which practice grounds a consciousness on the run. This education of the spirit is difficult to discern because of its necessarily mediated relationship to its objects. "They spurred their horses to a gallop," writes Mariano Azuela in *The Underdogs*, "as if in that mad race they laid claims of possession to the earth."[10] The whole question of revolutionary practice on land hinges on this seemingly inconsequential "as if," which in Azuela took on derogatory tints but which expresses the instance wherein the immediacy of experience seeks to lift itself up into a language of potentiality.

The heterogeneous nature of the power-space continuum in prerevolutionary Mexico (the relative lack of hegemonic relationships to express subordination) both conditioned and limited the revolutionary movement when it had to project itself onto a national scale. "Spatial displacement takes a psychological toll," writes Max Parra in his illuminating discussion of *The Underdogs*. It affects the very "meaning of the struggle." Everything that was immediate and verifiable at the level of actually lived injustices became "hazy and uncertain" when shifted to a larger stage.[11] The archive of revolutionary stories is rich in examples of this always puzzling encounter between the popular armies and the realm of hegemonic and instituted politics. A wonderful episode in Martín Luis Guzmán's *The Eagle and the Serpent* in which the Zapatistas confuse the presidential chair with a saddle (they share the same noun in Spanish, *silla*) shows this struggle to extend a set of references born from the locality of the revolt to that larger stage onto which the popular forces are thrust by the dynamic of rebellion.

If the revolutionary experience always found the key of its subjective unfolding in relationship to spatiality, how is the spatial itself reworked and reimagined so that it can both inherit and transform the passion that illuminated its existence for the first time? As the question suggests, inheritance and displacement take place together. The institutionalization of the revolutionary process brought about a reversal by which the cultural-institutional apparatus of the revolution claimed to inherit the same rights of encroachment that once belonged to the popular forces of the revolt.[12] A startling inversion takes place in which the principle that nobody and nothing is out of reach of the revolution is turned into the possibility that the revolution, once institutionalized, appropriates absolutely those exposed to its claim. Writing in 1947, as sharp a critic of Mexican political life as José Revueltas admitted that "all the different sectors that participated in the revolution, from General Calles to Mr. Luis Cabrera to the quiet Indian of Morelos's sierras, imprinted the Mexican Revolution with their seal and recognized the revolution as their own."[13] The act by which they "recognized the revolution as their own" is logically identical to the moment they became the subjects of that revolution.

One immediate goal of the postrevolutionary order was to reverse the long-standing Porfirista strategy of fictionalization through a process of national embodiment.[14] Since embodiment was the inversion of Porfirian fictionalization, it could not really do away with its embedded geopolitical preferences. Hence, the somewhat surprising result that followed the revelation of Mexico as a vast and sometimes unknown geography was reform projects centered on the all-too-familiar landscape of Mexico City instead of the relatively unknown countryside. Although the city of Mexico has always reflected the aspirations of various Mexican elites, the revolution presented it with a different challenge. At this point, and according to laws of representation that were indeed new and binding, Mexico City was asked to represent Mexico to the eyes of Mexico itself. The response to that challenge is one of the most dazzling chapters in the history of Latin American cultural imagination. Starting around 1919 intellectuals, artists, and cultural organizers abandoned themselves with unparalleled fervor to the task of imagining a country they barely knew. Mexico City became the site of innumerable "cultural experiments" that sought to endow the capital with the capacity to represent multiple Mexicos. Some of these experiments, like La Casa del Estudiante Indígena (discussed in chapter 3), were perplexing; others, like *La noche mexicana* and the first Exposition of Popular Arts (both discussed below), were staggeringly successful. A common denominator to all these expressions is that they took the city itself as an object and were unimaginable outside the parameters that the city brought into existence. It is with the city, then, that we are first concerned.

MEXICO CITY UNDER PORFIRIO DÍAZ

Porfirian ideologues of modernization were well aware of what, many decades later, would be called the "hybrid" nature of the Mexican nation. Obsessed with presenting a modern face to the world, Porfirian urbanists lived in constant dismay of the spectacle of poverty and deprivation offered by the streets adjacent to the Zócalo. As Edmundo O'Gorman noticed, it was a problem dating back to the original Spanish conquest of the capital. Immediately after the defeat of Moctezuma, Hernán Cortés divided the old Tenochtitlan into Spanish and indigenous neighborhoods, allocating to the former the sacred places of the latter. There were those who objected to the idea of building a Spanish city at the heart of the old indigenous town. It was not entirely advisable for Spaniards to live surrounded by a resentful and recently vanquished enemy. Cortés, however, prevailed, and what was separated at the level of habitation remained linked (or superimposed) at the symbolic level.[15] The descendants of this increasingly impoverished indigenous population and the successive waves of poor brought forth by the uneven development of New Spain became a familiar part of the city core.

By the last quarter of the nineteenth century, ridding the city center of its poor had become one of the obsessions of urban reformers. Faced with the disadvantages and even impossibility of that course of action (many of the impoverished were the rank and file of the service sectors), the planners opted for developing "an ideal city inside the confines of the real city."[16] The ideal city was connected to the Zócalo by the Paseo de la Reforma but extended west, away from the center and towards the manicured forest of Chapultepec. The Paseo de la Reforma had been opened by Emperor Maximilian in the 1860s with the goal of linking the Zócalo to the Chapultepec palace (today home of the impressive National Museum of History). By 1910 the Paseo de la Reforma had become the axis of the ideal city. It was decorated with different sculptures representing a historical progression. Closest to the Zócalo was a statue in honor of Carlos IV of Spain (known as El Caballito and found today in Plaza Tolsa) and then, at regular intervals, statues to Columbus, Cuauhtémoc (the icon of official Porfirist *indigenismo*), and finally a great monument to independence inaugurated at the centennial celebration: *El Ángel*. Plans to add a fifth landmark, a statue in honor of Porfirio Díaz as guarantor of peace and progress, were postponed and finally abandoned due to the dictator's hesitation in accepting such a tribute while still living.

The centennial celebration of national independence in 1910 provided Porfirismo with a chance to further its reformist aspirations. Modeled after the French centennial of 1889, the Porfirian festivities were designed to show the world how progress and modernization were the crowning jewels of the enduring pax Porfiriana. The Porfirian administration had been preparing for the events of 1910 for a long time.[17] The inauguration of several public buildings was timed to coincide with the festivities. Porfirian Mexico celebrated its one hundred years of independent life with the inauguration of a psychiatric asylum, an impressive school building to house the Escuela Normal Primaria para Maestros, and a complete overhaul of the national penitentiary—all the projects overseen by Porfirio Díaz Jr. The architectural gems of the centennial celebration were the Palacio de Bellas Artes (finished only some decades later) and the central post office building, both designed by the Italian architect Adamo Boari.

Using the celebration as an excuse, the government initiated a comprehensive cleansing of downtown Mexico City. Prisons were removed to the outskirts of the city. Hospitals were relocated to more spacious areas, and asylums were transferred away from affluent sections of the historical center.[18] Society was encouraged to actively participate in the events. Cocktails, parties, speeches, and receptions filled September. The Comisión Nacional del Centenario encouraged a variety of historical monographs to be written. The initiative produced a deluge of texts ranging from histories of pharmacology to manuscripts on archaeology to the role of women in Mexican history.[19]

Díaz wanted the celebrations to be popular and made a genuine effort to procure the participation of varying social sectors. Nevertheless, Porfirian Mexico could not produce figures able to incarnate and consecrate the popular. Above all, Porfirismo could not provide the popular with a performative space but rather conceived of it as something to be presented or represented. In the end, the only successful attempt to incorporate some popular elements into the festivities took place in relation to the centerpiece of the 1910 celebration, the traditional *desfile histórico*. The parade consisted of a massive representation of the three historical strata of the Mexican nation: the pre-

Columbian past, Spanish rule, and independence. The marked historicism of this representation, Annick Lempérière notes, proves that the real encompassing ideology of Porfirismo was a teleological notion of history completely dominated by an abstract idea of progress.[20] The selection of historical episodes at the parade sharply reflected the predominant values of the group in power. Lempérière remarks that insurgency—a generic term for the first badly organized revolutions of popular origin—was not as celebrated as could be expected, perhaps because of "its extremely destructive and anarchic character, which made an identification between those events and the style of General Díaz very difficult."[21]

References to indigenous people were made in terms of a transitional narrative that saw Indian culture as just an antecedent to Spanish rule. Thus, the episode selected for the parade was the encounter between Moctezuma and Cortés, signaling that the demise of Indian prowess was what in reality mattered most. Likewise, the promotion of the recently recovered ruins at Teotihuacán was framed in a historicist narrative that dismissed the idea of an indigenous present as irrelevant. Official propaganda presented the site, which had been cleaned up in a hurry and with such amateurism as to actually endanger its treasures, as an example of a foregone and superseded past. To stress the remoteness of this past more forcefully, some official documents alerted the visitors that they were in the presence of the Mexican equivalent of Egypt's pyramids. The Conference of Americanists that Mexico cohosted with Buenos Aires forced intellectuals to speak about the Indian. While on the one hand speakers at the congress displayed an uncharacteristic indigenous fervor, on the other most interventions showed a relentless racist discourse that often invoked indigenous backwardness on the basis of physiological theories and anatomical limitations. The monument built to honor Benito Juárez, however, posed an even more unique problem. Juárez's parents were Zapotecas, and his ascendance to the presidency had always been presented as an example of Mexico's social equality. There had in fact been a plan to build the monument in Zapoteco style, but it was later dismissed as a brave but improper means to honor such a lofty figure. The basic idea was that Mexico could welcome an Indian into its rule, but an indigenous style could not represent Mexico.

All in all, the centennial celebration was a highly Europeanized event in both taste and style, and there were few traces of what would be the rabid *indigenismo* of 1921. And yet, in the end, the celebration's emphasis on the historical brought about some unintended consequences. The main one was perhaps the interest elicited in the role of indigenous populations in the conformation of the Mexican nation. Curiously, it was Isidro Fabela—one of the most Europeanized men of the time, as a visit to his house-museum in San

Ángel could attest—who produced one of the few generalized eulogies of the indigenous by reminding Mexicans that Father Morelos had mobilized the indigenous people of Mexico in the fight for independence and suggesting that the indigenous properly represented Mexican ethnic identity.[22]

OBREGÓN'S MEXICO

In 1910 the festivities of the centennial of independence overlapped with Francisco Madero's call for a revolution to overthrow Díaz. At first, Madero's call was just an oddity to the eyes of the city dwellers. As Alan Knight summarily concludes, "The Mexico of the revolution was provincial Mexico. . . . The revolution originated in the provinces, established itself in the countryside, and after years of a costly war was finally able to conquer an alien and sullen capital."[23] As Knight suggests, the encounter between Mexico City and real Mexico was, by all accounts, not a happy one. Throughout the revolutionary struggle, the capital maintained a condescending attitude towards the revolt that was shaking and reshaping the country. By 1920, writes Mauricio Magdaleno, "The man from the city continued living according to patterns that had not moved in ten years. He feared to the point of massive hysteria the arrival of the Zapatist hordes—such was the language used in the newspapers. He feared with equal intensity the constitutionalist forces, which, commanded by Pablo González first and Álvaro Obregón later, occupied the city in 1915."[24] Mexico City existed as an affront to the revolutionary convention of Aguascalientes. When Vasconcelos announced that the convention had the sovereignty to decide the future of Mexico, the newspaper *El Liberal* replied with a poll of jurists and intellectuals who ruled that the convention lacked any authority whatsoever to direct public affairs in Mexico, since it did not incarnate the national will. Even in defeat, the haughty city refused to bow to the rights of the victors. The revolutionary armies, on the other hand, remained resentful of the capital's stubborn claim to political supremacy.

By 1921 it was clear that one of the imperatives of the postrevolutionary government was to defeat the centuries-old prejudice that Mexico City was all there was to Mexico and that the self-respect of the country would rise or fall according to the hopes and achievements of its impressive capital. This was not an easy task, in part because leaders like Obregón himself had a marked distrust for the city. Unlike his predecessor, Venustiano Carranza, who, after scolding the city for years, made himself quite at home in it during his tenure as president, Obregón left an unsavory taste in the mouth of its citizens during his first public appearance after delivering the city from the

Huertista troops. At his visit to Madero's tomb, he greeted a young lady—María Arias Bernal—who had vocally opposed Victoriano Huerta's regime. Unlike her, Obregón contended, the rest of Mexico City had silently accompanied the iron rule of the general. Obregón felt that the city had not fought for the revolution but instead had plotted and killed Madero. It had not openly rebelled against those who committed the crime and had abetted—through its irresponsible press—the demise of the former president. The same press, he noticed, was not as bold and antagonistic to Huerta as it had been to Madero. Claiming he could recognize bravery when he saw it, Obregón drew his pistol and handed it to Arias Bernal. A weapon that had served to defend the cause of the people, Obregón concluded, could only be entrusted to a woman in this city.

The portrait of a capital oblivious to the revolt and dismally beholden to its European linings is as colored by myth as the story retold so many times of Obregón's defacement of the city. Mexico City did not preserve its identity through the tumultuous years of revolutionary upheaval. It was both challenged and changed. It underwent an educational process out of which it emerged, by and large, a different city. As usual, purification was by fire. The city suffered a good deal under Huerta. Prisoners were routinely shot at the Convento de la Merced, and the spectacle of the wounded calling out to their mothers and wives while waiting for the *tiro de gracia* stirred commotion among the inhabitants. The permanent Zapatista siege and the destruction of haciendas produced a chronic food shortage. For months, bread and beans became luxury items and long lines of eight or nine hours had to be endured before securing the day's meal. The reduction in caloric intake combined with other deprivations led to a number of epidemics that multiplied the corpses throughout the city's streets. Francisco Ramírez Plancarte recalls,

> It was a terrible, macabre spectacle. Several men threw human bodies over a carriage as if they were logs. The bodies of the unconscious people who were still trembling and barely alive were taken to the common fosse. All sense of commiseration had disappeared. There was no remedy for them and they represented a danger to others. Furthermore, they were unconscious . . . which made the horrendous task of this vulgar euthanasia easier.[25]

Robbery and rape were common incidents tied to the coming and going of occupying military forces. Young and old alike were permanent targets of forced conscription. The practice decimated entire families. Meanwhile, those "selected" to fight the insurgency often did not get the chance to fight at all: they were placed at the forefront of the federal troops—although they had received no military instruction—and forced to charge first into the bullets of the enemy. Often even the weapons they were given were not in working order. At the height of the recruiting frenzy even the disabled citizens begging at the cathedral were levied under the sarcastic reasoning that "if you are not fit to fight, you are fit to die."[26]

Suffering made Mexico City resentful of Huerta, of the church, and of the well-to-do people who had fervently supported him. Be that as it may, there remained a gulf separating the ethics and mores of its residents from the crude customs exposed by the men and women of the triumphal revolutionary forces. Upon his entrance into Mexico City in 1914, Álvaro Obregón was greeted by a multitude elated over the end of the armed struggle and grateful because the first to occupy the city was a gentleman from the north rather than a vulgar peasant from the south. Still, at the parade the throngs cheering his name were overtaken with terror at the sight of the Yaqui contingent of the Constitutionalist army.[27] When the same Obregón was elected president of Mexico six years later, he would keep a solid group of Yaqui Indians as his personal guards. He always addressed them in Yaqui. Metropolitan ambivalence towards the Yaqui Indians and other indigenous groups is a reminder of a colonial situation that Mexican culture could not completely address in spite of all its attempts at founding a transcultural society. All through the 1920s the existence of strong ethnocultural prejudices hindered social coalitions that would have been both logical and necessary. The Casa del Obrero, an early representative of Mexico City's working class, showed nothing but hostility towards Zapata and his cause. Even those anarchists who were more inclined to befriend Zapatismo were dismayed at the religiosity and ceremoniousness of Zapata's troops.[28]

THE CENTENNIAL CELEBRATION OF 1921

By the time of his appointment as president, Obregón was an enormously popular and prestigious politician. His government, however, was besieged on multiple fronts. With scarce resources Obregón tried to appease the army through concessions and the middle class through economic privileges. Given its multiple economic interests in Mexico, the constantly overzealous United States was an unreliable neighbor. The city of Mexico had grown disproportionately in the years following the armed conflict, with some of its less affluent areas resembling refugee camps. Plans for reforming the city abounded but they were curtailed by permanent budget problems and the impossibility of a single group imposing its criteria on the question of urban reform.[29] In 1911 Madero reinstated communal jurisdictions in an attempt to further popular participation in the city council. The council became the site of a tumultuous democratic experiment as representatives of tenants from poor neighborhoods, street vendors, traditional shopkeepers (the family *talleres* that surround the Zócalo even today), union leaders, and myriad self-fashioned politically minded citizens converged on a single space. The constant disagreements and the practical impossibility of orchestrating city policies beyond the limits of the municipality made city government almost impossible. In the end, Plutarco Elías Calles would abolish the independent communal units in 1929, paving the way for urban reforms that continue to mark the face of Mexico City to this day, such as the development of the Colonia Condesa, where fortunes were made by revolutionary generals at the expense of fiscal lands and where Calles himself built a residence.

In the first years of postrevolutionary rule, the impoverished state contented itself merely with multiplying parks, strengthening public transportation, championing public hygiene, and renaming streets (a project undertaken during September 1921 for the celebration of the centennial of the consummation of independence).[30] Cultural politics was indeed one of few areas in which the government was not on the defensive. But even then most of the elements of this cultural politics were born outside its formal structures.

It is not clear who came up with the idea of a second centennial celebration to be organized in September 1921. While some sources suggest that the idea originated with the newspapers, others—like Vasconcelos, in his memoirs—charge Alberto Pani with fathering this "expensive joke."[31] Pani was, in fact, one of the most enthusiastic backers of the festivities and one of the members of the government who most forcefully articulated the need to erase from public memory the embarrassing display of pomp and snobbish imitation of European culture that had characterized the Porfirist centennial to the detriment of local expressions.[32]

If humility was a goal, the miserable material conditions of the country in 1921 all but ensured that the government's wish would be granted. Unlike its 1910 counterpart, the celebration of 1921 was put together in a hurry, backed by insufficient funds, and turned out to be, if not an utterly popular celebration, at least one in which society could claim the unprecedented role of supplying the event with meaning. This explains to some extent the disparity in the sources now available for the reconstruction of both events. While the 1910 celebration was minutely recorded in official memory, most of what we know of 1921 has to be pieced together from memoirs, direct or indirect testimonies, photo albums, and above all from the chronicles and articles that appeared throughout the whole year in the press.[33]

Although one result of the festivities would be to foster a new and more encompassing notion of popular and national culture, the activities most zealously promoted by the state did not contribute much to that goal. Indeed, Obregón's administration hoped to use the festivities to showcase Mexico as an example of institutional stability. If Porfirio Díaz had wanted to put peace and progress on display, the emphasis of Obregón's government was on peace alone. Mexico had not managed to gain diplomatic recognition from the United States or from European powers who questioned Obregón's grip on the country with a badly disciplined army of dubious loyalties. Not surprisingly then, Obregón took advantage of the centennial to commit the army to a more stable institutional role. The government spent 15 percent of the celebration's budget on new military uniforms, equipment, and horses, and the army was showcased in almost every single event during the celebration.[34] The fact that 1921 had to recognize the role of a conservative like Gen. Agustín Iturbide in national history was a thorny and explosive question. One should notice here the irony of a 1910 celebration in which an elitist government had to commemorate a popular revolt and a 1921 celebration in which a popular government had to celebrate an act whose republicanism was tainted by the poor revolutionary credentials of General Iturbide, a monarchist by conviction who proclaimed independence in part out of disgust for the liberal turn that public affairs had taken in Spain at that point. The revolutionary government actually reenacted the entrance of the triguarantor army into Mexico City, something rarely, if at all, staged in previous celebrations. While a number of conservative intellectuals used the opportunity to vindicate Iturbide and the Catholic Church, the national press was flooded with the opinions of those who, while supporting the celebration, expressed loathing for Iturbide. An eulogy of Iturbide cost Rámos Pedrueza, professor at the Escuela Nacional de Jurisprudencia, his post. After firing him an enraged José Vasconcelos remarked that Iturbide was the initiator of "our tedious history of military revolts."[35] Finally, the polemic reached the chamber of deputies, where Zapatista representatives Antonio Díaz Soto y Gama and Octavio Paz (father of the future Nobel Prize winner) proposed the removal of Iturbide's name from the Galería de Hombres Ilustres in the chamber. The proposition passed by an overwhelming 125 to 11 vote, and the hero celebrated on the streets was demoted within the inner circle of power.

Like Díaz before him, Obregón wished for a popular celebration. He instructed the president of the committee in charge of organizing the celebration, of which Martín Luis Guzmán was a member, to organize inclusive events able to represent all social strata.[36] But while Obregón knew what inauthenticity looked like, he was less clear what an authentic representation of Mexico might entail. In hindsight, we know that the identification of the popular with the indigenous was destined to be one of the most striking results of the celebrations. However, the idea was almost unrepresented in the official calendar of events. Rather, the state conceived of the popular through a sociological grid that situated class at its center instead of culture. Free meals were provided to the poor and free clothing distributed in lower-class neighborhoods, including infant clothes for newborns. There were excursions to Chapultepec for which the youth from poor areas were given free rides in automobiles. There were airplane and balloon rides. Following tradition, several hundred jail inmates were freed as part of the celebration. Near the Alameda installations were set up that offered free health care for working-class families, medical treatment for newborns, and a generous vaccination plan for children of peripheral neighborhoods. The dangers of alcoholism were given a prominent space in the campaign. There were many lectures given at facilities that included monitored play areas where parents of working-class origin could leave their children while attending the talks. The intense attention to childhood that would characterize postrevolutionary rule and many populist regimes throughout Latin America was a novel form of political intervention, although not perceived as such at the time.[37] The reason lies perhaps in the fact that another set of activities eclipsed those organized by the state. These activities originated in the private sphere and included some of the most brilliant and promising artists and intellectuals of the period. The events organized by these intellectuals—whom, following James Scott, I will refer to as high modernists—introduced a significant shift in the general conception of Mexicanness by replacing the Porfirian emphasis on the historical with the postrevolutionary accent on the geographical.[38] Instead, the stress now was on an ethnographic-aesthetic discourse designed to take charge of the heterogeneous composition of the country that the revolution had both unveiled and empowered.

The somewhat surprising promotion of art as catalytic of a national soul had already been announced by Manuel Gamio in his 1916 book *Forjando patria*. In its pages, Gamio argues that "art alone could be trusted" with the reconstruction of the country. Even "sociologists unconcerned with hearts" had come to the conclusion that unbridgeable differences in taste were both the origin of and evidence of a fractured society.[39] This preference for the aesthetic coming from the father of modern Mexican anthropology is intriguing, especially in light of the enormous centrality enjoyed by the social sciences in the constitution of an ideology of the national in Mexico. As an anthropologist Gamio was educated in the cultural relativism of Franz Boas, a relativism that often took the indigenous work of art as the surest proof of the native equality vis-à-vis other cultures. More importantly, Gamio's ethnographic practice made him aware that artistic or aesthetic valuation escapes the ethical dilemmas that plague the sociological or anthropological gaze. While anthropology seeks to recognize multiple forms of habitation in the world, this function comes at the price of an ethical misrecognition. This is the predicament known as the denial of coevalness exposed by Johannes Fabian. In ethnography the other is allowed a space of emergence that marks him or her as not belonging to the same present inhabited by the gazing subject.[40] For Mexicans the problem was how to combine respect for another source of the world (which is lived as a prior time) with the injunction of a national inclusion that needed to be coeval by definition. The aesthetic offered a way out of this predicament, because the beautiful demanded a common historical horizon for all those involved in the judgment.[41] Aesthetics became an internal criticism of ethnographic reason, a way to overcome the intrinsically Eurocentric features built into the notion of culture itself.

As for the artists and intellectuals who were in charge of implementing this aesthetic mediation between the popular and the dominant forms of socialization, none of them were organically related to indigenous or peasant communities. On the contrary, to a significant extent they were a genuine product of the Porfirist belle époque. Many of them had traveled and studied in Europe through fellowships granted by the dictator himself. Although their own artistic sensibilities were open to popular influences, they were fundamentally shaped by the experience of European modernism. Rivera had met Picasso and the most important Cubists of the time during his stay in Europe. Adolfo Best Maugard frequented Matisse, Cézanne, and Gauguin. The Guatemalan Carlos Mérida was deeply familiar with European formalism. He travelled to Europe to study the works of Paul Klee, Joan Miró, and, in particular, Wassily Kandinsky, whose influence would determine Mérida's abandonment of figuration in favor of abstract art in the 1930s. Roberto Montenegro studied in Spain and travelled to Paris to interview Georges Braque and Juan Gris. An important point to bear in mind, however, is that this metropolitan training was to a very important extent a training on the appreciation and vindication of indigenous and primitive art, a modality with which most modernist artists had been smitten for over fifty years at that point.

The events that these artists either organized or collaborated with are some of the most historically transcendental activities of the 1921 centennial. They represent salient instances in which "the change of values and perspectives brought about by the revolution process . . . take root in the collective imagination."[42] Each of the events I discuss below—the pageant competition to select the "*India bonita*," the first Exposition of Popular Arts and its catalogue, and *La noche mexicana* at Chapultepec Forest—were the subjects of intense journalistic interest and are regularly mentioned in commentaries on the period. If today they seem historical curiosities, at the time they held the key to understanding an affective configuration out of which modern Mexico was born.

The India Bonita Contest

The contest that crowned María Bibiana Uribe as the first *India bonita* enjoyed enormous popularity in Mexico. Her image reemerges in all kinds of media. Her name appears in the title of different theatrical pieces. We find her, shy and smiling, parading the streets or surrounded by Mexican officials in the photographic record of different formal receptions. Her image reemerges in Salvador Toscano's film *Memorias de un mexicano,* where she is referred to as "the most beautiful among those of her race."[43]

The contest was organized by Félix Palavicini, owner of the newspaper *El Universal.* The fact that a newspaper was responsible for one of the most popular events of the centennial speaks to the enormous purchase that journalism exercised in the first decades of postrevolutionary rule. Such a role may be surprising given the long association between illiteracy and the popular in early-twentieth-century Mexico. But in fact the revolution itself had functioned as a gigantic and chaotic literacy machine. Every important constituency had its own newspaper: *El Monitor* (Villa), *Tierra y Justicia* (Zapata), *El Radical* (Carranza, edited by Dr. Atl). The only one with relatively national reach was *El Demócrata* (which would eventually support the presidential aspirations of Álvaro Obregón). At the climax of revolutionary violence the country was flooded by several publications with an estimated circulation of fewer than ten thousand copies each. These newspapers, often written and produced by just one individual, constituted the most prevalent reading material for soldiers.[44] With the end of the revolution, these partisan newspapers lost their reason for existence and were replaced by commercial publications. The first modern Mexican newspaper was *El Imparcial,* founded in 1896; while its initial circulation was 65 thousand, it reached 125 thousand by 1910.[45] By the end of the armed struggle it was joined by two national newspapers modeled on American journalism: *El Universal,* founded in 1916, and its competitor *Excelsior* (1917). In 1919 Salvador Alvarado founded *El Heraldo de México,* which employed an important number of intellectuals like Martín Luis Guzmán, Xavier Villaurrutia, and Salvador Novo. To some extent, it was in the periodical press that the celebration gained a national projection, and it was largely thanks to the celebration that some newspapers acquired a national reach. Although individual states organized their own festivities, throughout Mexico people avidly read the different articles that on an everyday basis informed about the celebrations taking place in the capital. In *Recuerdos del porvenir* (*Recollections of Things to Come*) Elena Garro left a magnificent portrait of the interest elicited by the 1921 celebration in her natal Puebla.

Palavicini, a Maderista close to Obregón, explained his idea for the contest as a push for the recognition of Mexican indigenous values as well as a way to celebrate the beauty of lower-class women. Manuel Gamio acted as a judge for the contest but also as promoter of the event. Gamio proved to be an effective collaborator, rescuing the project anytime a fissure in its design endangered the whole enterprise. Even after the contest Gamio contributed a critical piece titled "The Indian Venus," where he explained the rationale behind the election of María Bibiana Uribe. As suggested by the extensive research of Rick López, Palavicini and his collaborators soon discovered that beauty was a characteristic that was far less intuitive than they had first imagined. When *El Universal* opened the contest to public entries, their offices were flooded with photos of white, middle-class women dressed as Indians. The notion of a beautiful Indian seems to have been preposterous to the newspaper's readership. Slowly, *El Universal* developed a canon to guide the searches. As part of this educational campaign, the newspaper published portraits of suitable candidates along with short explanations of how the depicted subjects related to the promoted ideals.[46]

The contest rapidly evolved from a journalistic trifle to a public phenomenon strongly implicated in the definition of a national culture. Once crowned, María Bibiana was introduced to the president and his ministers. She shared official banquets and celebrations, something, a witness of the time noted, that "would have been unheard of in 1910."[47] Clearly, in all these activities the question of her beauty was beside the point. She was questioned, showed around, consulted, and interpreted not because she was beautiful, but because she was *India*. And yet it was in terms of her beauty that she was first able to emerge as a valid subject of national presentation.[48] The iconic projection of María Bibiana as a representative of all *Indios* informed the interview conducted with her by Jacobo Dalevuelta a few hours before the vote in the offices of *El Universal*. Rick López correctly points out that Dalevuelta exoticized Bibiana, exaggerating "her Indian dialect, making her seem exotic, rustic, and uneducated."[49] Interestingly, the pinnacle of this exoticization comes with an exchange on happiness, a notion that Dalevuelta considers a primordial or universal feature of human life:

> "Are you happy, Bibiana? [¿Eres feliz, Bibiana?]
>
> Well . . . who knows, sir, who knows. [Pos . . . quen save, señor quen save.]
>
> Do you know what it is to be happy? [¿Sabes lo qué es ser feliz?]
>
> No, sir, what is that? [No, señor. ¿Qué's eso?][50]

Whether or not Dalevuelta's report was accurate is not much relevant to our case. Undoubtedly, the newspaper was prone to treat María Bibiana in exotic terms. She was described in close association with the world of nature: "She strolls through the woods . . . picking flowers as she goes."[51] More important, however, is the operation revealed in this representation. No feeling can be deemed more universal than happiness, yet María Bibiana does not know what happiness is. This fact alone confirmed her authenticity.

Enfranchisement through art confronts a peculiar predicament. It has to make familiar something (or somebody) who is presented as entirely other. This is why anytime that the aesthetic is asked to reveal the political (or the common) it stumbles upon the ethical (or the singular). What kind of conversations did María Bibiana have when she was taken to official ceremonies and the opera, to innumerable dinners and on city strolls? On these occasions, flanked by upper-class members of the Mexico City elite and often by high-ranking members of Obregón's administration, she was asked about her views on the revolution, politics, economy, and foreign affairs. Reportedly, most or all of her answers were in line with the ones that she provided to Dalevuelta. These clumsy answers confirmed, however, that she was the perfect representative of this other Mexico that Mexico so fervently desired. But it also confirmed the limits of a top-down engineering of the popular. If another Mexico could be brought to the shores of the public by an aesthetic act, it could not be brought into political coevalness by the mere exercise of an aesthetic option.

The Exposition of Popular Arts

While the India Bonita contest abstracted the indigenous from its world, the Exposition of Popular Arts took the opposite course, trying to wedge open a window onto the indigenous world through crafts and artistic creation. The exposition entrusted to Jorge Enciso, Roberto Montenegro, and Dr. Atl (Gerardo Murillo Cornado) by the Dirección de Antropología under the direction of Manuel Gamio, was accompanied by a catalogue authored by Dr. Atl which will be the focus of this section. In its 25 June 1921 edition, *El Universal* informed its readers in a language of loaded exoticism that "expeditions were dispatched to the four cardinal points of the country with the goal of recovering creations and utensils that could be deemed authentically indigenous (*netamente indígenas*) and representative of the civilization of our forebears (*ancestros*)."[52] In contrast, Enciso, Montenegro, and Atl did not use this exoticist language and preferred to refer to indigenous productions as simply art.[53] So, as in the case of the *India bonita*, the beautiful was put at the center of a strategy for political assimilation.

As the research of Rick López into the exposition shows, this characterization of indigenous production as art was far from obvious at the time. The use of the word "art" to describe indigenous crafts was a point of contention when the organizers tried to enlist the support of local officials in collecting the pieces. Baffled governors answered the organizer's request by plainly asserting that indigenous populations in their states produced no art. In the end, a combination of indoctrination and earmarked contributions to local states convinced authorities to send samples to the exposition.[54]

To the objections that Indians produced no art, Enciso answered that there was no region in the "vast territory" of Mexico where "the Indians do not offer manifestations of primitive art and talent, putting their hands to the products found in their native region."[55] Enciso's message contained a precise reference to the hermeneutic that guided the high modernists in their encounter with the popular: unlike Western art, which expresses the hopes and anguish of individual subjects, popular art is expressive of communal values. Moreover, it is itself necessarily attached to an immediate environment even if this environment does not exhaust or determine its meaning. Revolutionary nationalism would use this principle to judge all Mexican art, an attitude that lies at the origin of the enmity between nationalism and cosmopolitanism in modern Mexican culture.

Popular art is considered in a double movement: it partakes of the universality and detachability of art (paintings are supposed to lose little of their character for being stored in a museum), and it expresses the uniqueness of a relationship to the world through its assimilation to an anthropological rather than aesthetic notion of art. This intermediate position that imputed crafts simultaneously with the characteristics of the authentic and the detachable made of them ideal transitional objects. Mexico City dwellers were of course familiar with indigenous crafts. What was new in the exposition was the idea that these objects embodied and communicated a complex perception of the world that suddenly demanded to be understood on its own terms. The exposition was a tremendous success. It was widely covered by the press and people flocked to the exhibition. Obregón and his entourage enthusiastically endorsed the initiative, and the objects on display soon became familiar sights in the middle-class houses of Mexico City.[56]

DR. ATL'S *LAS ARTES POPULARES EN MÉXICO*

If, as many witnesses of the period remark, rural Mexico was a terra incognita for the local intelligentsia, the reader cannot but be awestruck before the impressive effort undertaken by Atl in the composition of the catalog for the Exposition of Popular Arts.[57] A cursory look at the index reveals Atl's zeal in covering a remarkable range of forms. There are chapters on pottery, toys, wood and metal crafts, textiles, woodcarving, architecture, painting, theater, popular music, lacquer, *charrería,* religious stamps, and ex-votos, among others. The profusely illustrated text included dozens of photos taken in the ethnographic style of informative photography. Atl was careful to provide notes regarding materials, contexts of production, and judgments on value. He also discussed the existence of literature in the local argot and extensively reproduced some engravings by Guadalupe Posada along with the original articles published by Antonio Vanegas Arroyo. Even after such a monumental effort, Atl lamented the omissions caused by the four scarce months allowed for researching, writing, and printing the book. The most important omission, he added, was the lack of any discussion of Mexican cuisine, to which he nevertheless devoted two excellent pages. Although Atl appeared as the only author of the catalog, it is plausible that he discussed the contents of the volume with Jorge Enciso, Roberto Montenegro, and perhaps Xavier Guerrero and Adolfo Best Maugard.

Atl seemed to assume that listing the different forms in which the popular is expressed, from serapes to food and recipes, would create a concept of the national by their simple addition. This organizational principle betrays a museumlike gaze. Atl's disposition towards the corpus of objects gathered in the exposition was ethnographic. By this I mean that Atl perceived these objects as emanating from the objective conditions of life as lived by what he calls indigenous people, which led him to postulate the seamless nature of the societies producing these artifacts. Atl writes, "I have spent many days among indigenous artisans in Puebla and Oaxaca. I have had the chance to admire the patience with which they work the primary materials, the methodic nature of their work, the tenderness with which they decorate their pieces and the dexterity needed to weave a serape."[58] These qualities are transposed into the crafts, and this is the reason why a correct appreciation of these crafts means, simultaneously, a correct appreciation of their makers. Only, locked in their regions and unaware of a larger constitutional body of practices called the Mexican nation, these artisans did not seem to truly belong to the Mexican nation. That these people are indeed the kernel of a Mexican expressivity is the point that the catalog sets itself to prove.

The problem with this argument lies in the intention of using the spiritual production of supposedly seamless communities to express a disaggregated modern society. If the conditions of production of the crafts are fatally tied to their forms, how can these vases and serapes represent the frantic and eclectic Mexico that around this time erupted in the work of the Estridentistas? Atl solved the problem by referring to these productions as art, since art is, after all, the name given to the suturing power of the spirit in the age of unsolvable divisions. However, the catalog is not consistent in its nomenclature. Atl calls the popular creations both industry (another word for craft but one with special emphasis on labor) and art. In a parallel fashion, its producers are referred to—also indistinctly—as both popular and indigenous. But these concepts mean quite different things in different contexts.

The very idea of craft as a form of art is a controversial point in the Western aesthetic canon. For Kant nothing born with utility in mind could be an object of aesthetic contemplation. The autonomy of art demands its disinterest.[59] Crafts may be judged beautiful—and in this sense, the aesthetic judgment still applies to them—but they are not art because they are not the free product of the spirit but the product of social and economic coercion. Actually, one of Atl's main goals in the catalog was to defend at all costs the autonomy of indigenous crafts by severing them from any notion of interest and even utility. This is not done, however, along the lines that sustain the autonomy of art in modernity, but rather by recasting the problem of autonomy in the language of ethnography.

The uniqueness of indigenous art is protected by a triple formation which relies on the identities of its producers, the economics of its production, and the temporal chiasm of which this art is itself an index. In terms of identity, crafts are the expression of an indigenous spirituality.[60] Atl wholeheartedly subscribed to (what will later be called) the ideology of Mexico as a country with a mestizo body and an indigenous soul. Except that for Atl, the indigenous component alone guaranteed the consistency of a possible national expression. Moreover, the economic function of the crafts further separates them from the utilitarianism of modern capitalist society. Atl convincingly argued that crafts were not commodities for their producers. Any cost-benefit analysis would indicate that the numbers did not add up. "No capitalist would be able to organize a business under this model."[61] Very likely, at stake here was an attack on intellectuals like Gamio who saw the mass production of crafts as a means to improve the economies of indigenous communities. Although Atl himself went on to promote the mass production of indigenous crafts, his despair before metropolitan interventions seems to have had some justification.[62] Ten years after Atl drafted the catalog, Paul Strand would send a report to the SEP with a dismal picture of the state of popular crafts in Michoacán. By 1932 the opening of local economies to generalized trade had resulted in "the production of objects completely alien to the life of the communities, such as powder compacts, jewelry boxes, and game tables; the imitation of pseudo-Greek, pseudo-modern, or pseudo-primitive motifs; and crass imitations of American cartoons."[63]

The final form of autonomy Atl attributed to indigenous crafts is the most intriguing. For Atl, indigenous art was worth collecting because these crafts were "set to disappear as soon as Mexico enters once and for all on the path of industrial evolution to which it is destined."[64] In the same space, Atl argued that popular art is a form of national expression that is destined to disappear. His reasoning hides a dissociation that the notion of beauty seems unable to contain: the image of crafts as material transpositions of a popular (and beautiful) soul cannot be reconciled with the popular as an actual agent of historical change. Nothing betrays this tension better than the visual record of the different pieces reproduced in the catalog. This visual record is marked by a strange anomaly. After dozens of photographs of objects from many regions of Mexico, Atl closed the book with a photo of Zapata. The photo was amply justified by Atl's observation of a rather scandalous and paradoxical revelation in the relationship between popular art and subjectivity. Atl notes, "It seemed to me that these men have done nothing but work and enjoy their work. And yet, all of them, without exception, belonged to this or other armed group that under constantly changing banners had committed the most ferocious deeds against the people of its own race."[65] Such was the very enigma of recent Mexican history: the double belonging of the indigenous and popular masses to the realm of masterful tranquility and the impatience of revolutionary ardor. While the first begot popular crafts, the second created the conditions for a unified nation.

For Atl, the time of the indigenous was doubled. It had to be doubled in order to explain its simultaneous autonomy—its nonbelonging and resistance to the mainstream of modernizing culture—as well as to show its exemplary role in the making of a nationality. This doubling was already inscribed in the notion of popular culture itself, in which the adjective refers to the always moving frontier of a political formation while the noun seeks to anchor this drift in the repose of a definitive idea. Atl was conclusive. This paradox was "the most Mexican of Mexico."[66] In a final analysis, the paradox is simply the one in which a well-organized order, within which everybody seems to find his or her place, is subverted from the inside by the bursting out of a political vocation. Atl "solved" the paradox by reinscribing it in an aesthetic of the second degree. The revolution showed that the temperament of the Mexican people was "essentially artistic."[67] Revolution and crafts necessarily coexisted under a logic in which the revolt became the expression of an intensity "without which the work of art would remain impossible."[68] Atl was not alone in this judgment. In a contribution to the SEP bulletin dated 22 September 1926, Alfonso Reyes—who took advantage of the occasion to defend the government in the Cristero War—commented on the itinerant Exposición de pintura de niños mexicanos in Paris. (The children had followed the Best Maugard method for drawing.) Reyes writes that "the same force that causes revolutions creates these works of art. It finds in them a final, appropriate language." What was truly characteristic of the national, then, was not patience but impatience. Or better yet, the condition of possibility of the nation is not so much the spirit objectified in art as the same spirit stirred by war. Atl stopped short of this conclusion, and hence, he stopped short also of pondering the structuring place that revolutionary sovereignty had in the constitution of the Mexican nation. In Atl's catalog, the disclosure of the popular is one with the attempt to cancel its political potential: its intrinsic belonging to a modern world into which, paradoxically, it needs to be integrated. The price for disclosing indigenous art seems to be the obscuring of the political vocation of its producers.[69] For the same reasons, his notion of the popular appears to be politically sterile, structurally alien to any play of alliances that could take it beyond the limits imposed upon it by tradition and geography. If Atl had had his way—which he did not—the notion of popular culture would have replicated the mutual alienation between forms of power and forms of authenticity that marked Porfirismo. At this point, the disregard that the catalog shows for the urban forms of the popular acquires particular significance. To announce that the cultural power of deep Mexico was doomed to disappear at the very moment when the center was being invaded by the forces of a newly discovered national territory was, to say the least, politically naive. Atl, who was so attentive to the relationship between cultural reproducibility and insurgency, failed to notice the conformation of a new wave of insurgency signaled by the slow but steady occupation of the symbolic center of the nation by masses of indigenous origin. Rooted as his thinking was in a positive and mournful conception of the popular, chances are that even if he had noticed this new form of insurgency, he would not have entertained any sympathy for it. But if the discovery of Mexican extension as the practical correlate of the essential equality of all with all was going to have any redeeming value, the popular as pedagogy had to give way to the popular as performance. This step was accomplished by Adolfo Best Maugard (despite his intentions, perhaps) in his *noche mexicana*.

La noche mexicana*: Theater, Parks, and Citizenship in the Field of Vision*

La noche mexicana, "an extravaganza of lights, food, and dance," in the words of Rick López, was one of the most massive events of the centennial of 1921.[70] Adolfo Best Maugard was put in charge of the gigantic "happening." Alberto Pani's idea seems to have been to use the festivity to showcase the newly extended electrification and lighting of Chapultepec Forest. But instead of producing an ode to modernization, Best Maugard populated

Chapultepec with different stands offering traditional Mexican food, hired a number of performers—according to some sources this was the first time that mariachis were part of a public festivity in Mexico City—and covered the newly installed light fixtures with stylized versions of popular and indigenous motifs. The centerpieces of the celebration were a spectacle of fireworks that Best Maugard supervised personally from a canoe on the park's lake and a ballet of fifty ballerinas who performed traditional Mexican dances against a complex backdrop designed by Best Maugard himself. He designed the beautiful stage following his own drawing method, whose inspiration dated back to his acquaintance with the different artifacts that Franz Boas and Manuel Gamio rescued in Teotihuacán.

La noche mexicana offered a balanced representation of different geographical areas of the country, and in that sense, it illustrates the desire to replicate the almost inconceivable extension of the nation within the limits of the representational ability of its capital. As reported by the newspaper *Excelsior*, those attending the celebration were invited to a historical and artistic tour that allowed them to tour the whole country in one night.[71] In a similar vein, *El Universal Ilustrado* summarized the event as a display "of authentic Mexican cultural expressions representative of remote and different places of the Mexican geography," and immediately added that "everything [took] place before the eyes of a bewildered public."[72] The bewilderment of spectators was occasioned by the staging of what a few years later would be deemed the most natural and Mexican of all cultural landscapes.

The celebration was so successful that the organizers decided to repeat it a few days later—on September 28—for a more popular audience. The mass character of the event surprised its own organizers. Alberto Pani and other officials expected a modest influx from the countryside for the festivities—discounted train tickets were offered for attendees—but were astonished when over one hundred thousand visitors poured in from the provinces to attend the various events. Rooms were in demand everywhere. In his diary, novelist Federico Gamboa registered the "noticeable increase in the number of outsiders (*forasteros*) coming from all corners of the republic."[73] The initial plan was to charge admission for the festivity of 28 September, a plan that was noisily challenged by the newspaper *El Demócrata*. Organizers could not completely make up their mind regarding admission when an estimated one hundred to three hundred thousand people flocked to Chapultepec for the celebration.[74]

Although popular and indigenous cultures were put on display at Chapultepec, there was no attempt—as in Atl—to link cultural production to a discourse of authenticity or even identity. Best Maugard's approach to cultural difference was mostly instrumental. He simply mounted what was simultaneously a spectacle, an installation, and a party, something with which he was rather familiar, having organized parties for millionaires in the United States. Best Maugard took popular culture by assault, forcing it into a kind of spurious sublation that was happy to preserve the form of the popular (middle-class women, dressed as Indians, selling *atole* in a stand) without paying much attention to whatever was left out of the equation. Unlike Atl, Best Maugard was completely unconcerned with the issues of cultural ventriloquism that would become so popular in years to come. In *Crafting Mexico,* Rick López criticizes this scarcely respectful approach to the popular and signals the political deficit to which it gives origin.[75] There was, however, a definitive sense in which an encounter took place at Chapultepec between aspirations grounded in the political visibility of the masses and the strictures of cultural codification. The masses of people did not just attend a spectacle—they were themselves the spectacle. The event simply allowed them to represent this exteriority of meaning that, through the diffuse yet still apposite name of "mass," began to define the new political subject of postrevolutionary Mexico.

The emergence of the urban mass as a reservoir of political meaning was one of the most important developments of the postrevolutionary period. To put the problem in perspective, let us recall that the capital's population went from 540 thousand in 1900 to 730 thousand in 1910, and it reached 900 thousand by 1921.[76] In twenty years, the number of city dwellers had almost doubled. This mass was composed of groups of individuals who coalesced around specific cultural, economic, or political forms of association but whose consistency was always elusive. They were the excess of the people over the people. Because visibility and representation were the rules that regulated their coming into being, they understood that visual representation was the ontological form of the social. They were everywhere and comprised the entire horizon even if few among the high modernists seemed to see them.[77] This failure to see shows the difficulties revolutionary intellectuals faced when the objects of their redemptive pedagogy turned into the actors of a performance of the popular. There was one more fold to the dialectics of space and recognition ciphered in the discovery of Mexico as extension. Through this fold the discovered cultures of deep Mexico brought to the city landscape a sense of insurgency that confronted the regimes of visibility proper to the metropolitan distribution of the sensible.

The movement that put the masses at the center of the urban spectacle was announced by the increasing purchase of theater as a medium and organizer of public opinion. The predominance of theater as a collectivized expression of experience began in 1915, when national unity itself and the existence of the country as a totality were a matter of doubt rather than a shared certainty.

That year saw the premiere of two of the most popular pieces of revolutionary theater: *Su majestad, el hambre* and *El país de los cartones*.[78] All through the 1920s an increasingly enthusiastic audience accompanied the emergence and consolidation of popular theatrical genres that, in opposition to the coyness and décor of the Porfirian era, did not shy away from the material world of appetites, desires, and antagonisms. As in other places in Latin America, this massive politicization of society through theater used as its vehicle popular genres of Spanish origin such as the *zarzuela*, *sainete*, and all the forms associated with the *género chico*.[79] By 1921 these spectacles were so popular that a reporter complained that "people could conceive of life without food, but not without *tandas*."[80] The reception of these plays in the press was rather ambiguous. Many admired the great popularity of the medium even as they lamented the nonsensical nature of the spectacle. Much of this criticism was of elitist origin and duplicated the marked ambivalence that the lettered city held towards the popular as a set of presentable aesthetic attributes (dances, crafts, food) and the popular as the imminence of political transformation. Even several years after the apogee of the *género chico*, *El Universal Ilustrado* would welcome the experimental Teatro de Ulises (linked to the group Los Contemporáneos) as "a very serious step in the direction of a depuration of Mexican theater."[81]

The postrevolutionary government, on the other hand, immediately realized the propagandistic potential of theater and tried to harness it for its own institutional goals. Gandhi Baca Barajas notes that whereas in the 1910 celebration "police fended off '*calzonudos, rotos y descosidos*'" from the city center, the 1921 festivities, in contrast, were marked by government subsidies for over a half-million theater tickets for "male and female workers" in addition to support for theaters so they could run their shows for eight uninterrupted days.[82] Likewise, the postrevolutionary regime favored local productions and their themes through the taxation of foreign companies and the financial assistance offered to local theaters. After 1921 a series of theaters like the Lírico (the favorite of Obregón and de la Huerta) or the María Guerrero (frequented by the muralists) opened a staggering number of brief sardonic pieces of political character. Obregón, de la Huerta, and minister of foreign affairs Alberto Pani would share a restaurant table with the most renowned playwrights of the time—like Guz Aguila (the stage name of Antonio Guzmán Aguilera)—and would suggest plots and jokes that were later transposed onto the stage.[83] Remarkably, some of these jokes would be censored by municipal inspectors.

Although *La noche mexicana* and theatrical plays were qualitatively different phenomena, they shared a modern ideology that saw the capacity for aesthetic representation as a precondition for figural or actual enfranchisement.

It was the Porfirian interdiction upon the poor to appear in downtown Mexico City in 1910 that suddenly endowed the image of the peasant with an immediate political meaning. But interdiction was not enough to turn the despised image of the peasant into a positive political force. Further techniques of representation and self-presentation were also required. These techniques could dialogue with forms of artistic representation such as theater, but in their essence they surpassed the limited sphere of artistic representation. Their stage was the street, the park, the bar, the market, and the modalities of their coming into being unveiled a sort of popular anatomo-politics—to use Foucault's expression. The common of the community was enormously expanded by the spectaclelike nature of the social. Perhaps the community itself—its purchase—only arises through this doubling, by which those acting see themselves acting. They become one in the disaggregating irony of this doubling. Significantly, the Aguascalientes convention that decided the immediate future of the revolution took place in a theater, the Teatro Morelos, but it was also in itself a theatrical spectacle of sorts. Every day, comments Ramírez Plancarte, "A multitude waited outside and as soon as the doors flung open they would run up the stairs to take their seats in the middle of crazy and noisy uproar." Once inside the theater, the public laughed at the "tortuous lucubration of some delegates, at their speeches plagued with idioms, popular sayings and often, utter nonsense. . . . The delegates' lack of knowledge about how to behave in an assembly, their multiplied ridiculous Daltonian gestures, and in general, the bizarre and maddening direction of the debates was a source of constant amusement." Admission, of course, was free and to everybody's joy, "a band played in the middle of laughs, clapping and screams."[84]

In the early 1920s popular theater and the spectacle of the masses met foremost around the streets and plazas of popular and working-class neighborhoods, where *carpas* lined the streets offering all kinds of shows usually charged with political comments and social criticism. The markets of Lagunilla or La Merced were full of street performances characterized by constant interactions with the passing public. Less prudish than the industrial cinema of the 1930s, these spectacles concentrated in a single plot or stage the various figures that made up the new social landscape characterized by mass migration and disorganized urban growth. The representation of new and often marginal social characters—such as prostitutes and slickers—combined with constant references to everyday events and a fluid dialogue between improvising actors and public produced a politically charged spectacle that called for a good deal of municipal supervision. Under Porfirismo municipal inspectors had expressly prohibited any interaction between public and performers, and while the authorities of the 1920s might have wished for a similar provision, it was impracticable in a social horizon characterized by the daily contestation of political positions and the popular classes' new sense of rights.[85] Of this other stage we have a very few, precious accounts. The spectacles of September 1921 were above all a lesson in self-representation. Through them, masses of people learned a choreography that often overlapped with their existence. Some extracted a source of pride from cultural configurations that had been previously despised, or at least sanitized as an element of the past, but that were now celebrated as the common language of the present. Perhaps to the surprise of the state, the indigenous identified with the popular came into focus as a potential site of state intervention and of a future "bio-popu-politics." We do not need historical hindsight to know that the vindication of the indigenous was partial, incomplete, and even hypocritical. But just as the popular was not the popular, the Indian was not the Indian, but rather the name or the concept of an unfulfilled promise. What was at stake in the construction of an operational notion of "popular culture"—and here the figure of the indigenous was essential—was the possibility of translating what was lived in actual experience as an emanation of "them" into a politically encompassing notion of "us." This operation did not simply trade on objects, forms of affect, or patterns of behavior. It was also and fundamentally a transmutation of life-forms into political forms. The negative without had to become the negative within. Such was the alchemy that the centennial celebration of 1921 found so difficult to perform and from which it extracted both its paradoxical success and its lasting appeal.

CHAPTER THREE

Depth

IN *DEATH AND THE IDEA OF MEXICO*, CLAUDIO LOMNITZ asks why, instead of adopting the posture of an enlightened and forgiving leader, Benito Juárez decided to execute Maximilian. His answer is tied to the two colonial wars that threatened Mexico with its disappearance: the Mexican-American War of 1846 and the French (supported by the British and Spanish fleets) intervention of 1861.

> The declaration of Mexico's second—post-imperial—independence was authenticated with an act of regicide, the execution of Maximilian of Hapsburg in 1867. . . . [Victor] Hugo proposed forgiveness and clemency . . . but Juárez chose instead . . . to present Europe with the spectacle of its own death, just as Mexico has been forced to ponder its mortality. The execution of Maximilian of Hapsburg at once certified the resilience of the postcolonial condition and sent a shuddering premonition of the end of colonial empires.[1]

For Lomnitz, the execution of Maximilian represents the dismissal of a form of sovereignty incarnated in the person of the emperor in favor of another one anchored in the immovable nature of the territory and the fatality of a population tied to it. When Juárez decided to execute Maximilian, he explicitly invoked the indigenous nation as the fundamental sovereign principle in Mexico. The regicide was "a vengeance against the death of Motecuhzoma and Cuauhtémoc," and the right to execute the foreign prince was grounded on the fact that modern Mexicans were "heirs of the aborigine Aztec nation," and as such "they will not abide by foreign rulers or judges."[2]

Now, the foreignness of Maximilian could not grant, by simple inversion, the land as the property of those who claimed it as their own. The imperfect rapport between land and people is a constant subject in the writings of travelers to Mexico at least since the time of Alexander von Humboldt in the early nineteenth century. Many of those foreign visitors doubted that the abject Indians that populated Mexico could in any way be related to the luminous races that had built the majestic pre-Columbian temples of Mesoamerica.[3] After the revolution, the protracted question of the correspondence between people and territory was once again on the table.

In chapter 2 I discussed how the discovery of Mexico qua extension resulted in an awareness of the importance of local differences. According to Enrique Florescano, the revolution uncovered "a veritable stratigraphy [the reference is to Gamio's stratigraphic method] of different cultures sharing the same political space."[4] How are these differences related to the political space they are said to share? Or more plainly: How do Mexicans belong to Mexico? The naturalization of the population—its anchoring to the land—is the specific problem addressed by the discourses of depth.

A postcolonial country after all, Mexico entrusted two distinctive discursive formations with the task of reconciling territory and habitation: Hispanism (or national philology) and *indigenismo*. The latter carried more weight in the early process of state formation, as attested by the several state institutions created for the purpose of facilitating the assimilation of the indigenous into the mainstream of modern Mexico.

Unlike other areas of Latin America, in Mexico literature did not play a fundamental role in the establishment of an *indigenista* discourse in the 1920s and '30s.[5] We do not find there an arch of authors comparable to the ones who provided Andean *indigenismo* with its remarkable political purchase. It will not be until the 1950s that a vigorous *indigenista* literature emerges with the so-called Chiapas cycle. But by the time Rosario Castellanos published *Balún Canán* (1957), thirty years of official *indigenista* discourse had brought together universities, state agencies, and political middlemen concerned with economic cooperation and development; these forces had already completely permeated and even modeled the notion of the indigenous in Mexico. So powerful was the construction of the indigenous in the terms dictated by the social sciences that, as late as 1954, a retrospective on *indigenismo* edited by Alfonso Caso had no section devoted specifically to literature; nor, indeed, was there any mention of *indigenista* literature in the different articles.[6] Whereas in the Andes *indigenismo* acted as a powerful criticism of the process of modernization, the relative lack of a similar movement in Mexico would have considerable consequences for literature and for state *indigenismo* alike. I say "relative lack" of an *indigenista* discourse because certainly there were works portraying the indigenous published in the years following the revolution. But they were understood, almost without exception, as belonging to a social rather than a cultural canon. Joseph Sommers rightly ascribes novels like *El Indio* (1935), by Gregorio López y Fuentes, to social awareness brought about by the revolution rather than to a proper *indigenista* movement.[7]

The construction of the indigenous undertaken by the social sciences answered to the most immediate political concerns of the time, and above all to the need to implement processes of political identification able to turn an amorphous mass of *gente* into a more or less stable political body.[8] The lack of a strong literary discourse to mediate this process meant, in practice, that *indigenismo* was not undertaken in Mexico as a criticism of modernity but rather as the confirmation of this modernity's core values. The goal of promoting an indigenous identity amenable to incorporation into the mainstream of Mexican life entered into direct conflict with the desire to flesh out the abstract policies of liberalism, something that could only be done by stressing rather than suppressing those features that set the Indian aside from creole society.

This dual orientation towards the indigenous creates some marked contradictions in the politics of the postrevolutionary state. Nineteenth-century abstract liberalism—to use Vasconcelos's expression—had banished the *ejido*, thus depriving indigenous communities of their means of subsistence. The 1917 constitution restituted the *ejido* but did not match its economic independence from liberal and capitalist forms of accumulation to any corresponding political form of autonomy. Instead, it engulfed the *ejido* within the larger juridical and political order of liberalism.[9] After the revolution, the municipality became the center of the political life of rural communities. Any alternative to the authority of the municipality was expressively prohibited. The goal of such a prohibition was to prevent the reemergence of the Porfirian system of "political bosses" (*jefaturas*) but in practice it made illegal the autonomous forms of indigenous self-government that had resurfaced along with the *ejidal* tradition.[10]

The goal of state policies was to recognize and respect indigenous differences in order to force these groups into modern governmentality. Hence, the indigenous were perceived as simultaneously malleable and unchangeable, immediately accessible and irremediably lost. What Luis Villoro describes as the antinomy of modern *indigenismo* in the work of Manuel Gamio "presents us with a double perspective: a culture completely alien to us that is perceived however as the source of our [cultural] uniqueness."[11] In the hands of official *indigenismo* recalcitrance and educability became two sides of the same coin. While indigenous imperviousness to change was the epitome of cultural authenticity, their essential aptitude for education made indigenous populations an ideal target of state pedagogy. It was the indigenous communities' constitutive inability to go beyond the most immediate conditions of existence that grounded their privileged relationship to the land. However, since, strictly speaking, these communities were not so much attuned to the land they inhabited as they were its prisoners, official *indigenismo* could also present itself as a battle cry for their liberation.[12]

The second discourse in which the function of depth was incarnated was that of Spanish philology, whose rank and file was constituted by the creole population of Europeanized outlook and sensibility. The colonial legacy played out quite differently in the case of the creoles. Unlike the Indian, who felt home at home, creole consciousness exhibited an anxiety around out-of-placeness that constantly betrayed its origin in the realm of colonial privilege. Far from providing a respite to this sense of homelessness, independence confronted the creoles with an even more pervasive sense of out-of-placeness. Alfonso Reyes never tired of denouncing the fundamental mismatch that characterized even the most successful of those nineteenth-century experiments in social containment: Porfirism. The word that pervasively appears to designate the rule of Don Porfirio is *fiction*. In "Visión de Anáhuac," Reyes opposes fiction to fiction in order to remedy the fundamental inadequacy of the Mexican in his or her home, and if the result seems deceptive from an ontological point of view, it can still be rescued from contradiction by the value of work contained in the operation.

Ricardo Pérez Montfort, among others, has voiced the conviction that throughout Mexican history, "*indigenismo* and *hispanismo* represented conflicting stances" insofar as they produced opposite valuations of the colonial experience.[13] As Pérez Montfort perceives, what is striking in this story is the relative lack of a transcultural mediation between scientific *indigenismo* and Spanish philology as privileged forms of inscribing subjects and populations in the thickness of the land. The concluding argument of this chapter is that this sort of transcultural solution is provided in the discourse (and realities) of architecture. To this end, I revisit the polemics that confronted the partisans of functionalist and colonialist architecture since the early years of postrevolutionary rule.

INDIGENISMO

In the postrevolutionary context, official *indigenismo* designated from the beginning a series of political, social, and academic practices that created an indigenous identity for some groups in such a way that the very existence of these groups authorizes—when it does not demand—state intervention in the countryside. This line of action was anticipated in *Los gran-*

des problemas nacionales, the book that Andrés Molina Enríquez published in 1908, which can be seen as the birth certificate of modern *indigenismo* in Mexico. The book offers a vindicatory discourse on the indigenous mixed with biopolitical recommendations grounded on a conceptual grid that pays special attention to environmental, physical, and alimentary variables of the Mexican population. Molina Enríquez presented here one of the first estimates of the racial makeup of the Mexican nation: of the 14 million persons living in Mexico, 4.9 million were Indian and 7 million mestizos. Twelve of these 14 million (almost exactly the sum of mestizos and Indians) survived on a diet almost exclusively based on corn and beans. Despite the sharp contrast Molina Enríquez drew between Indians and mestizos on the one hand and the white population on the other, it is clear that he saw the frontiers between the groups as mobile rather than as racially fixed. After the revolution, Molina Enríquez himself grew less concerned with the Indian and more preoccupied with the peasant, directing much of his efforts to consolidating agrarian laws, whose general blueprint in the 1917 constitution bears his mark.

In the 1920s indigenous issues, with all their conceptually slippery makeup, were put under the purview of two of the most influential intellectuals of the Obregón-Calles period: Manuel Gamio, head of the Dirección de Antropología at the UNAM and in charge of the excavation of Teotihuacán; and José Vasconcelos, creator of the SEP, who launched a vast literacy campaign that often targeted areas of dense indigenous population. In 1926 Gamio and Vasconcelos were invited by the Harris Foundation to offer their visions on the Mexican Revolution at a series of conferences held at the University of Chicago.[14] The opinions of the creator of the SEP and of the director of the Department of Anthropology could not have been more at odds. Vasconcelos's distrust and scorn for Gamio were never a secret. He resented Gamio's proximity to American culture, his training under Franz Boas, and even his doctorate from Columbia University. Vasconcelos's animosity was in part based on a deep disagreement about the true nature of the Mexican nation. Vasconcelos saw the essence of Mexicanness incarnated in a mestizo transcultural ethos whose glue was Catholicism. Gamio contested this picture of the country as simply unrealistic. There was no integrated Mexico; Indians were exploited and despised by their creole counterparts; and the Catholic Church had failed to unify the Mexican people. In a move that surely scandalized Vasconcelos, Gamio went as far as to champion the replacement of the Catholic Church by Protestantism in indigenous areas. While for Vasconcelos deep Mexico needed to be protected because it was the site of constitution for a unified, undivided Mexican political body, for Gamio it was necessary to intervene in deep Mexico because it was the repository of a system of cemented injustices which, if left unaddressed, would forever haunt the constitution of a modern nation. In Vasconcelos's view, Gamio's style of *indigenismo*—which would later favor the arrival of the controversial Summer Institute of Linguistics (SIL) to Mexico—was necessarily bound to a discriminatory outlook of Mexico. Moreover, he saw in the ethnographic passion of the early revolutionary period a biopolitical dispositive that would give access to deep Mexico to an array of bureaucrats and technicians who represented a centralizing Mexican state armed with intrusive forms of authority.

In practical terms, there were no stark differences between the agendas of Gamio and Vasconcelos, and both men were able to secure significant financial support from the Mexican government. Although costly, these interventions into indigenous and popular areas allowed the state to deliver immediate proof of its inclusive vocation.[15] If the Indian-other could become a citizen, the legitimacy that the state borrowed from the future was fully warranted. Additionally, an *indigenismo* thoroughly permeated by biopolitical concerns provided an immediate point of articulation for state disciplines to address realities that were perceived as chaotic and unformed. In few areas could the Mexican state enjoy the illusion of flexing its bureaucratic muscles with such freedom of imagination.[16]

Following the double matrix of the Indian as intractable and malleable, both Gamio and Vasconcelos understood their task as one of respectfully approaching a distant culture while actively intervening in its practical redemption. Vasconcelos's *misiones culturales* or Gamio's research in Teotihuacán were (at least theoretically) endowed with the authority to challenge and redraw social relationships out of tune with the fundamental principles of the revolutionary government. Vasconcelos requested his *misioneros* to provide information that ranged from social practices that could be perceived as feudal to allegations of corruption of local bosses. He personally oversaw the dismantling of prostitution rings. In Teotihuacán, Gamio distributed lands, founded schools, organized workshops where the indigenous communities learned to work the minerals that abounded in the area, erected theaters, and even produced a movie. He tried to enforce an eight-hour working schedule and implemented a vaccination campaign.[17] The political vocation of these initiatives explains the fact that, despite working in such a rich archaeological site as Teotihuacán, Gamio was unwilling to turn archaeology into the science of depth in Mexico and conceded that privilege to sociology and ethnography instead. The whole project of Teotihuacán—a project that began as archaeology but ended up as ethnography—showed the irresistible pull that the possibility of political transformation had for the intellectuals of the period.

There was an important obstacle to be overcome in this transition from archaeology to ethnography. The designation *Indio* was enigmatic in a country where aboriginal communities had been the subject of intense processes of miscegenation, most especially following the tradition, started in the sixteenth century, of forcing different ethnic groups into single pueblos.[18] Indianness was often the result of a laborious process of interpretation that sometimes, but not always, included processes of self-adscription. An Indian was an Indian, but he or she was also simply a peasant or a day laborer. In the 1930s, proficiency in an indigenous language was the sole criteria to identify somebody as Indian (with the complication that subsequent censuses would categorize the same person as creole if he or she succeeded in communicating with the census employee in Spanish).

VASCONCELOS AT THE SEP AND GAMIO IN TEOTIHUACÁN

The approaches that the SEP took towards the indigenous question changed considerably over a period of twenty years. They were more intuitive and humanistic under Vasconcelos's tenure as secretary (1921–1924) but became increasingly more "scientific" and better articulated with the state disciplinary apparatus under José Manuel Puig Casauranc (1924–1928) and Narciso Bassols (1931–1934). Vasconcelos's own involvement with indigenous education was brief and uninformed. As the creole ideologue that he was, Vasconcelos downplayed indigenous autonomy in favor of its rapid incorporation into the mainstream of Mexican society, or rather into what he imagined that mainstream to be. The minister encouraged his missionaries to liquidate the links tying the communities to behaviors perceived as atavistic and premodern. He was fiercely opposed to literacy in indigenous languages and attacked Yucatán's experiment with Indian empowerment under Felipe Carillo Puerto.[19] And yet, there was in Vasconcelos—as David Brading notes—a romantic kernel that greatly moderated his policies towards indigenous groups.[20] This romantic kernel is visible in his multiple calls to avoid the resettlement of Indians or to interfere as little as possible with forms of habitation that had become functional to the communities. Although Vasconcelos contributed very little to the formation of an indigenous discourse in Mexico, his missionaries produced the first reliable reports on indigenous communities, their ways of life, and the points of resistance to the pedagogical enterprise launched by the SEP.

While Vasconcelos started the first postrevolutionary policies towards indigenous Mexico, Gamio was busy with the excavation and restoration of Teotihuacán. Gamio's involvement with anthropology was facilitated by Franz Boas's arrival in Mexico for the opening of the International School of Archaeology and Ethnology in 1911. Boas was at that point the best-known proponent of cultural relativism and a strong critic of race-based theories of culture and society. Gamio collaborated with Boas and tried to apply his teachings to Mexico, although without fully renouncing eugenics as an interpretive framework. After the excavation of Teotihuacán and the subsequent publication of *La población del valle de Teotihuacán,* Gamio was awarded a PhD from Columbia University where Boas was teaching at the time. In 1917 Gamio was put in charge of the Dirección de Antropología by Venustiano Carranza. By that time, he was a well-known figure in Mexico, although many considered him to be an essayist rather than an anthropologist. In 1915 Gamio had won a literary contest organized by the newspaper *El Mexicano,* and in 1916 he published an acclaimed book, *Forjando patria,* that president Obregón recommended as mandatory reading in Mexican schools and of which he bought one hundred copies to distribute among his apparently many friends.

In *Forjando patria* Gamio announced that the science of anthropology was indispensable for the modernization of Mexico, since only an anthropological gaze could scientifically explain the reasons why a good part of the Mexican population was submerged in an economy of mere survival. Consequently, knowledge of indigenous populations was not predicated upon any need to build a true intercultural reach. Such knowledge was conceived since the beginning as part of an effort to modernize and transform indigenous groups. For this task Gamio enrolled two distinctive languages: a deeply transformed eugenic paradigm that bespoke the concerns of the state under a strong biopolitical tonality; and a culturalist ethnography put in charge of providing the communities with their own reflection. To this latter sphere belonged the extraordinary experiment of "synthetic theater," in which indigenous "actors" performed for hours their everyday chores before a mesmerized audience.[21] So, while Gamio the militant ethnographer deployed his cultural anthropology as a tool for transforming the valley, Gamio the state expert attempted to present the valley as representative of the dilemmas afflicting the whole nation along the lines of a modern governmentality.

The excavation, classification, and partial restoration of Teotihuacán was an archaeological feat whose achievements are even more notorious in light of lack of proper financial support and properly trained personnel for the task.[22] However, *La población del valle de Teotihuacán* was not a record of that achievement—not even a catalogue of the thousand of fragments and pieces (which would reach the millions with future excavations) that were recovered from the site. The book was a politically motivated ethnography of the current inhabitants of the valley adjacent to the archaeological site. Teotihuacán, Claudio Lomnitz observes, suited Gamio's intent to generalize the indigenous conditions in the valley and apply them to vast areas of the country.[23] The fluid frontiers between the indigenous and the nonindigenous favored Gamio's strategy.[24] As Gamio was always quick to point out, Teotihuacán was located no more than forty-three kilometers from the Zócalo. Right there, at the heart of the state of Mexico, a population left to its own—as Vasconcelos would have liked it—showed an astonishing index of malnutrition and infant mortality. While Gamio accepted that the frontiers between the indigenous and the mestizo were pliable, one of the goals of the study was to produce a reliable paradigm for categorizing a population as indigenous. To this end Gamio hastily educated a host of anthropologists to a view of alterity that was designed not so much to perform the scientific work of revelation as to facilitate state policies in these unassimilated areas of the country. *La población del valle de Teotihuacán* disaggregates the features of the indigenous culture into productive and unproductive, normal and abnormal, beneficial and pernicious. The idea behind this grid was that indigenous culture could be maintained, although some of its specific features—like alcoholism or diet—could be modified. For instance, since ceramics produced in the valley could not please modern tastes, they were hopelessly antieconomical and had to be transformed. For every ethnographic insight, there was therefore a corresponding piece of policy.

The perception of a seamless transition between ethnographic research and state building betrays the populist fervor of the political moment. Gamio wrote under the deep conviction that the postrevolutionary order that he represented stood in a relationship with the people that almost identified it with them. In 1921 government was, in Gamio's eyes, self-government. This is why he could simultaneously present his research as the groundwork for a project of governmentality and write that previous designs to manage rural populations had failed because they represented "governmental schemes that are imposed upon them."[25] Science could lend its own neutrality to the state as scientific discourse became the unavoidable companion to good government. In Mexico a politics that was not attuned to the deep truth of rural populations could only brew degeneracy or revolution.

Experimental Indigenismo

Like Gamio in Teotihuacán, Vasconcelos's teachers and missionaries were often confronted with communities that presented an uneven combination of creole and indigenous elements. The intractability that so often characterizes the idea of the *Indio* was somewhat attenuated in those locations. However, the confrontation with isolated and monolingual indigenous groups proved to be an obstacle that the SEP could not ignore. In a context marked by a sophisticated awareness of cultural difference, the intellectuals of the SEP soon came to the realization that an external agency was powerless to confront the stationary drive of the most removed indigenous localities. As José Carlos Mariátegui was also concluding at the time, only the Indian could redeem the Indian. This idea is at the base of one of the wildest cultural experiments of postrevolutionary Mexico: La Casa del Estudiante Indígena. This unique institution was a hospice located in Mexico City for carefully selected indigenous youth and designed to improve on the results of Vasconcelos's *casas del pueblo*. The *casas del pueblo*—of which Vasconcelos inaugurated some three hundred and which reached around seven thousand by 1932[26]—were also called *escuelas rurales*. The confusion was justified because these places of instruction and schooling were also conceived of as communal centers in which a whole pueblo could reflect on its cultural and economic practices and transform them. La Casa del Estudiante Indígena, active between 1925 and 1932, partially preserved this holistic view but sought to isolate its pupils from their original cultural contexts in the belief that proximity to the community could perpetuate some undesirable features of indigenous life. Conversely, removing students from their native environment could accelerate their transformation into leaders formed in the ideals of the postrevolutionary state. La Casa was conceived of as a sociobiological—even psychological (President Calles's designation)—experiment able to offer "incontrovertible proof of the Indian's capacity for assimilation."[27]

Alexander Dawson, who wrote the most authoritative study of La Casa, notes that the school—which accepted only young male students—both contested and confirmed the discourse of racialization, since it demanded "pure" Indians to prove in the end that purity could be easily overcome through education. Instruction did not take place in the casa itself. Instead, students enrolled in nearby schools. The rationale for having indigenous students taking classes in regular schools was emulation, biologically referenced as *contagio* in the official documents.

La Casa closed after a critical evaluation by an SEP inspector. The report pointed out that La Casa was a very costly experiment that was not delivering the results it promised. It was not that the institution had failed to integrate students into a creole lifestyle. If we discount those who fled or were expelled, it did so perhaps too well. The critical report lamented that students would not return home, "because they feel repugnance for rural living, and a repulsion for life amongst their brothers."[28] Posterior assessment of the school challenged these views and conceived of the school in a much more positive light. As the authorities of the SEP knew, similar institutions were implemented with some success in other areas of Latin America, such as Bolivia.[29] However, Mexico offered unique challenges since its indigenous population was more fragmented and less known than that of the Andes. Whereas in Bolivia equivalent institutions would deal with students of one or two linguistic groups—thus allowing instruction in native languages—in its first year alone La Casa accepted two hundred students representing twenty-four different linguistic groups at a time when it was estimated that there were around eighty indigenous languages spoken vigorously in Mexican territory.[30]

After the fiasco of La Casa, the SEP essayed the opposite move and sent groups of prestigious sociologists and anthropologists to live among Indians in Carapan, Michoacán. Led by Moisés Sáenz, the group opened the so-called "experimental station for the incorporation of the Indian." The strategy opposed the theory of "contagion" with a cultural and scientific embassy. The project was a resounding failure. All kinds of tensions exploded in Carapan, and Sáenz and his colleagues decided to abandon the station in view of an increasingly dangerous animosity against their presence. A deeply disillusioned Sáenz noted later that roads rather than schools could be the best way to favor indigenous incorporation into the mainstream of Mexican life.[31]

Faced with the evidence that both the strategy of bringing indigenous students to Mexico City as well as that of reaching out to communities through the *misiones culturales* had yielded poor returns, the SEP began to question its assimilationist project. In the early years of the 1930s, a group of pedagogues and anthropologists informed by the latest trends in education—especially the work of John Dewey—began to push for a culturally open, anti-assimilationist notion of indigenous education. An important step in this direction was the creation of the *internados indígenas*. The *internados*—as its name indicates—favored the containment of students who were now, however, located inside indigenous communities. As in the case of La Casa, the idea was to produce indigenous teachers and leaders able to help in the modernization of their own societies. The *internados* were farm schools of sorts where Indians (but once again the denomination was unstable at the best) of both sexes would live and establish an economy of self-subsistence that was as integrated as possible to local conditions. Material conditions in the *internados* often approached levels of absolute misery. Despite these difficulties, rural education certainly made its dent into the nonincorporated masses of deep Mexico. By 1936 the *internados indígenas* had produced thousands of bilingual teachers willing to return home as state employees. By that time the *internados* had changed their name to *centros de educación indígena* and had partly changed their function. Although communities resisted at the outset, in the inaugural years of Lázaro Cárdenas's government (1934–1940) over one hundred communities requested the establishment of new *internados* on their lands. In hindsight, one can see that the relative success of Cárdenas's administration to soften indigenous resistance to state education was based on the strategy of turning an educational and technical problem into a political one.

The enthusiasm over indigenous education in the Cardenista period was part of a political mobilization in which communities' relationship with the state was perceived to be a tool to increase the economic viability of indigenous pueblos. The failure of Sáenz at Carapan was in part due to his own misperception of the community as simple, undivided, and even atavistic. As Sáenz would later come to know, opposition to the mission was politically orchestrated in a community that already had a good deal of internal political differentiation. It was the image of the indigenous that Sáenz and his team had mounted that contributed to the defeat of their cause. When it came to local politics, Cardenismo never lacked regional experts on the ground. Cardenismo was able to build upon a previous politicization of the communities through a strategy that we now call "empowerment." It was Cárdenas's promise of trucks, machinery, and technology that made a partnership with the state attractive. Technology carried with it the promise of more, not less, autonomy, and in that sense it completely reversed the logic that efforts for indigenous education had followed so far. The tensions and negotiations that characterized the deployment of state initiatives in different localities created a dynamic quite alien to the idyllic image of the undisturbed indigenous community that had made it an ideal object of redemption in the first place. Mexico's consciousness of the indigenous problem was vastly transformed in the process—at a distance of less than fifteen years from those descriptions of María Bibiana Uribe picking wildflowers in her native forest.

Literature: A Just-in-Time Intervention

In 1950, Luis Villoro published a book of great intellectual subtlety, *Los grandes momentos del indigenismo en México*. In this work, Villoro, a philosopher by training and vocation, denounced the asymmetry that presided over the indigenous question: "We speak about the Indian. We measure him. We judge him. But we do not feel measured and judged by him."[32] Villoro is not saying that Indians do not judge the creoles, but just that the latter do not feel, *cannot* feel, the gaze of the Indian upon them.

Lecturing to his students in 1956, Alfonso Caso confirmed the accuracy of Villoro's diagnostic. When it came to the indigenous it was not useful to put much weight on history or archaeology, the well-established Caso told his audience. It was more important to "awaken . . . the conviction that we, modern Mexicans, have an ineludible obligation . . . to be sensible towards a problem that concerns at least 10 percent of our country's population."[33] In his conferences, Caso manages the feat of talking for pages and pages about *indigenismo* without using the word "*Indio*." In fact, Caso's conference on *indigenismo* is an almost pure example of Hispanism. The authors he quotes, reads, and discusses are all Spanish colonial authorities, and the Indians he envisions are statistical nuances best expressed in the language of percentiles.

Confronted by the mystifying effects that the discourse of the social sciences built around the indigenous question, one is tempted to reverse the traditional posture that sees cultural studies as a corrective to the intrinsic elitism of literature. In the case of Mexican *indigenismo*, the belated but essential flourishing of an *indigenista* novel came to the rescue of an image of the indigenous more or less completely fossilized, either in the reveries of film or in the dubitative abstractions produced by the alliance of academics and state functionaries.[34]

Given the unique development of Mexican *indigenismo*, it is understandable that when a vigorous *indigenista* literature finally arose, many of its writers were anthropologists or had some type of anthropological training.[35] Their most representative works are linked to what Joseph Sommers calls the "cycle of Chiapas." The cycle is rather brief—it extends from Ramón Rubín's *El callado dolor de los tzotziles: Novela de Indios* (1949) to Ricardo Pozas's *Juan Pérez Jolote: Biografía de un Tzotzil* (1952) to Rosario Castellanos's *Oficio de tinieblas* (1962)—and it comprises less than ten novels written by a few writers (Ramón Rubín, Rosario Castellanos, Carlo Antonio Castro, María Lombardo de Caso, Eraclio Zepeda, and Ricardo Pozas). The cycle owes much of its reputation to its testimonial impetus, which is skillfully combined with sophisticated narrations that seek to produce a nonexotic view of the indigenous.

Against these intentions, Rosario Castellanos presents an image of the indigenous colored by a recalcitrant and almost unsalvageable cultural difference in *Oficio de tinieblas*. In the novel an antagonism is neatly draw along the lines of a ladino culture and its urban center, Ciudad Real, and a Tzotzil counterpart. Indians and creoles seem to carry on a symbiotic relationship that is marked, however, by constant violence and a traumatic memory that often makes the origins of social frustration impossible to signify. Signification is the real business of this literature and ultimately the exclusive hero of its stories.

Set against the background of Cárdenas's land reforms, *Oficio de tinieblas* refuses to let this political framework become the hermeneutical key to the action—as happened with social novels of the revolution such as López's *El Indio*. Meaning itself is in dispute in the novel. Official, scientific *indigenismo* did not for a second doubt the intrinsic communicability of human reason. But official *indigenismo* was more reluctant to consider the possibility that such an optimism—progressive as it was—was simply an alibi for the forceful universalization of its own worldview. A novel like *Oficio de tinieblas*, on the other hand, makes manifest the multiple forms of exploitation and injustice suffered by the Chamulas, whose whole world appears incommensurable to the logic of cultural universalism promoted by the state. The novel places at the center of its argument the absence of a common language and the lack of bonds and linguistic affects able to translate between what are still, after all, worlds set apart.

Although intended perhaps as an attack on the official failure to recognize and address an indigenous situation, Castellanos's novel (she was a steady employee of the Instituto Nacional de Indigenista [INI]) exhibits also a marked ambivalence towards the intercultural dialogue that it proposes. While on the one hand *Oficio de tinieblas* belies the nationalist dream of a hegemonic seamless articulation of reality, on the other hand it shares with the whole postrevolutionary order the belief in expression as the ultimate ground upon which to constitute the postcolonial nation.

The situation is exemplified in the figure of Marcela, a young Chamula Indian who is sexually abused by a ladino while she tries to sell her merchandise in Ciudad Real. Catalina—the powerful *illoy* [a kind of benevolent sorceress] of Castellanos's novel—guesses what has happened to Marcela with just one look and uses this knowledge to take Marcela away from her abusive mother. Back at her jacal, Catalina introduces Marcela to her husband laconically:

> "She is estranged from her mother and she lives with me now."
>
> And then, faced with the interrogating gesture of her husband, she explains, "A Caxlan abused her."
>
> These words transform Marcela's inner world. Since the assault, the world has been hazy and unreal: she repeated the phrase over and over: "A Caxlan abused her." Yes. That is what happened. Something that was possible to say, something that others could hear and understand and not the vertigo, the madness. She sighed, relieved.[36]

The words are not new. They preexist Marcela and this is the reason she can understand them. She knew what happened to her, but this knowledge itself could not be expressed except negatively through some form of silence or conceptual abjection. It would always be possible to read Catalina's ventriloquism of Marcela's inner feelings as an invasive move in which the relationship between Spanish itself and the indigenous language is implicated. But I do not think that this is the case. By using the verb "to abuse," Catalina discloses a whole world whose complexity Marcela cannot simply reject as alien because qua the abused person she is already inscribed in its horizon. She is part of this world, not as a recognized subject of right, but as a recognizable one. She is, as a matter of fact, a member of two worlds superimposed by the word *abusó*.

Language plays an enormous role in *Oficio de tinieblas*, and at one moment or another all characters, Indians and ladinos alike, are captured in the frenzy of its evocative power. But in highlighting expression as a form of cure—Marcela gets over her trauma through Catalina's words—the novel also underscores a function of language that is intrinsically modern. As a function of speech, expression brings myriad subjectifying effects with it. Interestingly, the recalcitrance usually associated with indigenous discourses has to do with the lack of expression proper to them. Indigenous verbal repertoire is tied instead to functions that are confirmatory, therapeutic, ritualistic, apotropaic, or performative in nature but are rarely expressive. If the word *expression* still seems necessary, this is so in light of the notion of the indigenous fabricated by *indigenismo*, an image in which Indians are possessors of and possessed by a secret that defines them as proper objects of an ethnographic gaze. And this is the paradox of *indigenismo* as a discourse of depth: it has to reach its other through a language that cannot be uttered without violating the conditions of its authenticity. From this point of view, the project of *indigenismo* is not that different from that of Hispanism, at least as that project was incarnated in the figure of Alfonso Reyes, to whom I turn in the next section.

ALFONSO REYES: EXPRESSION AT ALL COSTS

It is perhaps the lack of extensive bibliographical references combined with the remarkable elegance of his prose that gives Alfonso Reyes's style—the best of all styles according to Jorge Luis Borges—its aura of effortlessness. Against this pretense, Robert Conn speaks of the creation of "a massive literary institution" that allowed Reyes to start an intellectual current that deeply altered the conceptual map of Mexican culture.[37] Reyes's work appears doubly implicated in a discourse of scientific aspirations—that of Spanish philology—and a search for expression to which his unique and evocative style is testament. His mastery of philological discourse provides enormous authority to his words and adds to the aura of his intellectual persona. His creative intervention in the archive of Latin American culture has been repeatedly signaled as containing the grain of political commitment that Reyes himself saw as unavoidable in a Latin American intellectual. And yet, it is Reyes the philologist that Carlos Monsiváis invokes when he argues that even those texts that pretend to address lofty matters are at the service of the consolidation of the postrevolutionary state.[38]

Reyes was not a lonely figure. A vast stream of philological enthusiasm ran through Latin America at the dawn of the twentieth century, when Latin American societies stirred in the current of massive internal migrations, increasing politicization, and the impact that modern forms of living had on the everydayness of their populations. It is in part to anchor the increasing feeling of instability associated with modernization that philology was activated everywhere, in Mexico no more than in Havana, Santiago de Chile, Rio de Janeiro, or Buenos Aires. In all cases, this or that variety of philological reconstruction took a predominant role in the establishment of national, linguistically based, and literarily grounded canons. According to many, Reyes exemplifies better than anybody else the figure of the intellectual philologist.

In an essay on the Mexican intellectual, Sebastiaan Faber sees Reyes's project as oscillating between two figures. On the one hand, Reyes appears to represent an already "extinguished species," true liberal humanists. Among them Faber lists Walter Benjamin, Stefan Zweig, and Erich Auerbach, intellectuals "fully devoted to the study and development of high culture, which they saw as the only effective barrier against increasing chaos and barbarism." On the other hand, the precarious nature of Latin American institutions forced intellectuals like Reyes to remedial, practical tasks that would devour their energies and signal new agendas for their efforts. While the first condition facilitates an image of the humanist intellectual as located beyond political divisions, the second often makes of him or her a social servant.[39] Intellectuals like Reyes and José Ortega y Gasset, Faber continues, are representative of a peculiarly peripheral form of unhappy consciousness that emerges from the unavoidable comparison between their lofty goals and the relative backwardness of their societies.

The most evocative statement that Reyes produced about this malady of consciousness is his famous diagnosis of the Latin American intellectual as having arrived late to the banquet of civilization. Reyes pronounced these words in 1936, in the context of an international conference held in Buenos Aires and devoted to cultural relationships between Europe and Latin America.[40] Jorge Luis Borges—to whom Reyes's figure so often invites comparisons—would have solved the problem by saying that there was never a banquet in the first place. And I believe that at some level Reyes echoed this strategy. The space that Reyes was willing to give to this doubt was minimal and yet it is pervasively inscribed in his subtle practice of irony. In the end, however, the Borgesian solution of an utter fictionalization of the primary scene of culture was unacceptable for Reyes. The ethical sphere weighed on him too much. He felt the urgency to respond to all the interpellations of his world. This is why Monsiváis's reading of Reyes as a state thinker is, although violent, completely legitimate.[41]

The standard interpretation of the missed banquet sees the Latin American man of culture arriving at a civilization whose main historical articulations have already been accomplished. This interpretation is correct but also superficial. When the Latin American intellectual arrives to the banquet, the banquet is over not because everybody left or there are no more ideas to be expressed, but because the unity of art and its utopian force lies in ruin. This ruin is not that of a Winckelmann seeking to generate whole the hermeneutics of a lost world from a deformed torso of Hercules turned almost unrecognizable by the work of the ages. It is a secondhand ruin that entails the shipwreck of art itself against a universe in which culture has ceased to point "to a single evolutionary process."[42] For us, moderns, culture is the name of the crisis that severed the realm of art from the realm of cultivation. It is the fact that we can no longer believe in the healing powers of art—a lesson that Vasconcelos learned at the British Museum—that accounts for the exteriority with which the Latin American intellectual is forced to engage with what remains nonetheless the most fascinating object of contemplation. Art loses its aura—and becomes to some extent culture—insofar as it no longer expresses universal attributes but rather the attributes of a class or a group. Reyes himself lived in a time (and a place) in which the banquet no longer served the circumscribed realm of high culture. Always a lucid thinker, Reyes's only exorbitant indulgence was to ignore this fact. Even if he could attribute to mere exoticism the interest that modernist artists visiting Mexico showed for popular crafts—something he certainly did not do—he could not miss the gesture by which culture refers to something other than the traditional shape of art. The impropriety of the creole intellectual exists now in a double register.

The man of taste reacts to impropriety with a daring act of style. The philologists—those forerunners of structuralism—used to say that the style was the man. We say the style is the subject. Reyes's position before the West as Other is not unlike the position of any subject who is born into a space marked and pervaded by an already apportioned cultural legacy. In the Lacanian tale, the emergence of a true subject is not tied to the discovery of something unique, but rather to patient appropriation through which the subject discovers himself anew. If the process is successful, at the end a style emerges as a compromise formed between the impossibility of a purely creative expression and the abjection of mere repetition. Style is a work of appropriation and, in the same movement, a form of self-foundation. Such is the only strategy left to somebody who arrives late to a place to which he already belongs.

Once a simple, lived identification with tradition becomes impossible, the rapport of the subject of expression to culture must pass through modalities of the disingenuous: irony at the level of expression and criticism as the only possible form of exposition. If the word were not so vacuous, I would even say that Reyes is a *critic*. But the general imprecision of this word is limiting and frustrating. There are literary critics, film critics, or art critics but not "something like a critic." The situation is not improved by saying that by critic we mean philosopher, because the figure—as we will see soon—may not be up to the concept.

The word *critic* was already a charged word in the intellectual circles in which the apprenticeship of the young Reyes played itself out. In an essay first published in 1914, Pedro Henríquez Ureña—the only master that Alfonso Reyes had—writes these disdainful lines on academic texts about literature: "The standard academic judgment, whatever its merit of patient and minute analysis may be, lives in the ignorance of the high functions of criticism."[43] Almost three decades later, when Reyes would write "La crítica en la Edad Ateniense," he showed no more sympathy for the appropriation of the word *critical* to describe literary exegesis.[44] What do these authors mean by *critique*? In Reyes, critique is almost always synonymous with the Enlightenment. Since he often uses the term with technical rigor, a reference to Kant is unavoidable. But Reyes's notion of critique is also clearly post-Kantian, which in this case means postphilosophical. Critique emerges in Reyes at the intersection of literature and philosophy. It renounces neither the claim to the actual nor the seductions of fiction. Even as the intrinsic answerability of the philosophical word seems to prevail upon the conscientious irresponsibility of the literary word, the thinking element cannot remain serene in the dogma of its form because literature has beaten it on its own terrain. Literature, not philosophy, is the real, presuppositionless discourse. Reyes underlines the antidogmatic nature of the literary anytime that a phenomenology of art is at stake: "A literature that champions the good or that avails itself of a system in the search for truth or that is interested in realizing the theoretical notion of the beautiful through strategies similar to those of the philosopher is, beyond doubt, a tendentious literature."[45]

The playful formalism in which Reyes confines the critical principle makes his whole operation hinge upon the mutual supersession of literature and philosophy. Critique wants to enjoy the irresponsibility of literature while exerting the vigilance of philosophy. Now, this critique is by definition devoid of generic consistency, and this is why in Reyes's hand it took the form of the essay.[46] Critique is an impulse that can inhabit the most diverse linguistic or poetic forms, and as a matter of fact, for Reyes it was a poet who took the critical emphasis to its furthest possibilities. In his essays, Reyes borrowed generously from philosophical vocabulary without remaining prisoner to the concepts. Conversely, his writings benefitted from fiction, but not in a restricted literary sense in which fiction is opposed to who-knows-what ghost of reality. They are fictional in the sense that they entail a vast reconfiguration of what counts as real and as fiction—fictional in the way in which they declare that we inhabit the fictions that we set out to analyze.

Reyes's strategy of a permanent siege of expression by lucid, rational thought—and, conversely, the permanent ruin of rational thought by the disseminating force of style—recalls the appearance of a modern (romantic) sensibility that is also simultaneously aesthetic and philosophical in nature. In the classical argument of Jean-Luc Nancy and Philippe Lacoue-Labarthe, the romantic crisis emerges once modernity makes impossible the restoration of organic communities, whose perennial model is the Greek city-state. According to Nancy and Lacoue-Labarthe, the open character of the work of art from romanticism to the present is an index of a new artistic disposition, one that acknowledges the necessarily incomplete character of any design, the irremediable loss of any sense of totality.[47] Like the Schlegels, Reyes found a solution to the decentering of his own standing in the world in the value of work. Obviously, the more than one hundred years that elapsed between the Schlegels' *Athenaeum* and Reyes's own Ateneo are bound to leave their mark in the argument. While work meant spiritual creation to the Schlegels, Reyes's painstaking construction of a position of enunciation through the work of style contains an unmistakable reference to work in its restrictive sense of labor. So, even if Reyes also took from classical antiquity the image of an ideal aspiration to totality, his theory of expression would not suffer any assimilation into its otherwise beloved classical model. As for the Greeks themselves, they did not work and perhaps for that reason they did not have, properly speaking, a style. Organicism was for them a given, and its enjoyment did not demand, as in the case of the modern subject, a share in the heroic.

In "La crítica en la Edad Ateniense" (which is itself the transcription of a series of lectures that took place at the UNAM in 1941), Reyes provides a picture of classical antiquity as resting on a notion of *logos*, or word as an incontestable sign of the consistency of the world. The Greeks "sincerely hoped that reality would follow their designs."[48] Reyes's Greeks want to talk ceaselessly about the existent without realizing that so much talk (so much hope, Reyes writes) will end up dissolving the object that their speech attempts to safeguard. The Greeks were true to themselves: seeking the permanent was the core of their expressivity. But the belief in such a substratum also sequestered expression from them. The experience of modernity, meanwhile, attests to a permanent dissociation of language from the world that makes a return to the kingdom of the *logos* impossible. Reyes advocated a moderate position before this loss of the transcendental. In the face of that loss, criticism becomes the only destiny of the word.[49]

"Rien n'aura eu lieu que le lieu": Mallarmé in Anáhuac

For Reyes, Stéphane Mallarmé represents the most radical actualization of the blending of the critical and the creative.[50] Written at the "mature" age of twenty-five, "Sobre el procedimiento ideológico de Stéphane Mallarmé," forms part of the volume *Cuestiones estéticas*. The appearance of Mallarmé in the general corpus of *Cuestiones estéticas* is enigmatic, surrounded as it is by a cohort of writers who cannot be possibly defined—except for Luis de Góngora—in terms of the radicalism of their artistic or intellectual projects. But, starting with this essay and up to Reyes's unfinished book on Mallarmé, the French poet remains paradigmatic for Reyes because of the open conflation of aesthetic sensibility (which in Mallarmé is inextricable from his attention to the immediate) with the work of writing. The radicalism of Reyes's reading lies in recognizing in Mallarmé's style the critical element as the constitutively unavoidable center of all modern expression. At first sight, it would seem that the general subjective disposition of Mallarmé points in the direction of a rehabilitation of the *logos*. Reyes observes that "without a philosophical concern in general there cannot be a work that is consistent or alive. Noble attention to ideas is the seal of the artist." Mallarmé's ideas are, however, puzzling because they are not, strictly speaking, ideas but rather their opposite. Mallarmé shows a clear and well-tempered sensibility for all the sympathies of the world. But the sympathies of the world are capricious and the subject is the site of their manifestation rather than of their constitution. The relationship of Mallarmé to these sympathies is—as it must be for a poet—of immediacy. To quote Reyes himself, "It seems that Mallarmé wrote nothing but his intuitions (*intuiciones*)." Therefore Mallarmé is a thinker "in the most immediate sense of the word."[51]

Intuition does not name an unreflective or inspired knowledge. Rather, the word is used in its Kantian sense of receptivity unmediated by concepts. Mallarmé, who is declared a quintessential poet, is declared also, and without interval, a thinker. With scrupulous Kantism, Reyes calls "thinking" the same process that elicited in Borges the opinion that his "memorious" Funes, so focused on the present reproduction of the recent, was unable to think. And Mallarmé is a Funes of sorts. The problem for both Funes and Mallarmé is that the world never comes to a stop: "If Mallarmé's task has anything that is portentous it cannot be contained in any technical dimension." It is a task that, like the happiness of the new Zarathustra (the image is Reyes's), "wants eternity . . . wants the deep eternity." This reading of Mallarmé, although informed here and there by a Kantian vocabulary, is, in the end, heavily Nietzschean. What Mallarmé confronts is that unnamable nature that the Greeks could not conceive. The passion for the Real (the formula is Alain Badiou's) defines the fate of Mallarmé's literary project, a project that "should out of necessity remain incomplete through its very realization."[52] Not even infinite time is enough for Mallarmé to complete his task because the world ceaselessly devours the reality that it poses.

Culture and crisis are two sides of the same coin. Of the two sides, Reyes will pick culture out of necessity but also out of political expediency. Despite his enormous and persistent admiration for Mallarmé, Reyes could not sympathize completely with a project that is antiexpressivist at its core—with a crisis that is not resolved at the level of some consistent version of the subject. In Reyes's hand, Mallarmé's intuition (*Anschauung* in the technical vocabulary inaugurated by Kant), will become a discursive construction, a sort of *anschaulich,* a word related to intuition but one that indicates what is vivid or brought to life, a vision in the exact sense that Reyes uses the word in his seminal essay "Visión de Anáhuac." It is here that Reyes's style—of which we have said nothing yet—becomes important.

What is this style? It is first and above all the style of the storyteller who tells all stories as if he had been present at the events and as if nobody had referred to them before: as if the world were coming into existence every time he opened his lips. His word is incantatory, demiurgic, and yet expressive. Reyes alludes to rather than quoting literary and even critical sources. In "Visión de Anáhuac"—the essay whose only and permanent subject is depth—the authorial voice slides effortlessly from Giovanni Battista Ramusio's maps to Bernal Díaz del Castillo's dazzled account of Mexico; from Bernal Díaz to the more calculative prose of Hernán Cortés; and then to others. Reyes's writing is a reading out-loud. Except in his most strictly philological texts (few people read them now), Reyes punctiliously avoids the practice of citing. His relationship to other texts lies in an ingestion of their materials. The procedure recalls those of the Brazilian *antropofágicos* whose members Reyes befriended during his diplomatic days in Rio de Janeiro. In his writings, Reyes becomes a ventriloquist of other voices who come back to us more noble and serene, but often also unrecognizable. I am not suggesting that Reyes refuses to acknowledge his academic debts; his intellectual probity is beyond suspicion. But in welcoming other voices into his arguments, he erases the borders that separate other discourses from his own. As in poetry, every word becomes his word. The reference to poetry is not whimsical.

This style is set to preserve the demiurgic and auratic power of the poetic in a time of no-poiesis.

Reyes blends literature and criticism in his description of the Aztec market. There, Cortés (or Reyes) tells us, the visitor is presented with "everything that could be found on earth."[53] The demiurge in Reyes conjures up the specter of Mallarmé—of a certain Mallarmé—to vivify an intuition that comes from the depth of a bottomless archive. Hence, the marked sensuality in the description of places, people, and merchandises. The mixture of a learned language with an orgiastic display of the texture of words anticipates the style of the most baroque Carpentier. Always vigilant, Reyes drops in passing the name of the protobaroque Flemish painter Denis van Alsloot, just to let us know that even the most subtle of connotations do not escape completely his attention. As we lose sight of the implicit references, we immerse ourselves in a dense network of words that often have a similarity to the logic of dreams in the playfulness of their construction. (If something characterizes Reyes's style, it is that there is always more than one person speaking through his words and more than one thing happening in his world.) In the description of the Aztec temple the sensuality of words and worlds is superimposed with—or coincides with—the critical intervention: "The Indian seller's breasts disappear among the browned vases. Her arms slide in the clay as if in their native element. They frame the vases, like handles, and slither down the neck of the colored jars. The jar's waists are colored with pigments of black and gold that resemble the necklace hanging from her throat."[54] We could spend pages deciphering this brief paragraph of voyeurism (Cortés's and ours) that is also, and without interruption, a scene of labor and a premonition of subjugation. By recasting Cortés's words in a language of appetite and desire, the style reveals a trait of the moment in which the mundane laws of sexual attraction hold the key to an entire historical configuration. Just as Reyes is talking about women and eroticism when he pretends to be talking of the merchandise, he is talking about the impending conquest when he seems to be talking about a woman. The text as a whole fuses recollection and criticism, analytic thinking and intense expression, through a remarkable act of stylistic condensation.

The ventriloquism of the past creates a crisis of authority: to whom do we owe this description of the Aztec market: Reyes, Cortés, or Bernal Díaz? Authority—or adjudication—is not however what is at stake here. It is by putting authority in crisis that the subject of enunciation asserts its laborious self. The storyteller works. He pays his rent with creation, as Reyes himself says elsewhere. The expression "paying rent" betrays the language of the shopkeeper. Reyes perhaps thought it too risky or too partisan to refer to the value of his own intervention in terms of the sphere of labor. And yet, it is work in the strict sense of labor that grounds the whole poetic undertaking of "Visión de Anáhuac." After a whole section devoted to an indigenous poetry that is "irremediably lost," the last section of the essay resumes a programmatic tone. Bending upon the pages he has just written, Reyes states his suspicion of any ethnic or cultural continuity: "I am not one of those who dream an absurd perpetuation of indigenous tradition; actually I don't even give much credit to the perpetuation of Spanish traditions."[55] Reyes's essay is structured in a circular movement that connects beginning to end and hides, to some extent, the supplement that holds the whole edifice together. How does Anáhuac work? This question can be rephrased as: How does Mexico exist? Reyes's answer is surprising. It works through work: "The drying of the valley starts in 1499 and ends in the year 1900. Three different races have worked on it, almost three civilizations. . . . Our century caught us opening the last ditch, holding our last spade still full of dirt."[56] The portrait of obstinate generations working the stubborn land of Anáhuac is a mirror of Reyes's work, a supplement to his own stubbornness. Without this work, there would be no tradition and scarcely any reality to talk about.

Let us resist for a second the power of the demiurge and take a step back in order to look to the whole scene from the outside. "Visión de Anáhuac" is an imposing title, a title that announces less the subject of its pages than the problem of who has the right to utter these words. Who can say: "I have a vision, a vision of Anáhuac"? It is a matter of saying and not of writing. A vision cannot be written. It has to be announced. And the person who announces the vision should be the one who has relaxed the stiffness of conceptual thinking with irony and controlled the capriciousness of creation with the vigilance of criticism. This is so, among other things, because Anáhuac/Mexico is not totally visible. It needs to be conjured. (Anáhuac itself designates a pre-Hispanic space whose exact etymology is in dispute even today.)[57] This person who speaks, who is not poet and yet demiurge, is the orator. In "La antigua retórica," Reyes contrasts Cicero to Quintilian and says that the latter "wants his orator to be an ethical prodigy. He wants the orator to be able to establish traditions and impose duties. A culture unable to reach that level will be always an incomplete culture."[58] Reyes's style makes it difficult to tell if the conclusive last sentence belongs to Quintilian, to his reading of Quintilian, or to Reyes himself. The moral of the story belongs, however, completely to Reyes:

> One understands that the orator needs to have before his eyes a vast human panorama that includes both past and present, without which

> he is a stranger to his species; and one understands too that this panorama includes what happened and what was imagined, history, legend, poetry, and actual experience.[59]

The figure outlined in this quote is none other than that of the possible author of a possible text entitled "Visión de Anáhuac." This narrative voice is not authorized by any romantic or neoromantic tradition, nor does it depend on a severance with the immediate context of enunciation. The position of enunciation is doctrinal in nature, a sort of civil credo in the style of Andrés Bello. Who authorizes this voice? What theater could be the most appropriate for the deployment of its statements?

The last pages of "Visión de Anáhuac" are luminously ambiguous when they come to answer the paradox of habitation. The question of the origin, openly stated at the beginning of the essay, runs as a submerged train of thought through the text and reappears at the end when Reyes tries to render the design behind his text explicit. The meaningful quote reads:

> Whatever historical doctrine we profess to link us to the race of the past, leaving aside the ties of blood, rests on the common effort to dominate our untamable nature, an effort that is the ultimate ground of history. We are also linked by the much deeper feeling of a quotidian emotion before the same natural object. The confrontation of sensibility with the same world tills, engenders, a common soul. But even if we accept neither one nor the other, neither common action nor common contemplation, let us agree that historical emotion is part of current life (*vida actual*) and that without its resplendence our valleys and our mountains would be like a theatre without light.[60]

This mythological land, in which poetry and testimony fuse harmoniously, has engendered, according to Reyes, a common soul. Obviously, ties of blood are not enough to sustain this construction, since, after all, one race has been killing the other for centuries. Reyes proposes two supplements: labor and contemplation (which itself contains a measure of labor). The tale works on the condition of work. But work cannot happen spontaneously: the nomadic principle must be already refrained. The same agency that represses nomadism is responsible for securing the labor destined to unite a transhistorical community. Reyes describes this agency as follows: "Three monarchical regimes, divided by parentheses of anarchy, are exemplary of how the work of the state grows and corrects itself, facing the same threats from nature and the need to excavate the same land."[61] The three monarchical regimes are the Aztec empire, Spanish colonial rule, and the rule of Porfirio Díaz. This genealogy poses a problem: If, for Reyes, all state power has thus far been monarchical in Mexico, does that imply that all state power is simply monarchical by nature? I think that the second option, representative of a sober Schmitteanism, is the case. Despite their differences, these monarchical regimes appear as an example of an overarching reality, the labor of the state. There is, then, a state beyond the state, a sort of immemorial principle already hidden in the fateful hour Huitzilopochtli ordered the Aztec priest to stop the tribe's wandering at the exact point where an eagle was devouring a serpent on top of a nopal. Monarchical regimes are merely examples of an antinomadic principle; examples of an *arkhé* in general. After all, it is the state that has enforced a common history, a history that now illuminates the space of the present regardless of the abject nature of its origins in sacrifices, conquests, and betrayals. But what about the revolution, the kingdom of anarchy in which sovereignty emerges without the sovereign?

Reyes devotes only one (but crucial) line to the revolution when, after summarizing the history of Mexico in a succession of monarchical regimes, he closes the cycle with the emergence of the social fright: "When the makers of the desert finish their work, social fright [*el espanto social*] breaks out."[62] In qualifying the "fright" as "social," Reyes seeks not so much to describe the emergence of the mob as terrifying (this is hardly his political point of view) but rather to signal a spectacular inversion in the agency of the historical from the state that forced the eyes (and arms) of the Mexicans upon the beauty (and land) of Anáhuac to the revelation of radical forms of democracy whose taming was everybody's task. Perhaps in this single line emerges better than anywhere else Reyes's attempt "to provide an account of the revolutionary moment itself."[63]

Throughout the whole essay we have seen Reyes pouring over old manuscripts, perusing the pages of history, facing the immensity of Anáhuac; the introduction of the social fright works as a reverse shot. It unhinges the narrator's calm and acknowledges the ethical horizon of his task. But, to continue with the cinematographic metaphor, this is also a continuous shot: past and present, repetition and event, are grasped in just one sentence. Reyes seems to be saying that even if the state as the guarantor of commonality disappears in chaos, the present is still enchained to a narrative form. It is in the name of this residual force that Reyes, an orator without agora, endows his words with a prophetic and even fatalistic tonality. The fright will subside for the simple reason that it is not outside the chain of history, just one of its most significant abysses.

Let us contextualize in a straightforward way. Reyes began to write this essay in the year 1915, the year, a famous description goes, when "salons housed horses and confessionals were fed to bonfires." The fateful year of 1915 was also and beyond all devastation the year of a revelation: *existía México*. Manuel Gómez Morín is struck by the resilience of a Mexican *thing*, by its obtrusiveness in the face of death. Reyes too is struck by the same discovery. The year appears playfully alluded to in the otherwise incomprehensible appendage to the essay's title, which Reyes even suggested as a possible title for the essay as a whole: 1591.[64] To use here Benedict Anderson's characterization of the nation, by 1915 Mexico appears to Mexicans as a mirror of a past, as a destiny. As for Reyes, he just devotes himself to showing the exact mechanism by which destiny is governed.

The overall subject of "Visión de Anáhuac" is fatality: the fatality of being asked if there are many trees in America, the fatality of conquest once Cortés sees the appearing and disappearing ghost of his desire between vases colored with the tonalities of the earth; but more importantly, the fatality of belonging to a land and the fatality of repeating a history. From the lost poetry of the Nahua people to an overlap of textual and visual imaginaries begotten by tradition, from Battista Ramusio's map of the orb to the tribulations of Bernal Díaz, Reyes traces a discourse, an illusory past—as Borges would say.

Generations of Mexicans have probed the unique alchemy of matching their words to a landscape that interrogates them with the same compulsory force that the sphinx used to interrogate Oedipus in the classical tale. But territoriality cannot be the only existing binding force because, as the orator teaches us, there is, strictly speaking, not a conclusive separation between the realm of brute matter and that of transmissible spirituality. There is also a mystical injunction that comes alive in the long history of cultural inheritance. Reyes understands that the injunction is best embodied in beauty, which here is, ambivalently, artistic and natural beauty. However, even nature as beauty is not enough to explain the civilizing process. Something has to force the gaze of the wandering people into an attunement with beauty. Could it be that the revolution acted as a supplement to the state function despite its apparently antisystemic nature? Has not Dr. Atl reached the same conclusion in his catalog of popular arts and has not Reyes confirmed this suspicion in his report about the exposition of Mexican kids' drawings in Paris?[65] In Reyes's reading, the revolution opens a felicitous perspective: the desire of the Mexican people can be one with the demands of sovereignty. At this moment, as Paz writes apropos Reyes, "Fatality ceases to be an exterior imposition and becomes a willful and intimate act of consent."[66]

The expressive injunction only demands work, work of desiccation and subjectivization. The Mexican orator holds up Anáhuac as an immediate vision before his eyes. This present will not be here and will not be present without the vivifying intuition of those who worked it through, either materially or symbolically. So, Reyes writes, echoing that Kafkian character who sat his entire life at the doorsteps of the law: "Even if this tradition proves to be foreign, it is nonetheless in our hands, and we are the only ones who can enjoy its full possession." To be owned by the tradition one strives to own is the highest point to which a theory of subjectivization can aspire.[67]

AN ARCHITECTURAL POSTSCRIPT

Derrida wrote that "inheritance is never a *given*, it is always a task."[68] We should not interpret this line in a literal or even anthropomorphic way, assuming too soon that inheritance is an affair of the individual. There are in Derrida's text enough indications that intentions and wishes do not count much when inheritance is at stake. Culture as inheritance is necessarily the inheritance of a mystery, of an unknown cipher that speaks to us in a language irreducible to our own language. It was well before the revolution, in the formative decades of the Porfiriato, that the colonial downtown of Mexico City appeared to the Mexican elite as an inheritance that they could neither refuse nor engage. Significantly, the architect Jesús Acevedo, who exerted an important influence in his fellow Ateneístas, referred to the architectonic treasure of the capital in an uncanny register: "A tradition of excellence lies dormant in our consciousness—dormant, not dead. A little bit of study and introspection is all that is needed to make it present in the depth of our being: because this immemorial tradition runs in our veins."[69]

When, in "Visión de Anáhuac," Reyes writes of an iridescence that illuminates the present, he could have not found a better example than an architectural legacy of four hundred years, which was nothing but the materially objectified dimension of the symbolic. In the order of inheritance, few things are as difficult to destroy or ignore. It is only in the infrastructural quality of the urb—at whose center tradition has always placed the house of the dead—that the present is confronted with a practical measure of habitation that cannot be diluted into any metaphysical notion of the past. How could this past be reconciled with the pulsating modernity that was also a defining trait of the emergent social order?

In the 1920s a bitter dispute broke out in the first years after the revolution about what architecture could best represent the aspirations of a revolutionary people. A dividing line was traced between nativists, who favored the colonial style, and cosmopolitans, who were partisans of modernity and functionalism.[70] Intellectuals like Vasconcelos saw colonialism as a proper style for representing the Arielist continuity of a Mexican soul. Functionalist architects, on the other hand, thought that little of this past should be preserved and that it was the duty of the revolution to break with tradition in favor of new concepts and especially new materials.[71] Both positions had the revolution as their background, but while the colonial style understood the revolution in opposition to the dangers of capitalist modernization, functionalism saw the revolution as a step forward in the destruction of the colonial habitus that had maintained Mexico in a state of widespread injustice.[72]

Acevedo—whose *Disertaciones de un arquitecto* exerted a perennial influence on Vasconcelos—attacked the modernizing architecture of the Porfiriato for its inability to carry on a fruitful dialogue with the past.[73] This tradition with the past cannot be merely cosmetic. For instance, Acevedo rejected as impractical the influence of indigenous Mesoamerican architecture given the simple fact that it was impossible to reconstruct the type of habitation the indigenous people imagined for themselves on the bases of the available archaeological ruins alone.[74]

Unsurprisingly, the postrevolutionary state had remarkably little to say (or do) when it came to writing its own truth in stone. At most, revolutionary governments remained content with inaugurating monuments, and even in this department production was far from significant. The first two decades of revolutionary rule produced only two meaningful monuments. The first, inaugurated in 1935, was dedicated to fallen elected president Álvaro Obregón. The second, which was finished in 1938 but never inaugurated, was Carlos Obregón Santacilia's Monumento a la Revolución.[75]

In the construction of the Monumento a la Revolución, Obregón Santacilia was forced to use the general framework of the dome for the legislative palace that had been planned but never completed during Porfirism. Meanwhile, Enrique Aragón Echegaray, the young architect in charge of Obregón's monument, was only limited in his design by the condition that the monument should be erected at the very place where Obregón fell to the bullets of José de León Torál. (Even the soil where the *caudillo* fell was preserved into the construction.) Both monuments are postmodern buildings of a sort, shunning the presence of visitors and remaining aloof and detached from their surroundings. Obregón's monument is especially interesting in this regard. Based on a pyramidal structure, the treatment of volume simultaneously points to the vogue of art deco and to a modernist reading of Aztec architecture. Ignacio Asúnsolo—who was Vasconcelos's sculptor of choice when it came to the statues that decorate the SEP—was trusted with adorning the monument with a series of motifs of his choice. Asúnsolo picked as his subjects popular figures of soldiers, peasants, women, and Indians. This sculptural group maintains an uneasy relationship to the monument as a whole. Asúnsolo's statues cover the base of the pyramid (and the uninviting and small interior), but they stop less than quarter-way up its walls. From a distance—and especially from the side—the monument resembles a cube of imposing but particularly uncommunicative lines. More tellingly, unlike most monuments of this type, there is no figure (or message) that crowns the construction. Accustomed as we are to read monuments in terms of how they support a certain ideology, the striking feature of Obregón's monument is the absence of any "message."

In the case of Obregón Santacilia's monument to the revolution, if a viewer is unaware that he or she is facing a monument to the revolution, there are few, if any, clues that would allow the viewer to decipher the meaning of the building. Eventually, the monument became a museum and a mausoleum. As Luis Carranza notes, a sign of the state's ambiguity towards the monument lies in the fact that the monument was never inaugurated or dedicated. The reason was not a lack of official interest in the project. Both the monument to the revolution and the monument to Álvaro Obregón enjoyed heavy bureaucratic supervision.[76] Although the communicational paucity of these constructions could be read as the instantiation of "empty signifiers" quite characteristic of populist regimes, what they communicate in the end is emptiness itself. Everything happens as if the postrevolutionary state had very little to communicate in the way of ideology, a problem originating in the state's dependence on the work of the high modernism to voice ideological messages.

Vasconcelos, for whom the meaning of revolution was restitution, sought to establish a sense of continuity with the past by having new buildings built in stone. Stone was a costly material and the necessarily low height that characterized the colonial style limited the number of projects that could be completed. Although Vasconcelos despised the 1921 centennial, the SEP inaugurated a great number of schools during the month of September, among them the SEP's own building, beautifully decorated with Rivera's murals and the statues of Asúnsolo. Perhaps the most emblematic building of the period, insofar as it synthesizes the postrevolutionary state effort to engineer a new society in Mexico, is the national stadium, an idea authored by Vasconcelos and placed almost entirely under his direction.[77]

The attack on the colonial style came from a group of enthusiastic architects well versed in international trends. The academy of San Carlos, where most Mexican architects were trained, continued favoring either a neoclassical or mannerist style. However, its library subscribed to the most prestigious architectural journals of the time, and through them the names of Le Corbusier and Frank Lloyd Wright, the propositions of Bauhaus and art deco, became widely available for architectural students. Although some architects favored the Californian style for the residential areas constructed for the new rich of the revolution, most young architects gravitated towards the modernism and functionalism that were prevalent in commercial buildings.[78] The building for the Secretary of Health and Welfare—an innovative design by Carlos Obregón Santacilia—represents a similar tendency in the sphere of public architecture.[79] In most commercial enterprises, functionalism—which favored new materials such as iron, glass, and reinforced concrete—was the dominant form of urbanization. The Nuevo Palacio de Hierro by Paul Dubois (1921), the department store El Correo Francés (1926), the Edificio Cidosa (1924), and the Woodrow Building (1922) by Albert Pepper were all marked by the emergence of functionalism.[80] It is important to note that unlike the Porfirist period, when most constructions were partially or totally financed by the state, functionalism emerged in close connection to a more dynamic and pervasive influence of private capital in Mexico, especially after 1925.

Functionalism organized its propositions along the lines of the establishment of a new fantasy; colonialism along the lines of a discourse of depth. What neither style could deliver was a transcultural production similar to the ones attempted by the cosmopolitan elite of artists like Best Maugard, Rivera, or Kahlo. Additionally, the slow but steady appropriation of popular motifs to further the ends of state propaganda complicated the relationship of the proponents of new architecture with the sphere of popularly inspired symbols. Increasingly throughout the 1930s, functionalists attacked what they perceived to be the ideological character of art and its mystifying forms of indoctrination. Vasconcelos famously proclaimed that the new SEP building had high ceilings in order to allow ideas to soar.[81] Meaning, not function, was paramount. The building itself was conceived as an intertext with Vasconcelos's *The Cosmic Race,* in good part through Asúnsolo's sculptural work.[82] For the functionalists, these justifications smelled of bourgeois metaphysics. To build in a postrevolutionary style—the first great Mexican functionalist, Juan O'Gorman said—means building at low cost for the benefit of the popular classes. Buildings do not need to save space for decorations or suggest any message in their form; the form itself was the message, and the message was that use was the only value. Art, O'Gorman contended, had always been the ostentatious signature of the rich. At the heated convention of Mexican architects in 1933, another functionalist, Juan Legarreta, launched into an even more blatant attack on the idea of a building signifying anything beyond its immediate functional form: "We will build the people's houses. Aesthetes and windbags—let's hope they all die—can come to their own conclusions afterwards."[83]

For a while it looked as if functionalism would carry the day, especially when it was adopted as an official form of state architecture in the 1930s. The project received help from the most unexpected of quarters, muralism. Diego Rivera trusted O'Gorman with the construction of his and Frida

Kahlo's studio house in San Ángel (currently the Frida Kahlo and Diego Rivera House-Museum). Although profoundly influenced by the strict functionalism of Le Corbusier, O'Gorman broke with his orthodox functionalist principles to allow his expressive side to take hold for at least part of the project.[84] The clearly divided two-body house reproduced and represented the detached marriage of Kahlo and Rivera. The building offered generous walls for mural projects or decorations so cherished by bourgeois taste. On the other hand, the construction's cost per square footage was equal to the characteristic cost of a worker's house. In 1932, a year after the completion of the project, Rivera introduced O'Gorman to the newly appointed minister of education, Narciso Bassols. Soon, O'Gorman became the official architect of the SEP during a boom of school-building in Mexico City. With O'Gorman on board, the SEP definitively abandoned the colonial style and any attempt at monumentalism in favor of comfort and cost-efficient architecture. O'Gorman built twenty-four schools in Mexico City in only three years. The total cost was only a fraction above the money spent by Vasconcelos for the SEP building.[85] Still, this did not mean that functionalism could so easily win general approval. For many critics, O'Gorman's style of covering bare necessities was indistinguishable from the perpetuation of an aesthetic of poverty and despair. Confronting his critics, O'Gorman famously proclaimed that his buildings were not about beauty but about hygiene, ventilation, playgrounds, and toilets.

In the 1930s functionalism began to make inroads in other areas of state-sponsored architecture. One year after wishing death on aesthetes, the young functionalist Juan Legarreta himself died, but not without first winning a national competition—overseen by Carlos Obregón Santacilia—for the construction of the *casa obrera mínima*. His project contained many references to popular architecture and was designed to allow the participation of the workers in the construction of their own homes. Although Legarreta won the competition, Juan O'Gorman's proposal ended up with the contracts, especially after 1940, when, under the presidency of Miguel Alemán, the state embarked on massive construction projects of working-class neighborhoods. At this point, history began to catch up with the functionalists.

Functionalism seemed to have triumphed over the nostalgic forces of the colonial style, above all because the architects could deliver the same space and accommodations at a much lower cost, something that was obviously important for a nearly bankrupt state. However, two issues began to crop up that would undermine the functionalist apogee. First, there was the question of a past that could not be simply obliterated in the name of modernity. The reconversion of downtown Mexico City into a historical district faced the functionalists with a challenge that was difficult to overcome. How was functionalism going to deal with the imposing baroque heritage of the city? How could functionalism become state architecture without duplicating the flight into fiction that had characterized the Porfirist remaking of the city?[86] Second, there was the question of the political valence of architecture, which took on a new dimension in the 1930s as many Mexican artists and intellectuals—O'Gorman among them—abandoned the loose ideology of revolutionary nationalism to embrace a more cohesive Marxist attitude. Along with the likes of O'Gorman, a new breed of leftist intellectual hit the stage of Mexican culture: the conscious, well-informed, paranoiac Marxist who wants to rebel against the system as a whole but who is, also, unwittingly a prisoner of a social order—the postrevolutionary order—that seems to maintain a schizophrenic double allegiance to socialist principles and capitalist development. Narciso Bassols himself, the great promoter of socialist education, believed—despite all the orthodoxy of his thinking—that education could counteract the structural effects of the economic. Functionalism was for him, as it was for O'Gorman, an antibourgeois statement because it incarnated the scientific, unbiased, and materialist look of the social. In this context, it is worthwhile noting that Rivera's most receptive attitude towards functionalism was perhaps inseparable from his visit to the Soviet Union in 1928, where principles similar to those of functionalism had been established.

O'Gorman championed functionalism as an "unmasking" of the long use of architecture for the glorification of the dominant class. For him, a house was not an investment but a "machine for living." Traditional architecture was condemned as necessarily trapped in the reproduction of capital. Decorations were synonymous with bourgeois expenditure; they indeed embodied the specific forms of capitalist surplus in the process of construction, since their only function was to improve the resale value of a property. By 1936, however, O'Gorman would effect a total reversal of his position. Knowledge of the growing economic importance of housing development projects in the United States—built in a functionalist style—and the increasing dependence of architecture in Mexico on private firms like the cement-maker Tolteca, led O'Gorman to adopt a critical position towards a functionalism that was establishing itself as the architectonic style of preference for capitalist profit-making. By 1938 O'Gorman abandoned the practice of professional architecture altogether to become a realist mural painter and a building decorator. Tellingly, his late projects, like his own house in El Pedregal, are the works of a modernist disenchanted with the world of rampant capitalism; they become assertions of private expression that show strong affinities with the work of Catalan architect Antoni Gaudí, above all in their lavish fusion of architecture and decoration.

O'Gorman's quandaries are a reflection of the puzzling character that capitalist development presented to those intellectuals embarked on a constructivist project in postrevolutionary Mexico. Vasconcelos did not mind the expenditure on buildings because he saw them as politico-economic investments representative of the nascent imperial order of the cosmic race. Of course, Vasconcelos completely misperceived the nature of the capitalist process, which engulfed, rather than depended on, the political fiction of the nation-state. The mirage seems to have particularly afflicted the proponents of the colonial style. The American architect Sylvester Baxter, who was educated in Germany and attempted to bring German architecture into the United States (and who also authored a book on Mexican colonial architecture), thought the colonial style was the best means to signify the increasing power of the United States. He was dumbfounded when, after a vigorous campaign, he was faced with the refusal of the nascent empire to embrace a monumental architecture. Like Vasconcelos, he could not see that financial transnational capitalism tends to abstraction and simplicity. Its heart was itself a functionalism of sorts.

The increasing affinity between capitalism and functionalism led O'Gorman and others to revaluate bourgeois and metaphysical positions such as those of Vasconcelos. This revaluation was not only political; it included also the painful realization that history and the past could not be ignored after all. At the time when O'Gorman was sliding away from functionalism, one of the most important Mexican architects of the twentieth century, Mario Pani (nephew of Alberto Pani), returned to Mexico from his studies in France. Unlike O'Gorman, who knew Le Corbusier from books, Pani held a French diploma and had direct access to Le Corbusierian circles and works. Pani was entrusted with some of the most important state projects of a rapidly developing Mexico, and his works helped to redefine the architectonic shape of the city. He was responsible for the first urban housing complex in Latin America in Le Corbusier's style (later demolished). In the 1950s, Pani was one of the four names to head the group of one hundred architects who built the Ciudad Universitaria, later named a world heritage site by UNESCO.[87] Knowledgeable of the debates of the 1920s and '30s, Pani tried to rescue some of the neocolonial concerns while remaining a minimalist and functionalist in terms of design. So, while Le Corbusier himself favored flat and smooth surfaces, many of Pani's buildings at the UNAM campus used rugged materials reminiscent of colonial and pre-Columbian architecture. It was actually the simultaneous rescue of both traditions that makes Pani's architectural style a sort of summa of Mexico's architectonic heritages. Interestingly, the site where the Ciudad Universitaria was built, marked as it was by volcanic rock and lava, had attracted the attention of Diego Rivera. It was there that O'Gorman, already converted to the thesis of the unavoidable weight of the past, built the impressive Anáhuacalli to house Rivera's collection of indigenous art. The Ciudad Universitaria also made heavy use of stone. One of the reasons, it is said, is that its construction almost depleted the reserves of concrete. But no shortage of concrete could explain the abundant references to indigenous architecture, and above all to the archaeological site of Teotihuacán, that marked the construction of the campus. Several buildings are organized around huge pedestrian plazas, with changing levels and flights of steps that evoke Aztec and other pre-Columbian ceremonial centers. Muralists like Siqueiros, although actively sidelined from the process of design itself, were in charge of decorating several buildings. Juan O'Gorman, along with two other artists, was responsible for the impressive mural at the façade of the UNAM's Biblioteca Central.[88]

This broad sketch of the defeat of colonial style at the hands of functionalism—but also of the indelible mark that the recovery of the past would play in any large cultural production in postrevolutionary Mexico—reflects the tremendous determination that all Mexican culture would suffer from the shadow cast by the initial invention of the popular in the first years of Obregón's government. At the time of the construction of the Ciudad Universitaria, the shape of the popular itself had changed, and its architects could content themselves with referring the whole realm of the people to an indigenous past that the middle class had learned to appropriate. They had even learned to feel it as a constitutive part of their own being as Mexicans, a tradition that, while foreign, was, as Reyes would remind them, nonetheless in their hands since they were the only ones able to enjoy its full possession. In the Ciudad Universitaria, space coalesced once again into time, and history was restituted into its place as the dominant form of ideological self-understanding of a culturally minded state policy. Space itself, however, always conveys the ghosts of the past, and the *pedregal* south of San Ángel, where the UNAM is located, can elicit in the visitor an eerie reminder of the always-contested process of material historical formation in Mexico.

CHAPTER FOUR

Life

The emergence of these new men in almost all the states of Mexico north of the isthmus was one of the remarkable features of Madero's revolution; in the space of a few months, as the winter snows melted and the summer rains began, a new political generation was born.

ALAN KNIGHT, *THE MEXICAN REVOLUTION*

IF, AS MIKHAIL BAKHTIN ONCE SAID, A WORD IS LIKE an arrow directed at its object, the word *life* is destined to be always off-target.[1] Equivocation is built into the meaning of the word itself. *Life* evokes what is most concrete and what is most abstract; what is most immediate and imposing (the uniqueness of my life), and what is most trifling and petty (all of existence reduced to a tiresome repetition of the rules of social reproduction). Throughout modernity the purchase of life increases at the same pace as the need to administer complex and variegated populations. Life as narrative, and even as economy, left its mark on a great variety of literary forms: picaresque literature, travel narratives, and letters and autobiographies. In all its different variations and intonations—biography, identity, exemplarity, martyrdom, sacrifice—life appears as a tool in whose name the unexpected is charted and even preempted. At the very moment of the consolidation of literature as a discourse of the contingent, life made its appearance on the scene under the form of the bildungsroman. The paradox that this emergence implied did not escape the most acute observers of the time. Somebody who cannot be charged with oversimplifying matters mockingly described the bildungsroman as a genre in which the main character "still gets his girl and some type of job, marries and becomes a philistine, just like everyone else."[2]

Of course, the genres of life are never read without suspicion. Did this really happen this way? What interests lurk behind that letter or that piece of autobiography? But the suspicion itself partakes of the economy of life. It seeks to amend, correct, and contradict, not to blast open the space of subjectivity that ineluctably inhabits every text. With his proverbial inconformity Salvador Novo exhibited this tension in his ironic comment on Jaime Torres Bodet, who "did not have a life, simply a biography."[3] Carlos Monsiváis reproduces this quote in his introduction to Novo's *La estatua de sal* and traces the ethics that would authorize Novo's irony back to the revolutionary upheaval.[4] The revolution, Monsiváis writes elsewhere, "disperses the structure of silences and omissions of the nineteenth century. . . . Massive migrations, the legion of fatherless children, the waves of prostitutes make it impossible to conceal the realities of desire."[5] One could expect that given the marked affinity between life and the narrative organization of existence that characterized the development of modernity—that characterized the forms of presentation and accountability linked to the bourgeois narrative that coincides with the emergence of capitalism—this type of narrative would crumble to pieces when faced with the anarchic dissolution characteristic of the revolution. Yet the opposite happens at the level of representation. Life as an organizing narrative principle (biography, in Novo's terms) traverses the entire landscape of revolutionary Mexico. It is active in all social strata and in almost every single narrative register, to the point that I feel entitled to say that life is perhaps the single most extended trope of the revolutionary narrative in all its different registers.

The motif is fundamental in pedagogy and education, as attested by the massive production of the first postrevolutionary textbook for primary schools, *Fermín,* written by Manuel Velázquez Andrade in 1927 and centered on the life of a child of peasant origin coming of age during the time of the revolution.[6] The emphasis on life is also present in the historiography of the revolution. Some of the most important historical studies of the revolution are organized around particular figures, such as Emiliano Zapata, Francisco Madero, or Salvador Alvarado. Of course the pinnacle of life as an organizing principle of the history of the revolution is Enrique Krauz's *Mexico: Biography of Power.* So intense is the trend that Friedrich Katz ironically titled his exhaustive study of Doroteo Arango *The Life and Times of Pancho Villa.*

Recent attempts to rescue a subaltern perspective on the revolutionary period adds to the list of narratives built around the normative use of life. This is so despite the fact that the very habitation of subaltern groups outside hegemonic socialized time is intrinsically refractory to this approach. A book like *Yaqui Women,* for example, uses the extrinsic temporality of "life stories" to reconstruct the experience of indigenous women.[7] Another example is Benita Galeana, the figure in whom Monsiváis sees the erotic nature of the revolution exemplified. Although Galeana was illiterate, she typed out her autobiography. In the text, her membership in the Mexican Communist Party provides the general guide for a narrative of life. However, the main contents of the book are entirely outside the accountability of life implicit in the Marxian narratology of existence. Perhaps the best-known (and most self-critical) example of this subaltern mismatch with the narrativization of life is provided by Elena Poniatowska in *Hasta no verte Jesús mío*.[8]

Why is it that at the very moment that all certainties crumble and all future is put within the reach of the present, when all moral codes are suspended and the possibility of appropriating one's own destiny is both at risk and at hand, such a teleological concept is mobilized to make sense of the disaggregated experience of the now? A first answer might suggest that this is precisely what the trope of life accomplishes: it reduces the multiplicity of existence to the category of the exemplar. Yet I would argue that this linear simplification is not what these people intended when they subjected the serendipity of experience to the stricture of life. Indeed there is no reason why *life* cannot be the vehicle for a complex and nuanced account. Henri Lefebvre once described a failed revolution as one that "has not changed life itself."[9] What does Lefebvre mean with the word *life* here? Certainly, something quite different from what Novo calls "biography." The problem is not just that a particular time of exacerbated violence lived out its own experience through the exorbitant demands of some form of superego, but also the fact that this ideology of life—this conformity of existence—is intrinsic to the hermeneutical modalities through which we read both the revolutionary event and its aftermath. Life can only become a sign in the chain of revolutionary meanings—rather than its disavowal—if we are able to wrestle this notion from the conformity that surrounds it in our everyday use and language. We need to extract life from what Roland Barthes calls "a psychology of unity,"[10] a psychology founded, we could add, on the obliteration of the subject in favor of the individual, the latter understood as a grid of juridical and moral attributes.

THE HERO

In *The Myth of Revolution*, Ilene O'Malley extensively describes the process of the mystification of revolutionary heroes. Although O'Malley attributes the heroic emphases of the Mexican pantheon to the ideology of the postrevolutionary state, such mystification reflects an understanding of the personal contemporaneous with the events themselves. Venustiano Carranza saw himself as already half-made in bronze and, according to Enrique Krauze, conceived of his own life as a reenactment of Juárez's history, which he avidly read and knew in all its smallest details.[11] Álvaro Obregón also understood his own life in terms of destiny, and as a proof he bequeathed to us the *vía crucis* of his eight-thousand-mile campaign trail. (A gifted speaker, Obregón was a hopelessly boring writer.) The tragic aura was certainly cultivated by the revolutionaries, but it was also an objective part of their stories. The fact that the lives of so many of them (Felipe Ángeles, Villa, Zapata, Carranza, Carrillo Puerto, Obregón, de la Huerta) ended so early and as much at the hands of their sworn enemies as at the hands of older friends and allies often adds an aura of tragic inevitability to their careers.[12] A connection emerges between heroic life and death—in their mutual implication, in their sheer inevitability. The narrative of the heroic life may indeed be telling us something about the experience of the revolution rather than simply eschewing its meaning through a narrative detour.[13] It is worthwhile, then, to take a closer look at the hero.

What do we mean by a hero? The hero is, in the proper sense of the word, an idiot. The nature of this idiocy was established by Bakhtin in exemplary fashion in his celebrated contrast between epic and novel. In his essay, the Russian thinker contrasts the linguistic and ideological limitations of the epic hero (who says what he is supposed to say and thinks what he is supposed to think) with the freedom that reigns over the characters of the modern novel.[14] Already written—himself a letter, as Foucault says of Don Quixote—the epic hero does not experience the world. He lives a prescribed plot in which he is always identical to the image that others have of him. What makes the hero heroic is precisely his undelivered submission to his destiny. I say *his*, because in the context of epic as well as in the context of the Mexican revolution, destiny is primordially a male ideology; female inscription into the revolution seldom follows the path of destiny. From the perspective of this opposition between epic and novel one can appreciate the oddity that most literature of the revolution takes the form of novels that display epic heroes. In the best of these novels, heroic life takes its meaning from a confrontation with—often a submission to—destiny, which often just means death. With this, I refer not to the banal fact of the character dying but rather, in the spirit of Freud in "Beyond the Pleasure Principle," to the way death acts as the actual engine of life and its narrativization. The quintessential example will always be Tiburcio Maya in Rafael Muñoz's *¡Vámonos con Pancho Villa!* Tiburcio's attunement to the revolution ends up confused with the search for death itself. And yet, what Tiburcio experiences as the almost total annihilation of a sense of selfhood is itself the binding character of the revolt. Muñoz expresses this binding character in the most abject of ways, making Tiburcio follow Villa even after Villa kills Tiburcio's wife and daughter. (Here, as in other instances, women are a hindrance to the idiocy of destiny.) Shortly before joining the revolution, Tiburcio walks arm-in-arm with some of his *leones*, singing: "If they are going to kill me tomorrow, they better kill me right away." The popular tune—whose first line is also the title of a collection of strange short stories by Muñoz—confirms the primacy of a death drive in the ideology of the heroic. The attunement to death prepares the idiocy of the hero. But insofar as this attunement stages a confrontation with the upmost limit of the human—with the absolute master—it can also prepare a movement away from destiny, a materialism of sorts. Why materialism? Because against all formalism, we affirm that the opposite of the heroic is not cowardice but sensuality. The heroic seeks to contain the sheer materiality unleashed by the prospect of death.[15]

FROM HERO TO SUBJECT

As often happens, the key to a hermeneutic problem hinges on the availability of a word. In our case this word is *subject*. A subject, we can say with Jacques Lacan, is that which seeks realization.[16] A subject is agonic by definition, often the object of a censored pleasure. However, the subject is not exactly the silenced body of enjoyment, although it has some genealogical connections to it. It is, rather, a message that tries to find its way among the debris of known sentences and well-weighted languages. The emerging subject does not establish a completely new relationship to the world: the world changes the constitutive frontiers that separate him or her from the thickness of reality. Things that were historical or political become intimate. This is the operation that Ramón López Velarde performs in *La suave patria* (1916) which, despite its civic title, replaces everything that is civic with references to an everydayness that was formative for the poet. In his essay "Novedad de la patria," López Velarde makes this substitution explicit when he dismisses the epic poet as being out of sync with the (revolutionary) times.[17]

Revolution, freedom, and subject are correlative terms. They disclose each other. For the emerging subject, the revolution is not simply a "fresh start," but rather a start constructed around a recollection, a gathering together of a scattered and sometimes repressed past. Ideas and ideologies are tried on and adopted or discarded with the ease with which one changes clothes, subjecting everything to the passion of the times. Through this process the subject can see that there is nothing specifically constitutive in the identity that came before or that was so recently appropriated. The subject comes to understand that the only property that inhabits him or her is precisely the possibility of appropriating. Without this understanding no revolution is possible or imaginable. This is why life, despite its limitations, is still so important for a narrative of the revolution. But this life is not a calculable life.

TWO WOMEN AND A MAN

Revolutionary and postrevolutionary Mexico was marked by an intense labor of self-invention. Gerardo Murillo was far from unique when he changed his name to Dr. Atl. Most of the artists and intellectuals of the time were obsessed with the horizon of possibilities opened by the revolutionary event. Self-design and self-production are not givens. The process can falter and derail. Nahui Olin (Carmen Mondragón) saw the photo that Edward Weston took of her in 1924 as a testimony of such a failure and cultivated a deep resentment for the photographer.[18] On the other side of the arch, we find Frida Kahlo, the most successful self-created character of the revolutionary myth. In 1932 she started making a painting for each year of her life, but even before then her own life had been the main subject of her art. Her self-portraits and representations are so meditated, so centered on the meaning of her body and her story, that one is tempted to deal with them in terms of autobiographical statements rather than in terms of artistic productions. Kahlo herself favored this type of interpretation. She said she was born in 1910 (although she was actually born in 1907) to make the beginning of her life coincide with the beginning of the revolution. She felt not only that she was living in a revolutionary time but also that the particular event of the Mexican Revolution was the condition of possibility for both her art and her performative self-production. Commenting on this self-production, Lola Álvarez Bravo said, "Frida is the only person I know who created her own life. She is the only person who gave birth to herself."[19] Interestingly, the prolific photographic archive on Kahlo confirms this insight and shows how dominant her figure is even when it was the object of a photographic act.[20]

One cannot say that Kahlo found it easy to reconcile the modernism of her art with the revolution that she staunchly defended. Instead, she was painfully aware of the contradiction between, on the one hand, a revolution that revealed the truth of Mexico as a recuperation of the indigenous and, on the other, the appeal of the modern that constituted the kernel of both her aesthetic and political convictions. The fact that modernization was conveyed in and by a revolution allowed her to establish a freer relationship to the past that is the temporal sphere from which Kahlo drew the fundamental elements for her self-design. Above all, it allowed her to borrow from that past without fear of falling into the inauthentic. She dressed in indigenous clothes, especially in clothes from the Oaxaca region, historically one of the most isolated regions of Mexico, but the region that from 1921 on began to incarnate the most authentic area of Mexicanness. Her necklaces, earrings, bracelets, and hair combs often imitated pre-Columbian forms and materials with sober fidelity. Her self-portraits painstakingly reproduce these attributes of her actual persona. As a consequence, Kahlo was able to solve the quarrel between nativism and formalism simultaneously at the level of art and at the level of life.

The story of Col. Amelio Robles Ávila, whom Frida Kahlo probably never met, is another impressive instance of self-design. There are few sources on his life. Most of what we know comes from the laborious work of a few researchers. A modicum of additional information can be obtained at his museum/house in Guerrero. Its visitors are rewarded with a well-preserved memory of the landmarks of the colonel's life; but the thrill and contradictions that marked his history are, by and large, absent from its halls. In 1912 Amelio Robles joined the Zapatista army. His military ability was rewarded with the admiration of his peers and the respect of his superiors. He served under different revolutionary leaders until he obtained the command of his own troops. In November 1919, after Zapata's assassination, he surrendered—along with 315 men under his command—to the military chief of Guerrero to become part of a new, unified military structure. In 1920 he fought alongside the Obregonistas in the rebellion of Agua Prieta that ended Carranza's government and signaled the full integration of the previously outlawed Zapatistas into the formal structure of the postrevolutionary state. By 1923 he was once again in the battlefields. This time he was recalled to fight de la Huerta's uprising alongside troops loyal to President Obregón. In 1974 the Mexican government recognized his decade of military revolutionary service and awarded him a medal as a veteran of the revolution. At some point in his life, he adopted a girl with his *compañera*, Ángela Torres. Both his daughter and Ángela would end up estranged from him.

Col. Amelio Robles was born Amelia Robles in 1889, in Xochipala, Guerrero, the only girl in a house of three children. As the young daughter of a middle-class rancher, Amelia was sent to Catholic school and by the age of twelve was well trained in the chores expected of a young Catholic girl—but even more well trained, perhaps, in the exciting activities related to the management of a ranch. She was a famed marksman and rider even before she joined the revolution. A story like Robles's could hardly go unnoticed in Mexico. His name is said to have traveled beyond the limits of his state. The Swiss journalist Gertrude Duby heard about Amelio Robles while traveling in Chiapas, near Guatemala, and decided to make the trip to Guerrero to interview the colonel.[21] In 1927 *El Universal* published her interview with Robles. Since his transgender identity was well known in Mexico by at least 1927, it was not simple oversight that led the Mexican state sometime in the 1930s to falsify Robles's birth certificate so he could legalize the adoption of his daughter.[22]

In her discussion of Amelio Robles, Gabriela Cano notices that "his radical change in gender and sexual identity was not simply due to a pragmatic desire to enjoy the social advantages of men, but rather the product of a deeper, more vital desire to radically transform the female identity."[23] Or any identity, we can add. We still know too little about Robles to establish the exact coordinates of his symbolic revolt against the backdrop of what we imagine are the strictures of gender allocation in Mexico. In part, Colonel Robles's aversion to interviews was one of the causes of the many lacunae in his story. In the interviews that he did grant, he appeared as a resolute, firm, but affable octogenarian (Robles died at age 95), who graciously entertained his visitors without letting his small Bible slip from his hands.

Around the time Colonel Robles was cementing his military and personal fame in Mexico, on the other side of the Atlantic a polemic was brewing within the psychoanalytic community gathered around the patriarchal figure of Sigmund Freud. The polemic was about gender—more specifically about women. Is a woman born or made? (Freud's theories regarding the Oedipus complex as formative of human sexuality provided the grounds for the question.) For Freud this question strikes at such depths that answers can only be provided with some level of hesitation. And yet Freud tried to dismiss the entire discussion with a simple aphorism: "Anatomy is destiny." Robles's story proved Freud wrong. Few things can reveal better the meaning of revolution than this clash with destiny. For Robles the revolution allowed life to return to that ecstatic moment in which, suspended in time, the subject can scout his or her own future instead of being offered to it as a mere sacrificial animal. And yet, we should temper our optimism if we do not want to fall in the same abstract subjectivism of the liberal humanist biographers of the revolution. It is not a minor irony that the end of Robles's courageous revolt against destiny finds a school named *Amelia* Robles and a museum that honors in her all Mexican women. Amelio Robles died in 1984 only to become Amelia Robles, an icon of the relationship of gender and revolution. It is tempting to see in this final trick of the symbolic a reversion to a female status he wanted to escape. Yet things were perhaps more complex. When he died, Colonel Robles expressed only two last wishes. He wanted to be buried with military honors, and she wanted to be dressed as a woman to meet the judgment of God.

While the sense of self-design in either Frida Kahlo or Amelia/o Robles has a direct reference to the realms of enjoyment and appearance (or even exhibition), if we try to find a similar form of subjective self-creation in men, most of the time we will be confronted with erasure and self-effacement. This is the destiny embodied in the so-called seven sages of Mexico, to whom Enrique Krauze devotes a conventional yet significant book. Perhaps the only element that makes *Caudillos culturales de la Revolución mexicana* memorable is the immense sense of failure upon which the book is constructed. It tells the story of a group of intellectuals who fashioned themselves as a continuation of the Ateneísta project and of a society that believed in the inevitability of this promise.[24] The seven sages thought literature was the pathway to moral criticism and to the reconstruction of society. During the years of the most intense revolutionary turmoil they did not let the rage and fire of the revolt extinguish the flame of spiritual creation. They founded journal after journal, wrote on poetry and art, and even created a printing house. They were would-be poets and would-be philosophers, would-be teachers and would-be cultural critics. But unlike their Ateneísta predecessors, none of them would write an unforgettable memoir like Vasconcelos or organize the exact space of Mexico within the general flow of the culture of the West as did Alfonso Reyes. Instead, at early ages most would become part of a group of stellar bureaucrats, if the expression is not an oxymoron.

This failed generation left a deep mark on the relationship between intellect and political expediency in Mexico. Samuel Ramos calls them "a ghost generation," and Octavio Paz refers to their resignation of an intellectual career as a sign of the worst asceticism, a negation of subjectivity that, while inherent in the intellectual function, inflicted "the most painful loss, the loss of the personal work" on the members of this group.[25] Krauze adheres: *Caudillos culturales* springs from a doctoral dissertation titled "The Seven against Mexico." In his mind, it was a tragedy.

Aware as we are of the deep personal transformations that the revolution imposed upon individual projects, the case of the seven sages appears exceptional since it implies not just a transformation but the total foregoing of their initial intellectual project, as with Diego Rivera, who goes from being an openly Cubist painter to a crypto-Cubist in the best of cases; or as with Adolfo Best Maugard, who renounces his muralist career after his encounter with indigenous art. The essential coordinates through which they prepared themselves to enter the culture of their time and the coordinates under which they actually entered the political arena are almost without relationship. Instead of transubstantiation there was violent conversion. A whole generation that based its commonality on the cult of letters and personal expression left only efficiency behind as its legacy. The fate of Amelio Robles, a fate in which the revolution allowed him to be who he already was, stands in direct opposition to the lives of the seven sages, for whom the revolution determined that they would never be equal to themselves.

One of the members of this lost generation, Manuel Gómez Morín, penned one of the most significant accounts of the year 1915. In the essay, titled simply "1915" and published in 1927, Gómez Morín argues that the year 1915 marked, for better or for worse, a complete renovation of Mexican life. In words that have often been quoted to characterize the year, he writes,

> It was a time when salons housed horses and confessionals were fed to bonfires; a time when the portraits of illustrious scientific dames were riddled with bullets and when stolen pianos were equitably divided with an ax. It was a time when trains were blown up and pedestrians hunted down, when church images were shot in the name of the Virgin of Guadalupe. It was a time when soldiers begged on the streets, their rifles in hand.[26]

In the midst of so much devastation the revolution managed to pull itself out of its own chaos and in 1915, "when the failure of the revolution seemed certain . . . a new orientation began to emerge."[27] Why? Simply because the revolution had created the people who understood it as the proper context of their social existence. For Gómez Morín, 1915 was the transitional year when, from the abyss of its own dissolution, the revolt projected itself into the future in a desperate attempt to redeem the devastation that it left in its wake. From that chaos, Gómez Morín concluded, a new Mexico was born and along with it, "a new idea of Mexico and a new value of intelligence in life."[28]

This new value of intelligence in life understands the political and social horizon established in the postrevolutionary period to be unsurpassable. To be a subject (to "realize oneself" as the adagio goes) means to be a subject inside the limits of this event. Insofar as this intelligence no longer seeks to transform the most general conditions of life but accepts that the change is, in its fundamentals, completed, the administration of life becomes more important than its invention. For Gómez Morín what was needed now from him and his generation was to secure the correct technical grounding for the new orientation. It would be a mistake to read Gómez Morín's declaration of the primacy of the technical over the political as a conformist statement that aimed not to muddy revolutionary waters. It is true that Gómez Morín was not a Jacobin. But neither was he conformist. The dissociation of technique and ideology—which Gómez Morín would turn into the dogma presiding over the Partido Acción Nacional (PAN) (which he founded in 1939 and which finally came to power in 2000 under the leadership of Vicente Fox)—was simply based on the conviction that a fight over the distribution of riches had ceased to be the moving force of the revolution. Gómez Morín, the conservative, embraced this reality to the point that he developed the financial instruments that made possible the extensive land reform that would take place under Cárdenas. This creator of a future neoliberal center–right party studied the agrarian laws and technical reforms of the Soviet Union with admirable consistency and drew from them most of his inspiration for the organization of key aspects of rural production in Mexico.[29]

All the threads that I have considered so far in this chapter come together in José Vasconcelos's autobiography. Vasconcelos's life is not perhaps the most interesting or important life of the revolution, but it is the best-written life. There is something of the seven sages in the way he ended up sacrificing all his bourgeois ambitions on the pantheon of state formation. There is something of Frida Kahlo in his intense investment in aesthetics as a means of personal and political unification. Finally, there is something of Amelio Robles in the history of a person who made and remade himself endlessly in the shadow of a big revolt with which he had a rather ambiguous relationship.

VASCONCELOS IN A THOUSAND PAGES

Between 1935 and 1939 Vasconcelos completed four autobiographical volumes of uneven quality. (There are five such volumes if we include *La flama*, published in 1960, a year after his death.) The first volume, *Ulises criollo* (1935), covers the period between Vasconcelos's birth and the assassination of President Francisco Madero in 1913. *La tormenta* (1936) is framed by de la Huerta's coup of 1913 and the assassination of Carranza in 1920; this volume recounts Vasconcelos's tormented affair with Elena Arizmendi, whom he names Adriana. The third volume, *El desastre* (1938), covers the years between 1921 and 1924, when Vasconcelos was at the pinnacle of his political influence and became a continentally known intellectual. The fourth volume, *El proconsulado* (1939), narrates his failed presidential bid of 1929 and his posterior exile. At the time of the publication of *Ulises criollo*, Vasconcelos was one of the most influential public men of modern Mexico. However, the publication of his memoirs turned him into a literary icon. *Ulises criollo* went through five reprints in less than ten months. Mariano Azuela considered the book to be the best novel of the revolution. (Xavier Villaurrutia joked that the honor corresponded instead to Vasconcelos's infamous *Breve historia de México* [1936].)[30] Vasconcelos became a legend through his own writings, and, as with every legend, a wide gap began to open up between the historical record and what he recounts in his texts.

It is doubtful that many readers have stayed with Vasconcelos through the more than fifteen hundred pages that comprise the five volumes. It is equally doubtful that reading the volumes affected the received image of Vasconcelos: revered by many of his contemporaries as the architect of modern Mexico, he was chastised by a posterior leftist intelligentsia for his conservatism and for his intellectual amateurism. Claude Fell observes that for a long time, until the centennial of his birth, Vasconcelos's name and work were the objects of an active forgetting, a sort of "remorse, a kind of bad conscience of Mexico."[31] With few exceptions—such as Fell's magnificent book on Vasconcelos—a certain intellectual laziness (in which the notion of life is not at all exogenous) fixed Vasconcelos in an image that, quite curiously, he himself helped to build through his memories. Writing in 1935 or 1940 Vasconcelos often falsifies the statements and the affects of the Vasconcelos who acted in the 1920s. Some positions that he claimed to have sustained all his life—such as his dislike of aboriginal languages and cultures, his lofty spiritualism, his recalcitrant Catholicism—were in no way the positions that he upheld at the time of the events being narrated. Fell speaks of a rupture in the chronological thread and a continuous temporal collapse. Sergio Pitol is more explicit: "Not only do the opinions of the writer not coincide with those of the character Vasconcelos, but they are, actually, absolutely opposed to the ones upheld by the historical Vasconcelos in letters, books, speeches, and interviews entertained before 1929."[32]

In bringing attention to this disjuncture I am not suggesting that we should proceed to contrast Vasconcelos the writer and Vasconcelos the character. This could never do justice to the extraordinary complexity that the becoming letter of his obsessions lends to Vasconcelos's style. Nothing was simple or unproblematic in his life; and the trait that matters most in a reading of his autobiography—the widely proclaimed inconsistencies—becomes at this point more central than ever. One of his faithful critics and biographers calls him "a sort of schizophrenic character" of the revolution, and many of his contemporaries underlined the way in which the word *contradiction* described his persona perhaps better than any other.[33] The memoirs do not hide but rather exacerbate this overwhelming feeling of conflict. A brief catalog of Vasconcelos's vehement assertions will be enough to illustrate the point. In *Ulises criollo* he praises Madero for defending the lives of recently vanquished federal officers, but in *La tormenta* he voices the demand to "put everybody, from lieutenant up, against the firing squad" following Madero's assassination.[34] He condemns Lucio Blanco for organizing the distribution of lands among peasants and blames other military officers for occupying the residence of de la Huerta's supporters, yet a few chapters later he informs the reader about the farm Las Rosas, near Mixcoac, that was trusted to him for an undetermined period of time.[35]

If one sentence displays his rage against the recurrent exchange of favors and gifts between state functionaries and generals, another one, almost on the same page, informs the reader about "a whole collection of diverse horses that were presents from some generals who were friends of mine."[36] There is the Vasconcelos who feels repulsion for Villa yet daydreams of kidnapping his secretary at the SEP (whom he calls Beatrice) "as Pancho Villa would do it."[37] There is the Vasconcelos who condemns all violence but who also rejoices in the possibility of seeing the houses of the anti-Maderista men plundered and their wives and daughters abused. There is the Vasconcelos who is rabidly anti-American but who seems not to take notice that he has made his small fortune defending American interests in Mexico. There is the Vasconcelos who fires a teacher for his Huertista past and yet recalls another Huertista, Ricardo Gómez Robelo, to work with him at the SEP. There is the Vasconcelos who attacks with almost racist anger the acculturated Mexican who has crossed the frontier and become a *pocho,* and yet it was among the *pochos* that he launched his presidential campaign and it was from the *pochos* that he received the initial financial support that made that campaign possible.

Against this background of gruesome contradictions and constant enmity with previous allies, it is not strange that Vasconcelos's participation in the government of Obregón has often been seen as an incongruity. Vasconcelos himself put some fervor into destroying his revolutionary credentials. The fact that he ended his life flirting with fascism and devoted to a frankly reactionary Catholicism raises the question of how genuine his involvement with the Mexican Revolution had been. His iconoclasm and confusion are often quoted as tangential proofs that this involvement was at best unintended. The construction is not without its uses, since it allowed many critical readers to score easy points by attacking a figure who after being hailed as an example of the committed intellectual was mostly remembered as an embarrassment of a failed liberalism.[38]

I take the opposite perspective here. I see Vasconcelos's story as exemplary of the inscription of the intellectual in the revolution. Against Vasconcelos's own words ("The best you can do with a revolution is kill her," he says in the opening pages of *La flama*), the revolution was never an obstacle that blocked the road to his personal and intellectual fulfillment. It was, instead, the condition that allowed the possibility of this fulfillment. Vasconcelos is one of the fantasies of the revolution. Even his most eccentric or conservative writings stand in a direct and causal relationship with the revolutionary upheaval. But this means that the specific form of inscription of Vasconcelos in the revolution has to be determined and brought to light—not by ignoring the interplay of passions, the outrageous remarks, the almost infantile belief in his own forces, the system of silences and false attributions that mislead readers and biographers alike, but rather by integrating them into a certain logic of the subject and the revolution.

Politics and Morality

In *Ulises criollo*, about the eve of an important political clash, Vasconcelos writes, "Above and beyond politics, ethics paraded its armies in preparation for the transcendental battle."[39] Vasconcelos's phrase aims to limn a stark opposition between politics and morality. Politics is interest, morality is the sublation of any mundane involvement in the name of higher ideals. The opposition between politics and morality is not only widespread in the memoirs, it is also the specific narrative device that Vasconcelos puts in place to explain the somewhat capricious path of his thinking and actions. Vasconcelos presents the tension between politics and morality under the familiar opposition between means and ends. The moral position sustains that no end is just if achieved by unjust means. Political reason, on the other hand, asserts that the justness of the ends may justify or at least redeem any injustice committed at the level of means. Thus, the uniqueness and even oddity of his position: Vasconcelos wants to present himself as a public man guided only by moral—rather than political—reasons. For Vasconcelos, a virtuous political goal that is achieved by virtuous political means is enough to take the whole process outside the sphere of politics altogether. This is how Vasconcelos understood his national campaign against illiteracy and this is why he could, in complete good consciousness, extend the grip of a secular and anticlerical state (an anticlericalism that, to some extent, he himself shared at the time) through a vocabulary reminiscent of the Spanish spiritual conquest. This is also the origin of some surprising statements in the body of the memoirs. In *El desastre*, Obregón's minister announces, "I don't care about political groups or parties. . . . Politicians nauseate me."[40] A few pages later, another assertion ignores its own conditions of enunciation even more blatantly: "While in the government, I preferred to stay away from politics."[41] Significantly, the conflict between politics and morality runs out of control in *La tormenta*, the volume devoted to the heat of the revolutionary moment that effectively destroyed the old order between the years 1914–1917.

The recourse to morality makes plain Vasconcelos's ambivalent relationship to the revolutionary struggle. If he had had his wish, the revolution would not have been necessary to wake the Mexican spirit. But once the revolution took place, he tried to tame its uncontrollable forces (which he often battled within himself) through a moral propaedeutic that he also correctly defined as an ethic. Significantly, this ethic does not oppose politics in the way the private opposes the public. Both politics and morality are forms of the public. This is not obvious at first sight given Vasconcelos's passionate defense of a private, bourgeois lifestyle. Through the whole autobiography Vasconcelos believes himself to be a lawyer; a financially independent man; and a centered, liberal mind comfortably resting on a successful liberal profession. This liberal self, rather than home and family, is his refuge. If affronted or unhappy with the business of the state, Vasconcelos immediately agitates the specter of a resignation and his return to the private practice that will bring him money and peace of mind. This is the Vasconcelos that he would have been had his path not crossed the path of the revolution. And yet, as the reading progresses, Vasconcelos is either minister or fugitive, presidential candidate or plotter, bitter outcast or resentful exile. The liberal self that he so often presents as the truth of his existence is in fact a leftover of an unlived life. Vasconcelos never retreated into it. Instead, he increasingly embraced the political dimension of existence, a dimension that he condemned in the harshest possible terms as being based on antagonism rather than cooperation and which invited deceit rather than truth, jealousy rather than generosity.

Now, the opposition between politics as calculability and morality as disinterest is, in the last instance, untenable: any inaction is a form of action and every silence could speak volumes. Once ethics is wielded as a tool in the realm of the social, it is forced into calculability by the very logic of its social deployment. In this process, ethics, the discourse of the obstacle, becomes morality, the righteous disavowal of all obstacles. In the case of Vasconcelos's autobiography, it would be relatively easy to prove that the replacement of politics by morality is never really achieved. At best, what we have is a mobilization of morality to rationalize decisions that are political through and through. In those instances in which the moralization of political decisions is simply unviable, Vasconcelos will have recourse to silence and omission. This is the reason why few approaches are more sterile to the reading of the memoirs than the attempt to correlate the text with historical events. Such a reading produces only the uncanny feeling that Mexico and Vasconcelos lived an intimate and yet completely divergent history.

Vasconcelos's opposition of politics and morals has strong genealogical connections with the vindication of culture as a tool for the creation of moral consensus, an idea that was, if not launched, at least authorized by Kantian transcendentalism. In his memoirs, Vasconcelos attributes Kant with facilitating an alternative conception of the world for himself and his companions at the Ateneo. The communal reading of the *Critique of Pure Reason* provided them with intellectual grounds for rejecting the then prevalent philosophy of positive facts.[42] Particularly appealing to Vasconcelos was Kant's grounding of both aesthetic pleasure and moral behavior in disinterest. Aesthetics and morality emerged as possible sites of redemption because they are located beyond the accountability that is intrinsic to economy and politics. Although Vasconcelos refused to speak their language, he saw both economy and politics as epiphenomenal manifestations of the modern capitalist world. As a minister in Obregón's administration, Vasconcelos had the chance to implement his view that art and literature could be vehicles of morality. He handpicked many of the books that the SEP reproduced for rural audiences. The instructions sent to rural teachers were predicated upon a view of art as a tool to control and subdue political passion. This aim was not to be achieved in an authoritarian way. As the directions that accompanied the remittance of the books made clear, the goal of those literary works was to jumpstart a process of discussion that would lead, more or less autonomously, to the valorization of a moral sphere. But it is not difficult to see that this altruistic use of literature to further morality is itself the product of a calculation, and hence, in its very being, a political act. Moreover, as we will see shortly, the project of enlightening the masses through art always risks being ruined by the geopolitical conditions of its deployment.

The Political Interruption of the Aesthetic

Like most of the members of the Ateneo, Vasconcelos held a deep admiration for the Greek past, seeing in that specific historical instance a time in which thinking and contemplation held primacy over the interests of the mundane and the power struggles of the political. He knew quite well that this was not the result of a natural or organic development but the product of cultivation and *paideia*. As Pedro Henríquez Ureña comments in his canonical "La cultura de las humanidades," the Mexican Ateneo was perhaps the first organized attempt to bring classical Greek heritage into active conversation with the most urgent social and political questions of the moment. Unsurprisingly, the small section that Vasconcelos devotes to the Ateneo in his *Ulises criollo* provides almost no insight into the group. Vasconcelos presents his own participation as marginal. Yet his Greekness was as bold as that of Alfonso Reyes or Pedro Henríquez Ureña. He had been the Ateneo's first postrevolutionary secretary and had even attempted to write a modern tragedy, *Prometeo vencedor* (1920), which was unanimously ignored. But along with a Greek communal ethic that would resound strongly in a Mexican intelligentsia disenchanted with fifty years of liberalism, Henríquez Ureña introduced also an agonic cultural motive through his lectures on José Rodó's

Ariel. Vasconcelos found Rodó's criticism of Anglo-Saxon utilitarianism obviously appealing, something that becomes readily apparent in the exquisite vignette "En la isla de los piratas" (In the pirate's island), included in *La tormenta*. The vignette centers on an official mission that Venustiano Carranza entrusted to Vasconcelos in 1914. The "mission" itself was nebulous and may well have been simply an excuse to keep Vasconcelos away and busy.[43] Vasconcelos was directed to obstruct the collocation of Mexican bonds in European markets by convincing investors in London and Paris of the fraudulent nature of de la Huerta's regime. The vignette begins with Vasconcelos on a steamboat on his way to London, lying on a couch and reading a guide to London museums. This image of the revolutionary connoisseur traveling to the radiant center of European culture by his own means and with both a political and a cultural agenda in mind is not surprising. Yet by the very first day in London, it becomes clear that the real goal of the trip was a dandy style of cultural tourism. Vasconcelos picked a hotel "strategically located" near the British Museum, and the next day he and Elena Arizmendi (the Adriana of the memoirs) hit the streets, deciding "to forget the century, determined to ignore the world in order to devote ourselves completely to the adoration of Phidias's sculptures."[44] The reader may be taken aback by the way Vasconcelos arranges his priorities. But as Vasconcelos himself protested, the visit to the museum was a precondition for writing his aesthetics, and his aesthetics would be, in turn, inextricably linked to the politics of the postrevolutionary state.[45] At the museum, Vasconcelos looked for confirmation of everything that he had held in esteem up to this point—Adriana, whom he lectured, was his witness. The most noticeable element of "En la isla de los piratas" is that it ends with the complete subversion of what Vasconcelos had praised as the social function of art. Once inside the museum, the aesthetic experience belied the canon through which Vasconcelos sought to contain it. Even as we are told about the religious rapture through which the beholder abandons himself to the adoration of art, the narration introduces an irreparable fissure in the apparently seamless realm of the beautiful. Political tension begins to mount at the lexical level as Vasconcelos reminds the reader that these beautiful statues that he beholds with ecstatic adoration "were ripped apart from the frieze of the Parthenon for the benefit of the British Museum."[46] The remark is not just an outburst of irony; it also prepares the way for a systematic exposition of the impossible reconciliation of art and politics. Before these statues, Vasconcelos says, the viewer experiences "a deep, virginal emotion."[47] But the presence of the sculptures at the museum is itself the product of a rape and an uprooting. The original aesthetic relationship cannot be really reawakened because it is already traversed by a colonial violence through which a utilitarian culture (evoked by the word "benefit") has turned art into just another form of gain. The title of the section has warned us beforehand of this development. Adding insult to injury, as he left the museum Vasconcelos spotted an "insolent" sign that informed visitors that these statues "were rescued by Lord Elgin and brought to England with the goal of saving them from the insouciance of the natives."[48] The scene triggered Vasconcelos's indignation and marks the beginning of a tirade against the British that reaches high levels of anticolonialist awareness. The serenity needed for the contemplation of art gives way to the rebellion of an oppressed political persona. In his wrath against "the new imperialism," Vasconcelos attacks "everything that is European, everything that belongs to the north, today in command."[49]

Vasconcelos did not abdicate the idea that art can be the instituting force of a new social paideia. He simply attributed the true aesthetic spirit to the Latino races, leaving the kingdom of interest to the Anglo-Saxons.[50] Since the liberating force of universal art has been co-opted by the development of modern imperialism, where could he turn to find the elements for an artistic education of the masses? It is at this point that Vasconcelos's general antipathy to modern art presented a hindrance to his educational project. The fact that Vasconcelos lacked even a notion of modernist aesthetics plays an enormous role in organizing the "reactionary" traits of his political persona. His rejection of the modern artist—epitomized in his disdainful remarks on Tina Modotti—pushed Vasconcelos further into a search for an Arielist paradigm of cultural production.[51] This paradigm was, in its essence, a crossover between canonical literary works (especially French) on the one hand, and, on the other, an emerging and evolving sense of cultural nationalism. Arielism became, then, a form of *criollismo*: in it the whole of classical tradition (represented by no other than Ulysses) has finally reached its (Latin) American destiny.[52]

Vasconcelos's answer to the pedagogical crisis of classical art is both nuanced and complex, although unfortunately couched in texts (such as *El monismo estético*) that are obscure and difficult to read. The problem that figures preeminently in Vasconcelos's discussion of art qua pedagogical tool is the democratizing effect of culture in contrast to the increasing authoritarianism implied in the subjection of the individual to the democracy of commodities. In his instructions to rural teachers, Vasconcelos makes clear that education is not about teaching "content" but rather about promoting a spiritual freedom without which there can never be true enlightenment. It is this search that gives priority to art—an open-ended form of expression—above all other possible cultural or scientific forms. As an educator Vasconcelos remained a rabid believer in the value of deduction. One can only learn what one has lived. Life (and, derivatively, feeling and sensibility) takes precedence over contemplation and transmission. In this his autobiography and his philosophical texts are, for once, of one piece.

Still in London a few days after touring the British Museum, Vasconcelos paid a visit to a monument commemorating Admiral Horatio Nelson, a column dedicated to "The English-Speaking People of the World." Vasconcelos found the monument impressive and overwhelming. He read in its inscription a reticent avowal of what British imperialism has always denied: that its foundation does not lie in the universality of the free play of market forces but is based on an ethnic community of race and language. British universalism has always been incarnated universalism. "As for myself," he somberly concludes, "I can only say that educated as I was in the hate of our Spanish blood, intellectually orphaned by a doctrine that presents Juárez as a savior, when all he did was deliver Mexico's soul to the Yankees; educated as I was to deprecate against Hispanic obscurantism while embracing an abstract liberalism, right there, before that monument to the English nations, I felt for the first time in all its unsoundable depth the bitter resentment for the defeat of the Invincible."[53]

The key word in this passage is "abstract." As a political doctrine, liberalism is abstract insofar as it has not managed to intertwine its principles with those of a lived culture. Liberalism is not false because it organizes a fiction but rather because it represents a failure to integrate the actual lives of the people into the logic of political representation. Arielism itself betrays a liberal component in its preference for classical culture. So, although art—as the principle able to guide any embodiment of abstract ethical standards—maintains its place in Vasconcelos's schema despite the loss of aesthetic universality at the hands of "those in command," his experience at the museum led Vasconcelos to the idea that, to be valid, the universalism of culture has to be rooted in conditions that are always local.

Ten years after his visit to the British Museum, already a minister under Obregón, Vasconcelos visited Zapatista Morelos, bringing with him, as usual, a cohort of artists and poets. The visit to Morelos entailed particular challenges for the minister. As often happened in postrevolutionary Mexico, the table brought together men and women representing castes separated for centuries. Past suspicions also contributed to the uneasiness of the meeting, in which a bunch of metropolitan intellectuals met the historical figures of popular Zapatismo, such as Gildardo Magaña and Antonio Díaz Soto y Gama. It is worthwhile to point out that at this historical juncture Vasconcelos was not the staunch anti-Zapatist he would become later. Still, he could perceive a disquiet in the meeting that was not just a product of differences in recent political allegiances. At this point, and following his aesthetic instincts, Vasconcelos asked the poet Joaquín Méndez Rivas to recite one of his compositions. The poet picked "Musa morena." Vasconcelos does not describe the poem but only the effect that it had on the audience (which is the only thing that matters to the ideology of the aesthetic state): "A shudder ran through the fatherless souls that we, all Mexicans, are. . . . That was Méndez Rivas's finest hour. His poem sealed the alliance between a new Zapatismo and our university, which readied itself for the task of reconstructing the national soul."[54]

Madero: Political Martyrdom

A practical man, Vasconcelos did not think that poets and museums could do the work of the state or politicians. However, the dominance of the political by the ethical was not a far-fetched utopia, since it had been incarnated in actuality at the core of the revolutionary process itself. The person who had achieved that balance was none other than Francisco Madero. In life, Madero was never the hero and the martyr he would become when the history of revolution was rewritten under the large shadow of the post-revolutionary state. On the contrary, he was vilified as president, harassed as a candidate, and underestimated (often by his own family) as a would-be revolutionary. To an important extent, it was Vasconcelos who launched a political canonization of Madero. For Vasconcelos, Madero was the father of modern Mexico, or at least of everything that was pure and good in that modernity. He was the hero, the martyr, the prophet, the saint—such are the words that the memoirs use to describe the deceased president. Above all, Madero was proof that a political life that was ethical in nature was possible and viable. It was Madero—Vasconcelos insisted—who exemplified the subjection of politics to morality. His actions were governed neither by economic interests (he was already rich) nor by political ambitions (he lacked the adequate political instincts). Against all historical indications, Vasconcelos argued that even the revolution qua social revolution (that is, the post-1913 revolution) received the foundation of its authority from Madero.[55] In a notorious text from 1914, his personal contribution to the Aguascalientes convention, entitled "La convención militar de Aguascalientes es soberana," Vasconcelos sustained that the sovereignty of the convention was based on two uncontestable facts: first, the convention was the expression of a people in arms; second, it was the legitimate heir to Madero's government.[56] The propositions contradicted each other. The legitimacy won by arms was opposed in fact to a legitimacy founded on the democratic event that made Madero president in 1911. It is interesting to note that by following this argument Vasconcelos retrospectively endowed Madero with a foundational revolutionary character. Madero never made such a claim, and even the Plan de Potosí specifically established that the Maderista revolution did not imply any break in the legal constitution of the Mexican nation—a constitution whose laws should remain in place, according to Madero, during the revolutionary process itself.[57]

However, as in the case of Phidias's statues, a thorough politicization awaited the figure of the martyr-president. The vignette "Política y negocios"—included in *La tormenta*—contains a measured but firm criticism of the limitations of Madero's policies as president. The criticism makes patent the inevitability of the political antagonism that Vasconcelos desperately tried to disavow through a permanent cancellation of politics by morality. Vasconcelos criticized Madero in three respects: his opposition to the disbanding of the defeated federal army, the confirmation of a few Porfirista politicians in key areas of the administration, and the lack of a practical gratitude towards those who had risked their lives for the revolutionary cause. With well-calculated ambiguity, Vasconcelos writes, "Unfortunately, Madero asked too much of the patriotism of the ex-soldiers of the revolution, throwing them into misery with just the consolation that 'the motherland is now safe.' A true politician should have understood the need to save and protect the most forsaken among his own supporters."[58]

The half-reproachful, half-benevolent tone of these lines is a surprise for any reader familiar with Vasconcelos's memories. Madero, whose historical figure eclipsed all others, is suddenly found guilty of political naiveté. If this is important, it is because for Vasconcelos naiveté was almost indistinguishable from hypocrisy. Not only had Madero asked too much of his soldiers, the revolution—the quote seems to say—asked too much of Madero himself. The recognition that ethical superiority is not enough to navigate the waters of a revolution seems to put into doubt Vasconcelos's moralization of politics. It is not enough to be good, he seems to say; one needs also to be astute. More importantly, is not Madero's real shortcoming the fact that he incarnates that form of abstract liberalism that Vasconcelos condemned in the figure of Juárez as he stood before the monument to the English-speaking people of the world?

The fight against abstraction is a constant leitmotif of the early twentieth century, although its roots are certainly older. Vasconcelos embraced a certain Romantic tradition when he tacitly asserted that morality is not a private affair. It enjoys an objective form of existence that Hegel names *Sittlichkeit*.[59] Values and morality are not abstract ideas used to measure reality. They are rather the embodied properties of a historical community. As we will see later, despite his ideological liberalism Vasconcelos too would base the morality of a possible Mexican nation on a tradition of social and popular autonomy.

In line with his ideology of incarnated forms of thought, Vasconcelos privileged action over thinking. Although he rarely used the word, *praxis* defines better than most concepts the core of his ideological and philosophical convictions. It is possible to find here, around the question of praxis, a conceptual break with Vasconcelos's former Kantian Ateneísta cohort. Some key Ateneístas interiorized Kant's advice on arguing as much as one wants but obeying as much as one needs. Their disagreements with the political establishment would be rigorously restricted to theoretical views while they devoted themselves to actualizing the aesthetic communitarian ideal either at a personal level or a level that could only be extended to a limited number of followers. For Vasconcelos, on the other hand, the satisfaction of the communitarian drive could not take an intellectual form because he understood, quite correctly, that this was a social desire that could not be redeemed in the personal sphere. Furthermore, revolutionary times had rendered the separation between intellectual and political labor unviable. The politics that he abhorred offered Vasconcelos an insight that he kept to himself but also one that dictated the direction of his life: whatever desire impelled him, it was one that would only find satisfaction in the realm of praxis. The status of this praxis is itself puzzling, since Vasconcelos seems to condemn so many avenues for political and social agency. Praxis here does not mean politics or even ethics, but creative activity. It would be possible to quote from Vasconcelos's philosophical writings to uphold this primacy of "creative activity" over either politics or theory. But his memoirs already offer abundant examples. Intellectual contemplation is always viewed with contempt by the minister. One has to take Vasconcelos at his word when in *El desastre* he dismisses intellectual work as the wrong strategy to cope with the problems of the world: "For God's sake, don't give me ideas," he tells an academic trained in the United States. "Ideas I can provide for myself or buy them at fifty cents apiece. Give me creative activity."[60] It is important to realize what exactly is at stake in this rejection of the analytical power of intelligence. It surely is not anti-intellectualism—one cannot accuse Vasconcelos of being hostile to the life of the spirit. It is rather—even if only half-glimpsed—the conviction that an idea that cannot be incarnated in reality is worthless in the context of a revolution. As for knowledge, Vasconcelos claims that one does not need to know the world to transform it, for the simple reason that the world's power to resist change had been weakened by the revolutionary act and was no longer a match for the transformative drive.[61] Vasconcelos recognized the moment for what the moment was. It was open to the designs of action. This remained true even if Vasconcelos ended up disgusted at the direction that his own master plan took, either at the hands of those in charge of implementing it (teachers, bureaucrats, cultural leaders) or at the hands of those who succeeded him at the SEP. In the same vein, the primacy of the transformative moment remained true even if the old world resisted all and each of these proposed transformations. What that world could not resist was the primacy of the political as the dominant form of sociability, a form into which the old world was swept to its utter disgust.

The Utopia of a Supposedly Apolitical Man

In 1928, after serving as minister for four years and spending another four in exile, this man disgusted by politics decided to return to Mexico and run for president. Vasconcelos's candidacy elicited an enormous enthusiasm in the vastly expanded intellectual circles of postrevolutionary Mexico. In *El proconsulado* Vasconcelos made almost no mention of his political platform in the campaign of 1928–1929. It was, however, far more leftist than the scant references in the memoirs may lead us to believe. Mauricio Magdaleno, who collaborated with Vasconcelos closely during the campaign, says that Vasconcelos's supporters were dismayed by the similarities between their own political platform and that of the Partido Nacional Revolucionario (PNR) in the election of 1929. Although both documents had been drafted independently, the program of the governing PNR, Magdaleno retells, "was our program minus two or three testimonies that were at the root of our beliefs and that made of us a better party."[62] Magdaleno does not say what these testimonies were, but perhaps no place is more suited to find the specific differences between Vasconcelos and his rivals than the memoirs themselves.

Land reform was Zapata's dream and isolationism was that of Villa. Obregón and de la Huerta cherished a vision of economic development to which Plutarco Elías Calles added a fervent anticlericalism. Madero was the martyr of transparent democracy. What was Vasconcelos's utopia? The utopia that underlined Vasconcelos's presidential bid was one grounded on a vision of the small Mexican pueblo: a provincial, multicultural, and multiclassist community organized around Hispanic rituals and put under the spiritual guidance of the Catholic Church. This utopia of parochialism was greatly at odds with the cosmopolitan nature of Vasconcelos's own lifestyle, and it was based on an idealized image of the small Mexican town that an uneven and chaotic modernization was putting rapidly beyond reach.[63] And yet this utopia was not merely nostalgic; rather, it presented an extraordinary challenge to traditional politics in Mexico.

As can be expected, Vasconcelos's examples of this community came from the world of his childhood. What was at stake, however, was not simply a sentimental longing. Not every provincial location would serve the purpose of communal redemption. Vasconcelos spent his infancy in Piedras Negras, a small border town in the north of Mexico across the Rio Grande from its American rival, Eagle Pass.[64] He attended school on the American side and grew up bilingual, a fact that would greatly help him in his professional career. On the frontier in the 1890s every sense of Mexicanness was mediated by its American counterpart. Life was life in front of a mirror. There, Vasconcelos experienced the existential urgency for which Arielismo would provide a name and diagnosis. He could ponder the prospectus of a total cultural annihilation of the Latino tradition by the invasive forms of modern, Anglo-American capitalism. As he was writing *Ulises criollo,* he needed only to recall the big sketches of his infancy to feel the devouring attraction of a frantic progress that threatened to swallow the soul of provincial Mexico. For some time, however, Piedras Negras looked more refined than its neighbor Eagle Pass. The public festivities on the Mexican side exerted a sort of aristocratic supremacy at the frontier. Slowly, however, "Eagle Pass progressed." In the blink of an eye, "New buildings appeared and the streets began to be paved."[65] The people from Piedras Negras developed the habit of shopping "on the other side," where everything was cheaper and more convenient. In his attempt to find a solid ground for the foundation of the community, Vasconcelos fled from the frontier, from that mirror that fractured his self from the inside out instead of returning a narcissistic image of wholeness.

A more integrative experience could only be found in deep Mexico. The opportunity arose when Vasconcelos's father decided to take the family on a vacation in Durango. Unlike the many Mexicans who boasted of taking their vacations in San Antonio, Texas, Vasconcelos's father took the road of "true civilization," where "the carved stone" prevails "over concrete."[66] Metaphors referring to buildings or to the materiality of existence are never innocent in Vasconcelos's writings. In a preface to a 1932 edition of *La tormenta,* he depicted himself as a cathedral to better underline the moral complexities that characterize any full life; and in his tenure as minister, Vasconcelos would make a point of erecting educational buildings in stone rather than other more modern (and cheaper) materials.[67]

Vasconcelos saw the trip to Durango as a return to that place where "our creole culture begins."[68] The vacation—circa 1892—overlapped with the festivities around Easter. Although colored by provincial simplicity, architecture also played a fundamental role in Vasconcelos's stay in Durango. The chapter entertains the reader with a description of the cathedral that is marked by an abundance of detail that could not have possibly been registered by the ten- or eleven-year-old witness. The narrator's gaze descends slowly upon the fiesta from the top of the cathedral bell tower. Vasconcelos cannot refrain from noticing how poorly the "elemental architecture" of Piedras Negras compares to the solid edifices that predominated in places like

Durango. Certainly the cathedral was unremarkable and unpretentious, but the power of the church reigned supreme nonetheless. "No one, in approaching the fiesta, asked who the name of the governor was."[69] Instead, everybody had their eyes fixed on the pomp of the ceremony and the gestures of the bishop.[70] The opposition between governor and church mirrors the one between politics and art that erupted for Vasconcelos at the British Museum two decades later. However, it would be too hasty to assimilate this eulogy of church to a conservative or even Catholic perspective. Strictly speaking, Vasconcelos did not oppose politics to religion but to the visible, affective, and communicative presentation of tradition. Religious festivity opposes a lived cultural tradition to abstract liberalism. Vasconcelos opposes "the laws of the Reform," which had banished "the exterior manifestations" of religion, to the vital "curiosity, fervor, and happiness of the multitude."[71] The fiesta unfolding around the walls of the church did nothing but enact the essential peoplehood that constituted the substance of the scene. The church actualized the *common* of the community, and it is easy to see how Vasconcelos's *casas del pueblo* were designed to wrestle this function from the religious space.[72]

The vacation in Durango is repeated almost exactly when Vasconcelos's family spends some time in Toluca. Vasconcelos perceived Toluca as almost unbearably parochial. The atmosphere "inhibited impulses and put a brake on thinking."[73] At times this parochialism seems to verge on biological determinism, as if life itself were coming to a stop as it approached the skirts of the volcanoes. However, "Toluca boasted of an intense religious life."[74] Vasconcelos recalls the hours spent in different churches and the intense religious devotion that pervaded everything in these younger years. The religious feeling does not take long to spill over into a more politically charged language and figuration. In the days of religious festivity, "a feverish trembling ran through the whole city. In the churches and the neighborhoods, from the bishop to the owners of commercial establishments, the whole town had in sight only the fiesta for the Virgin of Guadalupe four hundred years after her first revelation."[75] The usually quiet streets were now filled with pilgrims coming from every corner of the republic and also with a significant number of Indians from the highlands. All accommodations were taken. The poorest among the crowd spent the night in parks or around the stairs of the churches. Finally, the glorious day arrived with the ringing of bells and the noise of fireworks. The sun was bright in a cloudless sky, and a subtle breeze from the volcano cooled the people's exuberant faces.[76]

By eleven the cathedral was full. At noon the archbishop uncovered the image of the Virgin of Guadalupe, proclaiming her Queen of the Mexicans. At this point, Vasconcelos switches the narration to the streets and the verb tense from past to present tense.

> Outside, as in patriotic days, a multitude overflows from the sidewalks to the pavement. The carts with fruits and food attract passersby. Peddlers go around announcing their merchandise. . . . Light, heat, and colors, all castes confused, all indigenous dialects mixed, all kinds of clothes—the whole complex and mysterious Mexico was there, unified at least for an instant by a religious feeling subtly woven into a national destiny.[77]

Irony, the watermark of division, is completely absent from these pages. The communion of the community occupies the entire horizon of the narrative. The multitude enacts an instant of unification of castes and languages. These events, which take place several decades before the revolution, illustrate a realm of social cohesiveness that predates and owes nothing to the forces of modernization—an integrative Mexican *Sittlichkeit.* If the revolutionary state's most pressing project was to build up its own people, Vasconcelos strives to show here that the people have always been there, already joined in a primordial form of sociability that does not require the mediation of state forms to express its cohesive togetherness.[78] At least in his most disinterested moments, Vasconcelos's goal is to establish the unquestionable sovereignty of the people. A lawyer by training, Vasconcelos knows that popular sovereignty is a constitutional guarantee in Mexico, but as a political person he knows also that laws do not apply to reality by themselves.[79] The executive office—the one that he is running for—is the sine qua non condition of the sociability that Vasconcelos depicts in this festive day. He does not acknowledge this need for a sovereign mediation, perhaps because his intention is to discount the political altogether. But in this lack of acknowledgment he reveals less a contradiction and more one of the most intriguing and interesting aspects of his political thought. The Mexican pueblo was for Vasconcelos what the Greek city-state was for Hegel: an objective rendering of ideals that have not been detached from the mores of everyday transactions and as such are not in need of a reflexive foundation. As a matter of fact, Vasconcelos never speaks about communities but about "pueblos," and he means by that word the material distribution and inscription of bodies, buildings, and activities able to engender a togetherness irreducible to any political link.

If the popular is already constituted in its cultural ideality, why then did Vasconcelos put so much emphasis on his educational campaign? Education seeks to make constant what is episodic in the case of the church festivals. It is a matter of turning intensities into regularities. And in this case, Vasconcelos *saw* like a state. Conversely, even Vasconcelos acknowledged that the excesses of capitalist accumulation have had disastrous effects on the social fabric of small towns exposed to the tyranny of church and landowners. Despite everything that has been said or written about Vasconcelos's aspirations to educate peasant populations to the mores of high culture, the truth is that the SEP's educational campaigns always had remedial and utilitarian goals.[80] However, he also believed that culture in general, and aesthetic production in particular, was especially suited to creating a unified moral community. The enormous distance that always obtains between the people and their representatives could be lessened if representatives and represented could be made to conform to a more unified sense of the communal. In this project, religious feeling is only the cement—as Vasconcelos himself says—of that operation. Despite the religious references, a careful reading of these passages in *Ulises criollo* will confirm that for Vasconcelos culture and only culture, to the exclusion of everything else (including religion), is the fundamental sphere of political constitution. Indeed, there is nothing particularly Christian in Vasconcelos's evocation of either Durango or Toluca. In both instances what captures the writer's attention are the rituals of power and the life of a pueblo and its people in their utter visibility. Vasconcelos states it plainly when he observes that his father was a lukewarm Catholic who "adored religious rites that were for him the best form of art."[81] It is art, then, and not religion that is foundational. The communal festivities themselves were not—and they are not even today—strictly ecclesiastical occasions. Often the church does not exert total control over the ceremony, which is always open to different forms of hybridization between the religious and the communal. This type of festivity serves not only to reinvigorate communal ties but also to provide some of its members the chance to rise to prominence through institutions like the cargo. Through the cargo—which according to some historians dates back to the first years of colonial life but which was firmly in place at the end of the eighteenth century—influential members of the community (or those who want to become influential) finance a given religious festivity.

The festival in Toluca to which Vasconcelos was alluding took place, very likely, in 1895 on the occasion of the crowning of the Virgin of Guadalupe.[82] The crowning of a Virgin icon is a momentous act in Catholic rituals and is rarely seen in a lifetime. Often the pope himself performs the crowning. The crowning of the Virgin of Guadalupe that Vasconcelos may be recalling here was the culmination of a long process that started one hundred and fifty years before with an initial appeal that was only approved under Pope Leo XIII at the end of the nineteenth century. The episode had an enormous impact throughout the Catholic world. It was also a typical Mexico City affair in which the Porfirian government participated most actively. First Lady Carmen Díaz acted as godmother, raising a small fortune to pay for the thirty-pound, solid silver-and-gold crown used at the ceremony performed at Mexico's national cathedral, which was attended by President Díaz and all his government officials. While the church hierarchy was interested in a public demonstration of affinity with the government, this submission of the religious to the political was certainly resisted by some men of the church, especially in the provinces.[83] The fact that there was no mention of this metropolitan festivity in Vasconcelos's memoirs is due less to his nonattendance and more to his belief that it represented everything that is wrong in the use of the spiritual power for political calculation. As Vasconcelos knew quite well, the crowning of the Virgin was not only politically exploited in Mexico City, it was also the occasion for many forms of money making, as the church itself embarked on the selling of indulgences following a papal authorization.[84] In the case of the crowning of the Virgin at Toluca, Vasconcelos also writes of a crown adorned with rubies and diamonds, but he makes every effort to disentangle this representation from the one centered in Mexico City that dominated the event in the press at the time. The crown itself—Vasconcelos tells us—was the result of the effort of the community that celebrated its own unity and performance as part of the religious festivities. Vasconcelos saw in the provincial celebration, with its mixture of races and classes, an illustration of his own vision of Christianity as the transcultural ground of Mexican citizenship. The image of the Indians coalescing with the rest of the people for the celebration stands in stark contrast to the segregated nature of the metropolitan festivities, where the Indians were forced to attend mass at the cathedral on a different day than the creoles and the representatives of church and state.[85]

Finally, in Vasconcelos's story the description of the crowning of the Virgin of Guadalupe contains a veiled allusion to the question of sovereignty. As we know, the miraculous appearance of the Virgin of Guadalupe before indigenous eyes was the beginning of the cancellation of Spanish authority and the first step in the construction of a creole hegemony. The Virgin was first seen wearing a crown—Juan Diego testified to its existence in his deposition. The crown, always present in pre-1895 paintings, was erased from paintings after that year to make the (material) crowning of the Virgin possible. A crown, unlike a halo, is a signature of royal power—of sovereign power in one of its purest incarnations. This connection was not missed by the original propagandists of the cult of Guadalupe or by its posterior commentators, such as Edmundo O'Gorman—and even less, as we will see, by Vasconcelos.[86]

Outside the Fiesta

Vasconcelos wrote these passages on Durango and Toluca in 1935—six years after his failed bid for the presidency of Mexico. Obregón, the man who had introduced him to the high spheres of Mexican politics, had died in 1928, and Vasconcelos had lost a fraudulent election to an almost unknown official candidate: Pascual Ortiz Rubio. The possibility of an open presidential election was announced by President Calles—with whom Vasconcelos had formed a bitter enmity that went back to the years of his tenure at the SEP. Obregón had been the last *caudillo*. It was not—Calles argued—that there were not able men to conduct Mexico, but none of them had the kind of undisputed authority that came from having fought the decisive battles of the revolution. Power had to be institutionalized, and the president had to become more an administrator than a political guide to the nation. Simultaneously, Calles called for the formation of a strong opposition party (often referred simply as *la reacción*).

The fervent anticlericalist Calles considered that even groups linked to the church should have a voice in congress. They could not represent any real threat to the revolutionary government, since by then the system of interests created by the revolution outweighed the total sum of the interests of those opposed to the revolution. This assessment is rather puzzling, taking into account that it was almost contemporaneous to the raging fury of the Cristero War. This revolt started when the Mexican Catholic Church answered increasing state persecution (triggered in part by the church's organization of Catholic unions) with the suspension of cult (mass). The large, armed uprising of common people had revealed not only a wide base of unincorporated peasants, but also the continuous existence of a recalcitrant right-wing Catholic movement. The Cristero movement was composed of at least three different social strata. There was the ecclesiastical hierarchy, which did not participate actively in the war but was instrumental in both propitiating the hostilities and negotiating their cease. There was also the Mexico City–based National League in Defense of Religious Freedom, a loose group of professionals that had a more or less consolidated plan to replace the revolutionary government then in power with another one more receptive to the conservative demands of Catholic groups. Finally, there were the Cristeros proper, peasants who rose in arms with the suspension of mass and who abandoned the fight immediately when the ecclesiastical hierarchy reinstated religious services. In his depiction of the Cristeros, Jean Meyer describes them as "a piece of sixteenth-century Mexico that reacts against the revolution."[87] The Cristeros were simple, illiterate people, whose cultural baggage included references to the Twelve Peers of France and to orally transmitted stories that came from the chivalry books that were popular in the late Middle Ages.[88]

Both Vasconcelos and Gómez Morín heeded Calles's call for an opposition party. Gómez Morín began to organize PAN. Their invitations to each other to collaborate on the political undertaking may have crossed in the mail. Gómez Morín, however, did not plan to present a presidential candidate, and he courteously declined Vasconcelos's invitation to be part of the new crusade. In a respectful tone, Gómez Morín alerted Vasconcelos that the time of ideals had already passed and that power could be seized only by politicians well acquainted with the mechanisms set in place by the postrevolutionary government. Gómez Morín thought it impossible that just one man with a group of fervent followers could defeat the governmental machinery.[89] And even if they could win the election, it was unlikely that they would be able to stay in power. For Gómez Morín, Vasconcelos was risking his whole political capital in just one gambit. It was not time for an opposition, although that day would come. Its constitution would be painstaking. Gómez Morín was prophetic. Vasconcelos risked all his political capital on a single presidential bid and was left with nothing but a deep resentment against a people who supported so many adventurers yet did not support him when the future of the revolution was at stake.

Although Vasconcelos's project seems inspired by the figure of Francisco Madero, little or nothing of the idealism of the former president filtered through Vasconcelos's strategy. To begin with, his platform was far more radical and pragmatic than Madero could have possibly envisioned. It called for the nationalization of all means of transportation and oil reserves, and more generally for the nationalization of all sources of energy in the Mexican territory. The plan included a moratorium on and renegotiation of Mexico's foreign debt, the immediate implementation of the prolabor measures contemplated in the constitution of 1917, the enforcement of the women's vote, and the limitation of executive power by multiplying instances of communal control. Perhaps the most far-reaching proposal of the campaign was the idea to do away with state-level political organization, favoring the municipality as the main depositary of the political and financial support of the central administration.

The election of 1929 has not been the subject of a detailed study.[90] Although the recently formed PNR intimidated—even killed—Vasconcelistas and practiced different forms of fraud, it is not clear that the outcome of the election was determined by that fraud. The likelihood of fraud is sustained by the enormous popularity enjoyed by Vasconcelos during the campaign and the rather clueless performance of the official party. The PNR of 1929 did not even resemble what some ten years later would be the well-oiled machinery of the Partido Revolucionario Institucional (PRI).[91] It lacked a foothold in the working class or in the agrarian sector, and its actual structure was a sort of confederation of smaller political units representing *ejidos*, municipalities, or professional associations—coming thus quite close, ironically enough, to the democratic model of direct representation envisioned by Vasconcelos.

As I have already pointed out, the platforms of both Vasconcelos and the PNR were very similar despite having being drafted without mutual knowledge. Neither the PNR nor Vasconcelos could vouch for the viability of their programs. Both campaigns were mounted on a wave of disparate interests and a variety of political ideologies—including a good dose of reactionary conservatism on both sides—that would, sooner or later, complicate the proclaimed good intentions of the candidates. Vasconcelos's political strategy was based on gaining the support of intellectuals and the middle class—a task at which he was very successful. It is not clear, however, to what degree his following was in sync with the ex-minister. He attracted prominent figures of the Mexican intelligentsia but also a wave of middle-class professionals of deep-seated antirevolutionary credentials, who were obviously expecting to bend Vascocelos's arm after the election in case he became president.

Vasconcelos anticipated electoral fraud, but he thought that this fraud, if rightly manipulated, could bring a general uprising in the countryside that, mixed with the sympathies that his candidacy evoked among the middle class and some military ranks, would prove too much for the Calles faction to manage. To this end, Vasconcelos, whose Catholicism was no secret, had entertained several contacts with the leaders of the Cristero rebellion while also reaching out to a number of important army officers. The middle class would give him visibility, his influence upon the military would weaken the PRN's answer to the eventual revolt, and the Cristeros would be the actual fuel of the new revolution. While the Cristeros rose to the cry of "Cristo Rey," it is not by chance that his memory of Toluca recalls the Virgin of Guadalupe crowned as "Queen of all Mexicans." Vasconcelos was convinced that the negotiated resolution of the Cristero conflict had as one of its driving forces the fear of Vasconcelos becoming an Arielist president of Mexico. In *El proconsulado*, he writes, "The news of the enforced surrender of the Cristeros sent a shiver down my spine. I see [U.S. ambassador Dwight Whitney] Morrow's hand in it. He has in this way deprived us of all grounds from the revolt that the vote-rigging would logically have provoked."[92] Although perhaps this was not the only reason for Morrow's intervention, there are strong bases to believe that Vasconcelos's description is accurate by and large.

What is immediately interesting here is the relationship between Vasconcelos and the Cristeros. As a presidential candidate Vasconcelos reentered the country through Nogales, and his first public speech was unmistakably directed to the base of the Cristero movement. As already mentioned, the Cristeros were resentful of the interruption of religious services, and many of them looked with some horror on the state's appropriation of the style of Catholic rituals to serve as models for a variety of state-organized acts. The blatant anachronisms that permeated Cristero culture could not but upset

Vasconcelos, who was still and fundamentally a modernizing intellectual. His first public speech in Mexico introduced a clear note that distanced him from the Cristeros. Vasconcelos reminded his audience that "fanaticism is fought with books, not machine guns."[93] However, it is in the realm of the moralization of politics where Vasconcelos's hesitant association with the Cristeros shows the full force of the internal conflicts that had been fueling his life for over two decades.

As we saw, Vasconcelos attempted to address the tension between politics and morality by postulating an already existing organic community unified around Christian rituals. Although indivisible, this community is also multicultural and multiethnic (although not plurilinguistic). One of the defining traits of this society is how it distances itself from the powers of state manipulation every time it approaches its self-realization in the performative realm of the popular—religious festivity. Now, significantly, not only did Vasconcelos trust his political fate to an eventual revolt, he also thought of the Cristeros as a springboard for a jump into the presidency.[94] The people involved in the Cristiada were probably very like the ones that Vasconcelos paints in his utopian vision of deep Mexico. But if they are the utopian community, how can they be the objects of any political manipulation? The reduction of the Cristeros and their discontent to a mere means to political ends—of which they are mostly unaware—is incompatible with the political faith Vasconcelos claims to profess. He does not hesitate to ask for the sacrifice of the organic community for the more prosaic goal of political domination. That the end will justify the means was the conclusion he always opposed.

But all this Vasconcelos knew quite well. In a sober episode of *El desastre* Vasconcelos narrates his "last dialogue with Antonio Caso."[95] Caso shared with Vasconcelos an Ateneísta past and an intermittent but intense friendship. They were for decades the pillars of a spiritualist philosophy invested in contesting positivism and Darwinism in each and all spheres of thinking. Caso was, at the moment of this "last dialogue," the director of the Escuela Nacional Preparatoria and came to Vasconcelos's office to present his resignation. Vasconcelos had recently dismissed Caso's brother, Alfonso, for just signing, along with other professors, a petition for the reincorporation of some suspended students. Vasconcelos resorted to their long friendship to convince Caso to withdraw his resignation. He tried one, two, three, a half-dozen times. Caso remained inflexible. To every argument mounted by Vasconcelos he replied with a laconic, "But Alfonso is my brother."[96] When Caso finally decided to leave the office, Vasconcelos grabbed him by the arm and offered a last, completely different explanation: "Look Antonio, let's put aside our friendship. . . . Let's consider the issue man-to-man, as if we were enemies and not friends."[97] Political truth partakes of a moment of fiction, but it is a fiction of antagonism fueled by interest and resentment: "as if we were enemies and not friends." The fiction of enmity is the fiction of the political (or of the political as *necessary* fiction) insofar as what is at stake is the practical overcoming of the essential dissymmetry of human actors in any given situation. Politics in that sense can be defined as the attempt to disrupt the quiescence characteristic of every kind of ethics and morality. The fact was that Vasconcelos was very reluctant to reveal the real reasons for his decision to dismiss Alfonso Caso. That these reasons can only be explained assuming an antagonistic relationship reveals his obstinate, heroic fight to reconstitute politics and morality, interest and disinterest; but simultaneously it confirms the centrality of war in any political calculation, the same war against which his intellectual project was first raised into existence.

Martín Luis Guzmán—whose role is not exactly minor in the vast universe of Vasconcelos's memories—offered an incisive portrait of the future minister around 1914. By that time, Guzmán says, Vasconcelos was already well known for his unsucessful battle against the rebellious body to which his soul was destined.[98] But the tensions that had their origin and cipher in the revolutionary turmoil spared no one. Guzmán himself suffered the same ambivalence he denounces in Vasconcelos, although he was able to hide its consequences behind the ironic and detached pose of the impartial observer. Vasconcelos knew neither irony nor detachment. Guzmán was right about one thing, though: Vasconcelos felt in his persona this clash between drives that had to become political in order to survive and dreams that had to prove their worthiness in the most crude dimension of materiality if they were going to be redeemed. It is a destiny less singular than it appears. In *The Century*, Alain Badiou contrasts two modalities under which the relationship to the uncharted political future is imagined in the nineteenth and the twentieth centuries. The nineteenth century, says Badiou, was the century of the imaginary: a century of well-defined dreams and ideals, a Platonic and Apollonian century of sorts. In arts as in politics, a yet unbroken confidence in the power of humanity to bring about a rational order prevailed. Socialism and the Russian Revolution were still a dream during that century. Meanwhile, the art, politics, and revolutions of the twentieth century brought about a fascination with the real—with the meaningless, the abject, and, in the end, with death itself. The French philosopher concludes, "The passion of the real is the touchstone of twentieth-century subjectivity."[99]

The Mexican Revolution transits between these two modalities: between Madero, the dreamer, and Francisco Villa, the man of the unnamable acts. Vasconcelos, who outlived both of them, had his share of both destinies. Like the Mexican Revolution itself, he danced between the abysses of the Apollonian (to which he tried to submit the political) and the Dionysian (which, in the form of political passion and erotic longing, persecuted him his whole life). This is the story told at great lengths in *La tormenta*, the book that followed the calm and yet unsteady pace of *Ulises criollo*. The book is a tale of two storms, says Enrique Krauze: the first was the storm of revolutionary Mexico; the second was the tempest that still raged in 1935, when Vasconcelos "writes about a love affair that was then twenty-five years old."[100] The pace of the narrative accelerates while Vasconcelos intertwines his mad attachment to Adriana with the passion that consumes his liberal self within the torch of the revolution. These are the agitated days of the Aguascalientes convention, of Vasconcelos as a short-lived minister of Eulalio Gutiérrez, and of the cheerful occupation of the National Palace, where Vasconcelos sits at the table alongside Villa and Zapata. They are also the days of the desperate, miraculous escape to the United States following the entrance of Obregón's army into Mexico City. Nights and days of cold and thirst afflict the fugitives as they traverse miles and miles in a caravan of runaways who pretend, nonetheless, to be the legitimate government of the Mexican nation. They are almost killed more than once. Adriana goes along, with all her charm and, if we believe Vasconcelos, all her caprices. (Several witnesses and later commentators objected to the picture of Adriana in the memoirs.)[101]

Then came the peaceful stay in Washington, DC, and New York, in whose library Vasconcelos embraced Greek philosophy as the most certain representation of the lost motherland. Are they really two storms, as Krauze says? Badiou would doubt it. Revolution and love partake of a similar logic.[102] The break with Adriana makes Vasconcelos's world crumble: "The city became a ghost city. I don't understand the language of those speaking to me. Time passes or stands still, but nothing changes inside me."[103] He spares her in his prose but charges as a blind man against her new lover, whom he nicknames "the hunchback" but whom we know to be a man of irony, Martín Luis Guzmán.

Arizmendi's break with Vasconcelos was grounded on her understanding of him as a figure completely bound to fate: "I have to prepare for my own life. You don't need me. As soon as the call you are waiting for comes, as soon as somebody offers you a position that will allow you to make true your many projects and desires, I will become an obstacle. . . . You are one with your dreams—I don't have space for existence there."[104] But Vasconcelos did not rest happy with his idealizations—not even with the idealization of Elena/Adriana modeled after the image of his own mother.[105] Perhaps Adriana was mistaken in believing that she was the figure of passion and Vasconcelos's political vocation was the call of reason and conformity. Certainly, Vasconcelos did attempt an Apollonian domestication of the political. But the political took for him a shape that did not allow the personal any refuge. Against a world that revealed itself as a string of passionate attachments, Vasconcelos could only oppose the aesthetic relief of his own prose or the images of bygone eras of maternal affection and religious rupture. Certainly at the moment of the statement, Vasconcelos knew very little about his own passion. But the scene of writing was entirely constituted inside its dialectic. The year was 1914. Deprived of any "creative activity," Vasconcelos consumed himself in his own rage—as he would do twenty years later when writing the often sour pages of his political failures. The storm of New York, recounted so minutely in 1935, may have made the tumultuous years of revolutionary engagement appear as an oasis. Vasconcelos could not renounce either of his storms. The two became one at a distance of two decades. Such a distance may have given him perspective, revealing, actually, the truth of his subjective and political composition. His contradiction was as much personal as it was epochal: a contradiction that marked his figure with a singular irony according to which, he, the last thinker of the imaginary, had to be also, and without mediation, the fist lover of the real.

CHAPTER FIVE

Fantasy

Sigmund Freud, the first person to use the notion of fantasy in the sense intended here, conceived of fantasies in correlation with the traumatic. Fantasies are contraptions that narrativize an impasse that happens at the level of almost unmediated experience. Increasingly throughout the twentieth century, commentators began to emphasize the idea of the stage as a metaphor able to explain the function of fantasies. A fantasy, write Jean Laplanche and J.-B. Pontalis in their classic dictionary of psychoanalysis, is an imaginary stage (*scènario imaginaire*).[1] The metaphor of the stage brings by association the figure of the actor. A fantasy is not, however, a stage where a preformed actor displays his or her potentials and limitations. Rather, a fantasy builds a world where there was none before. That is why Slavoj Žižek says that, contrary to popular belief, a fantasy is not about the realization of a desire but about staging "desire as such." Since desire is not something "given in advance," a fantasy is needed in order to "learn how to desire."[2]

For life to reestablish its pace after the revolution's destructive force had cancelled all previous orders, a new stage was necessary. But what was to be the grounds for such reconstruction if the revolution had implied the destruction of every condition? It is here that the radicalism of fantasy and its ultimately ungrounded nature becomes of interest to us. Revolution and fantasy belong to two different orders. The social, political, and cultural codifications that obtain between them should not be analyzed in terms of necessity, but rather in terms of freedom, responsibility, and overdetermination: in terms of freedom because the event does not formally determine the subjective answer; in terms of responsibility because the event cannot fail to elicit an answer; and in terms of overdetermination because the main traits of the fantasy that is constituted as a response to the event are never the whim of their producer(s). They are inscribed in a history, and they receive the coordinates of their own organization from that history.

A fantasy strives to create what Jacques Rancière calls a new sensible: that is, a way of understanding hierarchies in the world that reflect a given social mutation.[3] No cultural mediations were more important in postrevolutionary Mexico than those of the muralists, and no fantasy of Mexico was as far-reaching and convincing as the one Diego Rivera presented in his murals. And yet the Mexico that arose from Rivera's murals was the culmination of a long historical process that included other fantasies—some triumphant, others defeated. I begin my discussion of fantasy, then, not directly with Rivera but with the production of fantasies in a more general—and less elitist—sense.

POPULAR AND ELITE FANTASIES: AN UNEASY NEGOTIATION

In the context of the revolution there are many fantasies. As a rule they are difficult to retrieve. Many of them are subaltern fantasies obscured by the path taken by the social imagination in the years that followed them. In rescuing them, it is vital to relax the historicist's bias that demands paying attention, above all, to those features of the past that came to fruition in the present. Still, regardless of their elite or popular origins, all revolutionary fantasies share an interpretive kernel that betrays their basic commonality.

One of the best illustrations of the fundamental revolutionary fantasy comes from that endless reservoir of revolutionary motives that is Martín Luis Guzmán's *The Eagle and the Serpent*. At some point in the novel we find Guzmán and his friends sneaking back into Mexico from their exile in Texas. In a melancholy tone, the narrator notices that the trip "from El Paso, Texas, to Ciudad Juárez in Chihuahua is . . . one of the greatest . . . humiliations that human geography had imposed on the sons of Mexico." Compared to the clean and modern streets of the American side, the Mexican city appears as a "pigsty." But when the revolution wins, an enthusiastic Guzmán says, "We're going to clean it up. We'll make a new city, bigger and better than the one across the river."[4] What is fantasized here is not the future, the clean Mexican city to be built after the revolution—this is just the incarnation of an ideology of progress—but rather the will itself. The empowerment of the revolutionary subject is the first fantasy of the revolution.[5] Memoirs and accounts of these years written by people as diverse as Alberto Pani, Diego Rivera, José Vasconcelos, Manuel Gómez Morín, Daniel Cosío Villegas, or José

Alessio Robles all testify to an obsession with building, doing, constructing, erecting—always in a modality of urgency and immediacy. Usually such activity demanded great physical exertion. According to Jean Charlot, Diego Rivera's average workday lasted eighteen hours as he painted some of his murals. Dr. Atl completed his path-breaking atlas of Mexican popular culture—*Las artes populares en México*—in just four months. Francisco Goitia produced a staggering number of precise illustrations for Manuel Gamio during the excavation of Teotihuacán. This profusion of cultural producers was fueled by a fantasy of a subject for which the whole past was open to appropriation and the whole future to construction. Some of the most transcendental fantasies of self-foundation are often located in provincial Mexico: for example, the Estridentistas' occupation of Veracruz under the government of Heriberto Jara in 1925 and the progressive experiments of Felipe Carrillo Puerto in the Yucatán.

Popular fantasies are much more difficult to retrieve. Unlike elite fantasies, popular fantasies lack specific authors. This fact alone weakens their credibility. Conceived as the domain of the multitude or the anonymous—and often the unanimous—the popular becomes a fertile terrain for interpretation. To say that we are dealing with representations of the popular rather than with the popular itself is not enough to put this pseudoproblem to rest in an age in which speaking for the other or making the other speak has come to signify the very business of cultural analysis. This much we accept: each and every unveiling of the subaltern voice is marred by the implicit ventriloquism that the operation supposes. But this begs the question of the validity of the authorized voice. The task at hand is not to retrieve the voice of the true subaltern but rather to discover how hegemonic expressions—as marked by ventriloquism as any other—ultimately achieved the status of the voice itself. With this caveat and disclaimer, I will introduce the question of popular fantasies of the revolution through a representation twice removed from the thickness of actual and historical popular agency: Paul Leduc's cinematographic rendering of John Reed's *Insurgent Mexico* (1914). I will supplement my observations with a commentary on the "Corrido de Pancho Villa," a popular composition about Gen. John J. Pershing's punitive expedition against Villa in 1916.

In his loose adaptation of Reed's testimony, Leduc describes the visit of the American journalist to northern Mexico around 1913. As Reed begins to interact with a group of soldiers under the command of General Urbina, some of them become curious about Reed's background. After learning that he studied at Harvard, one of the revolutionaries proclaims, "When I am done killing Huertistas, I will also go to Harvard to study." The idea here is that any place (Harvard in this case) is accessible in terms of the will alone. The revolutionary subject inhabits a space of fundamental equality vis-à-vis other human beings. Another soldier, Longino, asks Reed if the subject of technology was important in his academic formation and is disappointed when Reed suggested that *la técnica* may not be such an important part of an elite education. It is the same Longino who best expresses how contact with technology stirred the imaginations of largely peasant armies. Longino launches into a complex explanation of how to attach cartridges to a free-standing wheel in order to create a permanently firing, moving machine. While the bourgeois fantasy of the revolutionary is shaped around verbs like *erecting, constructing,* and *cleaning,* the story of the Villista soldier introduces an intense interest in and awe for the emerging world of technological innovation. For Longino, the fantasy of unbounded possibilities that the revolutionary triumph will open is inextricable from a desire to fuse his own story with technological trends. The revolutionary soldier who has just had his power revealed to him seeks to exponentially increase that power by coupling it to a machine. If this is still a fantasy, it is because what is unveiled by this invocation of the technological is the soldier himself and not the world of technique, just as what was enacted in the managerial fantasy of the well-to-do revolutionary was not the world but a new position of the self.

Although the technological fantasy was not an exclusively northern fantasy, the fact that it was uttered so candidly by a Villista soldier is significant. To an important extent, the figure of Villismo was bound to this modernizing image of the triumphal machine. The proximity to the United States—a society for which Villa professed true admiration—had a strong impact in the ethos of Villismo, an impact ranging from the uniforms and weapons of the Division of the North to its leader's flirtations and contracts with American studios like the Chicago Mutual Film Corporation. In the context of the enormous purchase provided by technology in the revolutionary horizon, we can appreciate the subtlety with which technology and revolutionary agency are intertwined in a *corrido* that was composed on the occasion of Pershing's punitive expedition, launched in retaliation for Villa's attack on Columbus, New Mexico.

Pershing's expedition served as a general rehearsal of war tactics and equipment soon to be deployed in World War I. It was also a resounding failure. Pershing entered Mexico on 16 March 1916 and for eleven months unsuccessfully tried to engage Villa's dismembered army. The punitive expedition was composed of fourteen thousand regular army troops. It was the first time that sizable trucks and airplanes were used for a military operation.[6] The trucks proved to be useless on roads that existed more as good intentions on a map than as realities and whose scarcely delineated routes blurred and disappeared after the first rain. The airplanes did not manage to navigate the strong winds of northern Mexico and proved equally unable to ascend the mountains in which the astute Villa had hidden his forces.

It is against this background of technological nightmare for the Americans and relative amusement on the part of the invaded Mexicans that we can appreciate the cat-and-mouse game portrayed in the *corrido* in terms that are unmistakably technological in nature. In the *corrido* the Americans cannot find Villa because while they use horses, Villa uses airplanes:

> Those on horseback no longer could sit down,
> And those on foot could no longer walk,
> While Pancho Villa flew over them in his airplane
> and from up there told them, "Good-bye!"[7]

The *corrido* is representative of a frontier sensibility in which the other is also a mirror image. As Americans try to behave like Mexicans while going after Pancho Villa on horseback, Pancho Villa appropriates not only the staples of the other culture (in this case the technology represented by the airplane) but even its language. In another version of the same *corrido*, Villa dresses his troops in American outfits and invites the airplanes to land, after which he seizes them for his own army.

The prominent place of technology in the imaginary map of revolutionary Mexico speaks of a widespread experience of alternate forms of worlding. In a way evocative of Walter Benjamin's criticism of auratic forms of production, the reproducibility guaranteed by the machine stands in marked contrast to older and more venerable forms of reproducibility like the ones tied to the cycles of nature and life, or like those forms of reproducibility that had been subjected to theological forms of surveillance for centuries. In this context, it is apposite to notice that the theist faction of the revolution—Zapatismo—was also one of the most reluctant to explore the fantasy dimension of their own fight.

The import of technology in revolutionary fantasy would wane to the extent that the intelligentsia's construction of a national imaginary was increasingly bound to the emblems of deep Mexico. (But technology would endure a second life in the form of film.) The consolidation of a national imaginary around the auratic figures of the peasant and the Indian gave way to a somewhat contradictory situation: while technological fantasies ran rampant in the most removed areas of the country (like Yucatán or Chihuahua), Mexico City–based intellectuals ended up producing a national imaginary that was formulated on a counter-technological version of the countryside. When Frida Kahlo painted *Self-Portrait along the Borderland between Mexico and the United States* in 1932, the opposition between Mexico and its rival United

States had been totally reworked along the axis of a criticism of inhuman modernization on the one hand and an uplifting view of the same backwardness that had been frowned upon only years before on the other. In this portrait, Kahlo stands on a pedestal between a Mexican and an American landscape. The Mexican side is dominated by the forces of nature and the cycles of life. Both worlds are connected underground however. An electrical generator operating on American soil seems to draw its power from the roots of the plants that emerge on the Mexican side. Placed at the viewer's left, the Mexican landscape comes first in the arrow of time. Not only is it more primordial, it also signals the endurance of the past: a stubborn resistance to the supposedly binding laws of developmentalism that Kahlo flatly equates with the ignominious laws of capitalism. The subject, Kahlo, stands at the center or, one could say, at the border. Straddling the border, she *is* the border, the meeting place of past-present and future-present. This border is always unstable and made of many layers.[8] As a modernist painter, Kahlo is simultaneously attracted to technology and innovation while also being disappointed with its results on a human scale. The tension between the two worlds nearly obliterates her figure. The inconspicuous pink dress she wears belittles her presence. Her body itself remains minimized, almost de-realized. Although the emptiness of the central figure could betray the disappointment over a failed pregnancy, it also shows the complexities involved in imagining a scenario in which a postrevolutionary subjectivity could unfold and come into its own.

RIVERA'S ROAD

In Rivera's murals the problem of a stage able to encompass all the extremes uncovered by the revolution is tackled head on for the first time. The criticism of the first murals at the SEP and the National Palace indicates a tense and ambivalent relationship between artistic representation and predominant conceptions of the social. Rivera's murals were both shrugged off as wild inventions and vilified with a passion that is only reserved for the existent. These reactions—scrupulously registered by Jean Charlot in *The Mexican Mural Renaissance*—are a vivid testimony to the fluid nature of the new sensibility. Posterior criticism—including academic criticism—has not fared much better when confronted with the representations that cover the courtyards of the SEP or staircases of the National Palace. A certain prejudice traceable to the time of their composition assumes that an art about and for simple people should be, out of necessity, a simple art. The social function that Rivera himself attributed to his paintings encouraged a critical style that concerned itself above all with the referential accuracy of the paintings. To understand the murals as fantasy, however, would mean that their significance cannot be established through a one-to-one correlation with the world they are supposed to transcribe. While it is true that Rivera aimed for minute historical reconstruction in representation, the fantastical aspect of the murals does not lie in the representation of individuals. The fantasy appears instead at the level of staging. In this sense, the fantasy that Rivera advanced in the murals is not present *within* the composition, but rather in the very composition itself. Rivera paints the textuality of the revolution. What the murals produce—what they are about—is an interpretation of the specific modality of existence of social life in the aftermath of the revolt and an exegesis of the historical dynamic that led to that situation. The superimposition of these two intentions gives the murals their pictorial and theoretical tension. We know from other artists such as Sergei Eisenstein or Tina Modotti what exactly enticed and defied the aesthetic gaze in Mexico: it was the almost surreal coexistence of heterogeneous modalities of life, the simultaneous emergence of the old, the untimely, and the partly-realized. Rivera's daunting project was to make a true social phantasmagoria visible through a poetics of everyday life. Such a poetics had to convoke potentiality and actuality in the same stroke. This conceptual duality is matched by a stylistic duality as Rivera's trace combines Edvard Munch and Jean-François Millet. The sudden brushing of codes and elbows that characterizes the social landscape of postrevolutionary Mexico is simultaneously portrayed and ordered. This duplicity has largely been overlooked in the critical appraisal of Rivera's work, but it surfaces in the contradictory statements used to characterize it: naïve referentialism and wild, ungrounded invention; aesthetic complacency and serious distortions in the portrayal of the real; banal caricatures of the everyday and false rendering of the most salient features of the present.

Although Rivera understood the task of art in the historical process as a search for a workable fantasy of the revolution, for some time he misconceived his own position in this process. Writing in 1923 in *La Falange*, he describes the revolution as a turmoil in which "all personages, positive as well as negative, of this as yet minute movement, are impelled by a deep force: the aspirations of the masses which shake the surface of the country like an earthquake." He concludes, "Let us hope that some artist or group of artists manages to give such aspirations a voice."[9] The expression "give such aspirations a voice" can be misleading. There is no such direct path between the aspirations of the masses and the sanction of representation. Indeed, the condition of Rivera's own invention of Mexico is the product of a complex negotiation of influences and determinations.

A previous attempt at mural painting took place in the context of the

1910 celebrations of independence, when Dr. Atl, at that moment a leader of the young artistic scene, requested and obtained some walls to undertake his project. The revolution cut Atl's project short. When Rivera and David Alfaro Siqueiros returned to Mexico in 1921, they quickly overshadowed Atl. Like Atl they would sustain a thorough criticism of academicism, but the origins of their criticism lay in their firsthand knowledge of the European avant-garde. Simultaneously, the muralists of the 1920s built for themselves a national tradition able to feed their own artistic processes. The three 'greats' of Mexican muralism claimed to be indebted to José Guadalupe Posada, an engraver who sustained himself by illustrating different leaflets depicting current affairs.[10] As the muralists further elaborated the theoretical and ideological bases of their project, their resemblance to Posada grew. Posada was as much an artist as he was a craftsman. He always took a political stance of clear opposition to the abuses of the Díaz dictatorship and identified with the struggles of the Mexican people.[11] Finally, he was able to produce a truly popular art that was also connected to persistent motifs in the history of Mexican cultural expression.

Particularly significant in terms of political commitment is the role of Siqueiros. Although Siqueiros's artistic contribution in the early phase of muralism was not significant, he introduced a consistent Marxist tonality in the discourse of the modernist avant-garde.[12] Siqueiros met Rivera in Paris in 1919, and some guidelines of muralism sprang from this encounter, which Siqueiros described as the meeting between "the new fervor and ideals of the young Mexican painters . . . who had joined the armed struggle" and "the representative of an important period of the formal revolution in the plastic arts."[13] This contact led Siqueiros to publish an important document in the history of muralism. The text in question appeared in 1921 in the only number of the journal *Vida Americana* (published in Barcelona), under the title "A New Direction for the New Generation of American Painters and Sculptors." In this manifesto Siqueiros eulogizes Paul Cézanne and the Cubists for providing tools for an art able to grasp the present moment while retaining a fruitful contact with all of Western tradition. The manifesto includes a strong condemnation of the "decorative" tendency that Siqueiros saw as the dominant force in Mexican art. It also praises primitivism.

The muralists who started their work at the Escuela Nacional Preparatoria included Rivera, Siqueiros, Jean Charlot, Fernando Leal, Fermín Revueltas, Xavier Guerrero, and Amado de la Cueva among others. José Clemente Orozco was not invited in the beginning because of his previous collaboration with anti-Maderista newspapers. Some of the muralists were experienced painters, like the Frenchman Jean Charlot; others were surprisingly young, like eighteen-year-old Fermín Revueltas. Painting murals is a complex and demanding undertaking for which none of these painters had specific training. Technical issues plagued the movement from the beginning.[14] Most of the paintings they produced were later destroyed or painted over with other murals. The sketches, photographs, and reproductions available today testify to a dismaying conservatism. Antonio Rodríguez observes, "One cannot help wondering why painters who started the revolutionary movement in the Escuela Preparatoria, a school which was preeminently secular, should paint virgins, religious festivals, theological virtues, landings of the cross, proletarian women with wings, etc. The contradictions become even more obvious when we observe that, next to the woman with wings, Siqueiros painted an enormous sickle and hammer."[15] Siqueiros is a case in point, because he was, among all artists, the one "with the greatest revolutionary experience and the greatest theoretical knowledge of socialist doctrine." However, Rodríguez concludes, a painting like *The Elements* shows him "possessed by a kind of inertia."[16] As for Orozco, when he was finally called to work at the Preparatoria he produced a mural of which only the panel called *Maternity* remains. The section—spared by time and the axe that Orozco took up against his own work—shows unmistakable Renaissance influence: virgins, children, angels. Although Orozco insisted that the virgin was in fact a mundane mother, little of the everyday world emerges in the representation. Rivera painted the only mural that is fully conserved from that first period, *Creation*, an important composition painted on the walls of the Anfiteatro Bolívar. *Creation* was inaugurated in 1923 and Rivera grew increasingly disappointed with it. The mural covers a surface of 110 square meters. As always with murals, Rivera had to accommodate his designs to the architectural possibilities and limitations of the buildings on which they were painted. Unlike other murals, in which the nature of representation diverges from the design of the building, with *Creation*, Rivera aimed for a smooth transition between building and work of art. The mural portrays two naked human figures, one male, one female, who stand for the native Mexican race. Over them hover allegorical figures of the arts and sciences such as Dance, Music, Song, Wisdom, Knowledge, Fable, Tradition, Tragedy, and Justice. While the subject and treatment of *Creation* were obviously in line with the aesthetic preferences of José Vasconcelos (who prided himself on directing Rivera in the design of the mural), the mural was quite removed from the paintings that Rivera would favor in coming years. More importantly, insofar as *Creation* was just an evocation of an existing ideal, it completely lacked the dimension of fantasy that would give Riveras's later murals their uncontestable historical solidity.

Maternity, *The Elements*, and *Creation* are beautiful murals in and of themselves, but they bear little relationship to the political convictions these painters so noisily professed. The muralists were acutely aware of the problem and addressed it with astounding diligence. The task was not easy. They would have to unlearn the formation that had turned them into traditional *artists*. A certain (excessively Italian and somewhat Baroque) ideal of beauty was the first casualty of their explorations. As soon as Rivera, Orozco, and Siqueiros began transforming their own styles through a desperate act of self-criticism, viewers started asking not only if what they were doing was art, but also if it held any connection to beauty whatsoever. The hesitations and ruminations one reads in the reviews of the works-in-progress were just preludes to other, far-reaching confrontations between the muralists and their urban critics. As long as they painted virgins and winged angels they did not attract much public hostility. But when they started to cover the walls with popular references, social satyrs, and political proclamations, a good deal of conservative Mexico City turned against them. The lettered city reacted with anger. Poets were often the most vociferous of critics. Vasconcelos himself, as he left the SEP, regretted the fact that the muralists had fallen "into the abjection of covering the walls of Mexico with portraits of criminals."[17]

After his first mural at the Escuela Nacional Preparatoria, Rivera worked at the SEP, where he painted *The Courtyard of Labor* and *The Courtyard of Fiestas*, a group of murals representing traditional forms of work, farming, and mining as well as customs and traditions. In 1929 he started his best-known mural, *The History of Mexico*, at the National Palace. *The History of Mexico* was punctuated by Rivera's multiple commitments both in Mexico and the United States. In artistic terms perhaps the most important of these commitments is the 120-foot-long fresco that he painted at the Palace of Cortés in Cuernavaca, to which I will return later.[18]

In *The History of Mexico*, the subject of the mural was no longer the folk forms of Mexican culture, as it had been at the SEP. Instead, Rivera depicted historical developments from the perspective of nation formation. Before the eyes of the visitor the whole history of the country unfolds according to a chronology that, while not entirely linear, is dominated by the theme of colonialism. As viewers ascend the main stairway of the National Palace, they are presented with an idealized depiction of life in pre-Columbian Mexico. They then pass the crucial political and cultural junctures in the country's history (conquest, the wars of independence, Maximilian and the French occupation, the rise of liberalism, Juárez, Díaz, Madero, Zapata, the revolution). Finally, when viewers reach the top of the staircase, they face a utopian section entitled "The World of Today and Tomorrow," in which the figure of Marx crowns the history of Mexico as he points the way to the future. The conceptual richness of the mural is stunning. Rivera plays on a complex dialectic between Marxism and indigenousness (between Marx and Quetzaltcoatl in the mural) to propose a highly idiosyncratic and novel conception of history.

The history of Mexico depicted in the murals was not merely propagandistic, as simplified criticisms of Rivera's production never tire positing. Even if Rivera's murals at the National Palace were put to pedagogical use, it is disputable that they present us with a straightforward argument about the history of the country and the position of the popular classes in it. Rivera's strongest statement regarding the nonpedagogical nature of the murals comes in the strategic central panel. This panel, Leonard Folgarait comments, relinquishes any attempt at indoctrination: "The historical episodes on the central wall can be seen as merely mixed and juxtaposed, next to and amongst each other because they belong in that history all at once as equals, and not necessarily positioned by order of occurrence or historical importance."[19] After emphasizing that this quality "is not shared by the two side walls," Folgarait remarks that "this refusal by the mural to compose according to the linear narrative properties of episodic history . . . creates [one important effect]: the mural is not, in spite of its site and subject matter, in spite of its 'purpose,' didactic in any explicit manner. . . . Each separate knowing produces its own telling/viewing."[20]

Unlike Folgarait I do not read the central panel as a collage of different possibilities of identification from which the viewer can choose. Taken as a whole, the central panel seems to say that *in history* one cannot choose. If an affirmative politics can actually exist, it should take its cue from the materialist admission of the totality of existence. Rivera includes in the murals characters with whom he could not have possibly identified, people whom he actually abhorred: bankers; ruthless, exploitative emissaries of the Spanish empire first and of the American empire later; Luis Toral, the Catholic fanatic who killed President Obregón. If the now is going to redeem all past sufferings and misgivings, nothing of this past can be renounced. Yet, it is not a matter of looking to the past objectively, so to speak. To the contrary, it means overcoming the difference between the subjective and the objective. All that stands as mere data to be observed has to be carried into the present, made the stuff of the viewer's life. This process, through which an alienated past becomes the stuff of an emancipated present, unfolds in the dimension of representation: a word to be taken here *à la lettre* rather than in terms of art as mimesis. The history that has merely happened needs to be brought back to life in the light of the present. The past is not represented with the air of the closed and unquestionable but turned instead into a site of constructive reproduction that engenders both past and present in mutual determination. The viewer has to make pre-Columbian civilization, the heroes of independence, the anonymous backs of peasant Indians, and the recognizable figures of the forefathers of the revolution his or her own. Even the Inquisition, even Porfirio Díaz, has to be accommodated into the picture.

It is not enough to say that Rivera placed the revolution within some kind of historical perspective. We have to clarify what type of history is the one we are invited to contemplate. This historical perspective was not the one pushed by a group of influential postrevolutionary intellectuals such as Alfonso Reyes, for whom the revolution of 1910–1920 had been the third and last phase of two previous bourgeois revolutions: those of independence and reform. Against the implicit triumphalism of this argument, there is in Rivera's murals a recurring insistence on defeat and injustice, through whose windows something like an alternate history crawls into the scene. Evoking Walter Benjamin, we can see in this recurrence of contingency and defeat the mark of tradition rather than history. We approximate in this way what is, in my view, the kernel of Rivera's imagining of the historical development of Mexico. In the murals the problem of the history of Mexico is fused with the problem of an impossible history of its people. Why impossible? Because in Rivera's mind the truth of the people is constituted as an intermittent act of insurgency.

Rivera's Three Voices

I see Rivera's work at the National Palace determined by three overlapping but not completely supplementary injunctions. As an ideological thinker—as a member of the Communist Party, we can say—Rivera obviously thought that the political activities of the masses had to be referred to the dimension of instrumental politics in order to be effective. The murals had to propose recognizable situations, names, and identities. As a Latin American intellectual of the twentieth century, he was also quite conscious of the transcultural and heterogeneous nature of Latin American societies. In other words, he was conscious that a process of subalternization is inherent to any representation of the popular. Finally, as an artist, Rivera worked under a permanent demand for singularization; modern art is not an example, it is the thing itself. How this demand for singularization intersected with his political convictions is, beyond any doubt, the kernel of all interpretations of his work so far. The problem of the murals is how to strike a compromise between two heterogeneous narratives: a history of political accumulation that is eminently social in nature and an ethics and aesthetics of irretrievable singularities without which political accumulation would be meaningless.[21]

Rivera's first voice, then, is focused on the question of the people qua people of the nation(-state). This is the people as already represented or as subject to representation. As we know, in Rivera's work the masses are made to appear on the stage of history under two strategies: metonymically through recourse to enumeration, and metaphorically by postulating the indigenous as the historical constant in the intermittent emergence of the people into history. In *The Courtyard of Fiestas,* no one figure stands out as allegorizing or symbolizing the joys and sufferings of all. The landscape, so important in some scenes in *The Courtyard of Labor,* is minimized as Rivera frantically covers every last inch of the wall with popular figures. It is impossible, even in compositional terms, to arrange the multiplicity of figures according to a system of values. As a trope, enumeration allowed Rivera to accommodate his own political radicalism under a form of aesthetic populism that was irrefutable insofar as it also constituted the "official" ideology of the revolution, at least in those moments when the revolution was thought to have an ideology.

However, enumeration carries with it problems of its own. Enumeration creates the semblance of signifying the totality. It entices us to think that everybody is counted and that everybody counts. More importantly, it leaves the problem of what concept determines the totality completely open and, as it were, up for grabs. As much as Rivera wanted to imagine the popular in its autonomy and to question the role that the elites had played in building the country, it is doubtful that enumeration could have provided the solution. When enumeration extends for too long it coalesces into a symbol and ceases to be enumeration. This is exactly what happens in *The History of Mexico* with the introduction of the famous colored eagle at the center of the composition. The eagle itself is modeled after an Aztec monolith known as the *Teocalli de la guerra sagrada* (Temple of sacred warfare), a designation popularized following a publication by Alfonso Caso in 1926.[22] Even if Rivera intended the *Teocalli* to symbolize indigenous persistence, it is clear that the symbolic articulation per se places it in the realm of an identification with state function. The history of the symbol itself suggests such a development. At least since the seventeenth century, the *Teocalli* has been used in double reference to the indigenous and to imperial power. Now, if on the one hand there is a symbolic identification of the *Teocalli* with imperial history, there is on the other hand an identification of the *Teocalli* with the defeated empire of the Aztecs and the oppressed indigenous masses. Was Rivera's *Teocalli* a reference to the principles of nationalism or to the subterranean masses that make history? It is perhaps impossible to choose one possibility over the other. Rivera referred to this painting under two different denominations: *The History of Mexico* and the *Apotheosis of the Mexican People,* thus with its title duplicating the ambiguity of the representation.

We stand on familiar—even if uncomfortable—ground: the indigenous masses appear in an irresolvable tension between an ethico-political demand for coevalness and an equally inalienable demand for recognition that is loaded, as all demands for recognition are, with the asymmetries of specific historical and political situations. In order to really show that Mexican history is not just colored by but also determined by the (indigenous) masses, Rivera had to name them and show them. But this presentation endangers the very principle of the people as an intermittent force pushing against the walls of sovereign formations.

Rivera's second voice belongs to his attempt to singularize the people at stake in his representations in both ethnographic and pictorial terms. This happened in two steps. In the first step, Rivera's strategy to avoid an objectification of the indigenous masses consisted of a deep "scientific" engagement with the landmarks of their culture. This confidence in an objective approach is responsible for Rivera's relentless vocation of knowing the indigenous other. Immediately following his return to Mexico, Rivera acquired an exceptionally deep knowledge of ancient Mexico, reading frantically, interviewing dozens of experts (Manuel Gamio and Alfonso Caso among them), and traveling to archeological sites. This knowledge was transposed to the murals, which display "the remarkable range of [Rivera's] research into his country's archaeological past."[23] By the time of the composition of *The History of Mexico,* "the empirical and accurate reference" to the past had become "an obsession" for him.[24] Rivera murals included minute descriptions of pre-Columbian architectural trades, everyday life, and geography that historical analysts have found unobjectionable. His passion for the Mexican past also showed up in the impressive collection of indigenous artifacts that he amassed over decades—some sixty thousand objects by the time of his death—which he housed in a three-story museum, the Anáhuacalli, built on the outskirts of Mexico City (see chapter 3).

In the second step, elements of an indigenous artistic worldview were allowed to enter into the composition of contemporary art itself. As we know, Rivera incorporated into his painting some aspects of indigenous pictorial traditions by borrowing a figural schema that often contradicted the historicist narrative style proper of modernity. The murals painted in 1930 in Cuernavaca at the Cortés Palace drew from the codex *Lienzo de Tlaxcala* and the *Matrícula de tributos* scroll as well as from Aztec sculptures housed at the national museum and publications of codices held outside Mexico.[25] At Cuernavaca the organization of space recalls the scroll in its use of superimposition rather than perspective to suggest spatial depth. In many of Rivera's murals, the painting behaves as a scroll, grouping different themes or periods in codified clusters of meanings and using an additive system of representation to display different characters and symbols in an arrangement that admits different routes of reading. But how does all this differ from the canon of modern art in which Rivera was educated? Is not Rivera's reference to an indigenous schema a covert reference to European artistic modernism?

In *Los privilegios de la vista*, Octavio Paz observes, "Without Western modernism, whose artists appropriated the style and visions of non-Western cultures, the Mexican muralists could have never understood the Mexican indigenous tradition. . . . Artistic nationalism was a consequence of early twentieth-century cosmopolitanism."[26] Paz's position looks historically sound. In his essay-manifesto from 1921, Siqueiros had already vindicated primitivism as one of the foundational influences in a future and revolutionary Mexican art. The appeal of primitivism has been a constitutive force in modern art at least since the last quarter of the nineteenth century. By 1870 several European painters had heralded the strong formalization of the human body and the grotesque impressionism of primitive art as allies in their antinaturalist and antirealist crusade. Edvard Munch saw *The Scream* as thoroughly determined by his acquaintance with primitive art and paintings by children. The Paris Exposition of 1889 had already offered the opportunity to appreciate primitive art from Asia, Oceania, and the Americas to an important number of European artists like Munch, who had travelled from Oslo for the occasion. And even before that event, different artists had been exposed to these alternate forms of depicting the human world in the ethnological museums that flourished throughout Europe earlier in the nineteenth century.[27] By the beginning of the twentieth century, there was almost no modern painter who was not influenced, in one way or another, by a desire to "go primitive." Paul Gauguin carried the movement to its final consequences when he abandoned Paris for Tahiti. Likewise, explorations of primitivism permeated the works of Klimt, Cézanne, and Klee who were constant points of reference for the Mexican artists of the period. By 1910 artistic pieces coming from Africa, Oceania, and the Americas were so common in Europe that most painters had important collections of these objects. Vlaminck, Matisse, Picasso, and Kandinski were all well acquainted with brokers of primitive art and decorated their studios with pieces from all parts of the world.

However, Mexican primitivism was not just an offshoot of its European counterpart. In several ways it was more consistent, better developed, and more deeply imprinted in the composition of the artworks than its European counterparts. As John Goldwater notes in his seminal study of primitivism in modern art, perhaps the only formal trait that modern European painting took from primitivism was the lack of psychological connection among the figures of the composition.[28] Mexicans, on the contrary, borrowed generously from an indigenous schema that they strove to decipher and develop further. Rivera, as we have seen, integrated the logic of the pre-Columbian scrolls into the design of his murals.[29] Carlos Mérida made stylized use of Mayan motifs in his paintings. Some of Siqueiros's compositions, such as *Madre proletaria* and *Madre campesina*, drew generously from an indigenous schema; and the post-Cubism of Rufino Tamayo owes much of its identity to the treatment of volume in Aztec art. More importantly, unlike their European counterparts, Mexicans were not merely colonial collectors of peripheral oddities. They felt that they were brokers and purveyors of a treasure that promised immediate political relevance; the viability of a new social pact hinged upon the correct promotion and appreciation of this treasure. While there is a sense in which the European vogue of all things primitive is inextricable from the colonial figures found in museums, in the Mexican case the relationship with the primitive was tinted with the urgency of a clearly circumscribed political configuration.[30] Siqueiros expressed the thought in unambiguous terms in his 1921 manifesto: "The art produced by the Mexican people . . . and its tradition are our biggest possessions."[31] The existential weight of the experience of the primitive often led these artists into activities that were decidedly ethnographic in nature. The best example remains, of course, Adolfo Best Maugard, whose whole career as a would-be painter was "ruined" by his encounter with indigenous schema while working for Franz Boas. In compensation, he was able to elaborate, based on his knowledge of the indigenous schema, the famous Best Maugard method for drawing.

Now, and this will constitute my second "correction" to Paz's description of the elective affinities between the European and the Mexican avant-garde, even a cursory glance at Rivera's murals will tell us that the destructuring influence of primitivism is—barring a few exceptions—absent from his compositions. The fact remains that most of the references to the indigenous that we find in Mexican art (and even architecture) are not, strictly speaking, forms of primitivism. In European modernism, primitivism was expected to provide a critical vantage point from which to deconstruct the habits of perception that permeate the cultural evolution of the West. In the case of Rivera's murals, the figure of the Indian was not invoked to upset dominance, per se, as much as to create a new dominance. A factor that greatly facilitated this constructive rather than critical use of the indigenous tradition was the fact that the schema that Rivera borrowed from the indigenous retained the figural language and codes of powers already imperial. The indigenous models Rivera transposed to the murals have little to do with an emphasis on the simplicity of perception. On the contrary, they bear testimony to the artistic acumen of the great Mesoamerican civilizations. Interestingly, the New York Museum of Modern Art exposition on primitivism in 1984 excluded Mesoamerica. As William Rubin, the editor of the exposition's two-volume catalog, explains, Aztec and Mayan art does not qualify as primitive art but rather as court art. It is, Rubin argues, a form of art that evokes not a reawakened primitive contact with the world, but rather points to ideals already completely immersed in the symbolic organization of a well-developed political formation.[32] When Rivera encouraged young Mexican artists to study the Aztec or Toltec tradition, he never referred to those traditions as primitive but rather, establishing the exact distinction that Rubin would introduce some fifty years later, as classical.[33]

Actually, the element that allows us to speak of the murals as fantasy proper—that is, as the creative translation of an untranslatable relationship—only emerges in reference to Rivera's third voice. This third voice corresponds to the question of masses that act partially independent of any apprehension in a state form and even beyond any possible inscription. To this register belongs Rivera's hesitation concerning the actual face of the popular. His images constantly move between the overlapping and yet noncoincidental figures of the Indian, the revolutionary fighter, the worker, and the peasant. The Indian occupies a privileged position, since Rivera understood the history of Mexico as marked, above all, by the colonial experience. The intractability of the signifier *Indian* in the present of the composition—the impossibility of ascribing certain traits and practices as definitively indigenous in nature—made it difficult, however, to sustain this privilege in conceptual and figural terms. The problem of presenting the people as an excess *over* the people reaches a conceptual climax when what is at stake is the popular qua insurgent.

The seemingly unbridgeable gap that exists between the masses as a subterranean force and the masses as a visible and namable subject of political action is not just a historical accident, but we can consider it a practical and logical problem. When the people or the masses are considered in their historical becoming—as agents of political transformation—a certain process of desubjectivization necessarily ensues. The peasant or the worker who engages in a political struggle does so by abandoning and relinquishing forms of behavior that characterized him or her as peasant or worker: for instance refusing to work, abandoning some duties, or simply acknowledging that they no longer want to be who they were. This is why Jacques Rancière repeatedly observes that, strictly speaking, the poor are never the poor and the people are never the people.[34] Politics—or to say it with Rancière, true politics—always seizes its subjects in a transient state.

Now, the work of Rancière himself is testimony to the fact that it is awfully difficult to conceive of and even more so to show this becoming, and it is perhaps even more difficult for a painter than for a writer. So, to paint the people—to give a voice to the aspirations of the masses—is synonymous with *not* painting *the people*; although a painter, for sure, has to paint something. The only solution to this representational quandary seems to be to encapsulate the masses in an insufficient image or symbol and then to complicate the symbol as a means of evoking the always evanescent becoming of the historical. Such a task can only be done by showing that the essential political subjectivization of the people stands always in excess vis-à-vis the established forms of political individuation. One of Rivera's most dramatic discoveries is that the impossibility of tracing a history of the people qua insurgents springs not only from their defeats but also, perhaps more persistently, from the history of their false redemptions. In the case of Mexico, the dominant instance of a false redemption lies in the institution of Christianity.

The public present at the inauguration of the murals that Rivera painted at the SEP were astonished by what they perceived to be an odd mixture of socialism, Marxist critique (condemnations of private property, exploitation, and colonialism), and allusions to Christian iconography. One panel, *Exit from the Mine,* shows a worker being searched by mine officials; he stands with outstretched arms that unmistakably evoke crucifixion. Another climbs a staircase towards the surface, wearing a hat that the stylistic disposition of the painting invites us to confuse with a halo. In these and similar panels Rivera draws on Mexican popular religiosity to bridge the chasm that separates his revolutionary art from the masses.

It may seem ironic that the muralists, some of whose members boasted of a militant atheism, borrowed a perceptual schema from the religious tradition in order to relate their paintings to the revolutionary event. There are of course disciplinary reasons that made painters aware of the possibilities afforded by Christianity in relationship to emergent social movements. Christian religiosity pervades the history of painting in a way that is totally absent in the intellectual tradition of modern liberalism that forms the core of the Latin American intellectual field. But in using Christian imagery, muralists were not just slavishly following a Western tradition with which they had already broken in so many violent and yet imperceptible ways. The Christian tradition gave muralism a dignified version of the popular classes, a version that considered the popular sector to be exemplary of the category of humanity in general, elevating these groups to a universality thus far negated by the Mexican political establishment. What muralism borrowed from Christianity was not its iconographic tradition (in which a certain figure carries an already codified meaning) but rather a figuration. The elevation of the neglected people to prototypes of the universal did not detach them from their place and their time. It entailed, rather, a carnivalesque inversion of religious imagery. Instead of these peasants and indigenous peoples becoming more "saintly" and ethereal, "saintliness" became more mundane and embodied. By recognizing the formative role of Christianity in the configuration of a tradition of the oppressed, Rivera refused to depict Christianity as a form of false consciousness, even if, in the same stroke, he refused to grant to Christianity the role of the historical voice of the oppressed. The ineluctable existence of a Christian redemptive discourse means in the end that even aesthetic reproduction is no match for the long process of reinscription by which the intentional acts of the past have been concealed by a strand of movements acting in the name of the people, but from which their proper name itself is absent. The painter suspects that these acts of giving voice to the oppressed have resolved themselves into a betrayal of intention. The obvious answer is that we will never know. However, this not-knowing is not simply ignorance but rather the very condition of possibility of a redemptive justice. Let us read David Lloyd's treatment of the same problem in *Irish Times*:

> Only in remaining out of joint with the times to which the dead are lost is there any prospect of a redress that would not be concomitant with the desire to lay the dead to rest. . . . The paradox of redress is that the catastrophic violence of history can be righted only in relinquishing the desire to set it right, in order to make room for the specters in whose restlessness the rhythms of another mode of living speak to us.[35]

Rivera recognized Christianity as that language in which generations of oppressed people safeguarded the singularity of their own earthly lives. The clergy and the church are certainly denounced in the murals, and Christianity is put on trial. Yet the popular allegiance to religion is absolved. Christianity is not only accepted but also respected as one of the most powerful embodiments of the tradition of the oppressed. It is respected in the hope that as a language, it has indexed and included all the clamors that it rescues, all the voices that it obliterates. The enactment of the political is never simply—as I take Rancière to suggest—a happening of a consciousness that comes so close to the absolute good that in this very act it changes the whole constitution of the visible, the sensible, and the thinkable. This Platonic realm of transformation is always mediated by the history of oppression itself! It is not just that political subjectivization implies an abandonment of past individuations, but that the individuations of the past are often the material that fuels the subjectivizations of the present.

JOSÉ CLEMENTE OROZCO

Why did Rivera's fantasy become the grounding fantasy of postrevolutionary Mexico? I believe that part of the answer lies in the historical nature of representation in his murals. History itself is offered as a principle of intelligibility for a subjectivity that is, in the same movement, charged with becoming responsible for the totality of its past. The appeal of Rivera's murals does not come from that historical rendering of the past. It comes rather from his recognition that the popular subject is, as is any subject, already split. Now, this was not the only fantasy offered to the Mexican people, and as audacious as Rivera's reconstruction of a Mexican imaginary was, it was not after all the most radical of alternatives when it came to dealing with the question of fantasy. At this point a reference to the work of Clemente Orozco is in order.

The work of the three great muralists of the revolution did not take place at the same time. Rivera, the oldest and best trained of the three, the one most willing to compromise with the increasingly consolidated postrevolutionary state, enjoyed a dominant position in the 1920s and 1930s. As their work matured, both Orozco and Siqueiros would become increasingly critical of Rivera's murals. For Siqueiros, Rivera misused his great artistic acumen in favor of a naïve and objectivist reconstruction of popular mores and traditions. In his own murals, Siqueiros sought to purge the romanticism (Gauguinism) that he perceived in Rivera in favor of a quasifuturistic rendering of the encounter of the masses with modern technology. Orozco, on the other hand, leveled the opposite criticism against Rivera: Rivera's emphasis on the indigenous was in reality a historically unsound reconstruction. Few traces of true indigenous presence remained in Mexico, since all original indigenous traits had been lost—through transculturation—in the course of four hundred years of colonial rule.

Orozco's yearning for truth is not easy to read in the stylistic features of his art. Unlike Rivera, who spent many years in Europe studying the classics of Western art and witnessing the emergence of the avant-garde, Orozco had an important background as cartoonist that gave his work not only an uncompromising agility but also a "corrosive" satirical impulse. He joined the other muralists in 1923. A year later, when Vasconcelos departed from the SEP, most of the muralist movement came to a halt. Only Rivera was able to negotiate his permanent place on the project in a successful way. Orozco found himself unemployed. He returned to the SEP in 1926. In 1927 he emigrated to the United States, where he lived until 1934. In these years he painted his famous murals at Pomona College in Claremont, California; at the New School for Social Research in New York; and at the Baker Library of Dartmouth College in Hanover, New Hampshire. In 1936, back in Mexico, Orozco started the most productive period of his artistic life. In Guadalajara he painted the hall walls of the university campus, the staircase of the city hall, and a series of frescos at the Hospicio Cabañas chapel. In these paintings Orozco yielded to his anguished and violent vision of Mexico's history as a perpetual marginalization of the poor, portraying the incomprehensible horrors of conquest and the tragedy of Mexican figures, painted as men on fire, shrouded in flames, consuming themselves in their own passion and impotence. These are the paintings that made Orozco famous and won him the title of the most powerful aesthetic force of Mexican muralism in the eyes of many critics (among them Sergei Eisenstein, who transposed several spatial schemas that he found in Orozco's paintings into the mise-en-scène of his film *¡Que viva México!*).

At first sight, it may seem that Orozco's paintings do not bear too much resemblance to those of Siqueiros and Rivera and that even in his political and personal passions the painter from Guadalajara was quite removed from the urgent calls from history that seem to have obsessed both Rivera and Siqueiros. Some biographical elements tend to underline this misguided perception. Orozco, for example, destroyed all his first murals at the Escuela Nacional Preparatoria. (Only portions survived and were incorporated into later paintings.) This perception is superficial, however, because no other muralist can be said to have confronted the revolution as an irreducible event as directly as Orozco did in his unsettling murals.

In Orozco's paintings the revolution is not celebrated in the clear lines that characterize Rivera's murals. Everything is both more nuanced and ambiguous. Actions are colored not so much by heroism but by the incomprehensible rules of a fatality beyond understanding. This effect is produced, above all, by subtracting any transcendental ground in the represented figures. *The Trench,* painted on the walls of the National Preparatory School, is a powerful illustration of these qualities. The painting shows three men in dramatically arrested poses. Their clothes are mundane (they are revolutionary fighters), but the composition clearly suggests a rupture between the sphere of human decisions and a "beyond"—let us call it history—in which these figures are taken in as in a nightmare. In Eugène Delacroix's *Barricade,* Antonio Rodríguez writes, eliciting a comparison between two revolutionary paintings, "Men seem to be fighting with the hymn of liberty on their lips." Nothing can be further removed from *The Trench,* in which Orozco presents us "with the bare essence of war."[36]

The utter unavailability of a historical redemption able to subsume the singular pain and distress of the revolutionary subjects gives Orozco's paintings their sense of nakedness. This aspect of his art, and his many derogatory remarks about the relationship between art and politics, could lead to the false impression that Orozco was unable or unwilling to cope with the revolutionary event. But one can also argue that Orozco was in fact the artist most obsessed with naming the blind impulse, the secret energy that was shaping Mexico at that time. By refusing to stage a fantasy of the revolution, he insinuated that realm of no-meaning from which all fantasies arise. This enigmatic revolutionary impulse appears not so much coded as contained inside the bodies of the figures, bodies that appear always on the verge of expression but also consumed in their isolated and irreducible solitude. The relationship of the composition to historical time is not only more complex than in Rivera's work, it is also the real center of these paintings where, as many critics have said, an eerie stillness prevails. This stillness does not represent a flight from the ever-changing nature of historical reality, but rather evokes a deeper immersion in it insofar as it contributes to a sheer (or naked, as Rodríguez puts it) presentation of the present. If in Orozco's paintings time is almost frozen, and if this impedes the development of his contained figures, it also subtracts them from any facile incorporation into the siren songs of the nationalist and modernizing culture of the time. The stillness of the figures combined with the exodus of any transcendental dimension in the paintings (an absence that can be marked as presence—for example, by heavy, meaningless Christian crosses) seems to leave the people in the paintings in a state of poetic orphanhood. Even opinion, perhaps the most shocking feature of Orozco's caricaturesque style, has no voice in paintings like *The Trench* or *Revolutionary Trinity*. These paintings emerge as a criticism of the fantasy-making aspect of muralism. But they do not replace a wrong version of history with a correct one, as many critics have suggested. Whoever loves the truth falls into the void. Orozco perceived quite easily that fantasies, by nature, always end in unproductive repetition. The fantasy that arises to occupy the space left open by the demise of an old world is always an alibi. The only truth of fantasy is its own anchorage in a region that is outside and beyond any positivity and that no number of images can placate. These paintings, which are neither sad nor optimistic, figure the traversing of the fantasy of the revolution. Orozco could well be the painter of the stillness of the revolution, not as a negative indecision in the face of reality but as the codification of an afterlife of the revolution in the subterranean force of bodies tortured by the demands placed upon them by history.

CHAPTER SIX

Synchronicity

PART ONE: THE TASK OF SYNCHRONIZATION

"In nineteenth-century Mexican photography," writes Carlos Monsiváis, "there are no equivalents to the works of [Eugène] Atget in France, Julia Margaret Cameron in England, or Mathew Brady and Jacob Riis in the United States. In Mexico, photography does not look for the originality of those portrayed. It looks, instead, for those gestures able to inform about social status and attitude. . . . The rigidity of a pose is thus elevated to the condition of a natural landscape."[1] The revolution rendered art a favor when it shattered the acquiescence of the present. A forgotten everyday, onto which the spectacle of a revolt was superimposed, became the tenacious object of a new wave of photojournalists. By 1915 over one hundred photographers were covering the Mexican revolution. Gifted professionals like Walter Horne and James Hare crossed the border to cover the fight for different American publications. As the pages of *Collier's Weekly*, *Leslie's Illustrated*, and, to a lesser extent, *Harper's* filled with photos of revolutionary generals, troop movements, and military preparations, the war postcard became a genre that attracted dozens of freelance photographers willing to produce "souvenirs of the carnage and destruction in Mexico."[2]

Agustín Casasola, the unofficial photographer of Porfirio Díaz, dominates the Mexican side of photojournalism. In 1911 Casasola organized the first Mexican photographic association. He made a habit of acquiring negatives from other photographers, a collection that, along with his own photographs, formed the core of the legendary Casasola Archive. In 1921 he began the publication of the *Archivo gráfico de la Revolución mexicana*, a project that, although truncated, uncovered the difference between the horizontal composition that prevailed before 1910—devoid of both drama and surprise—and the dynamism that characterized the photography of the revolutionary period.[3] Acquired by the Mexican government in 1976, the collection was integrated into the archives of the Fototeca Nacional in Pachuca, which remains the primary source for photographs of the revolutionary period.

Photographing the revolution was a daunting task. Equipment was heavy and difficult to transport. As a rule, photographers were barred from the battlefields and only arrived at a battle site several hours after the action had ended. This is why some of the most dramatic photos we have of armed conflict come from the Decena Trágica (9–18 February 1913), an event that took place inside the limits of Mexico City.[4] Finally, although photographers were organized early on in Casasola's association, their ability to protect the intellectual ownership of their work was limited. As a result, an enormous majority of photos of the revolution come to us classified as anonymous, and many of the photos credited by tradition to the main lenses of the time (Jesús Abitia, Hugo Brehme, Casasola) have proved to be falsely attributed.[5]

Despite all difficulties, these photos constitute a dazzling archive of undisputed quality. Olivier Debroise has remarked that not only was the Mexican Revolution far better documented than World War I or the Russian Revolution, but also that the register of the European conflicts lacks the dramatic quality that often shines through in the photos of the Mexican conflict.[6] Even in the case of Russia, where the popular component could not possibly be overlooked, the results are often disappointing: "The revolution looks like an organized labor movement. . . . The leader—Lenin or Trotsky—is always at the center of the image, haranguing the crowds that appear as a sea of upturned heads."[7] The Mexican Revolution, on the other hand, presents us with an unscripted reality that lends photographic productions an intensely dramatic quality, one that has spawned more than a few interpretive problems.

Although the photography of the revolutionary period is overwhelmingly journalistic in nature, its function is far from being merely indexical. There was something intrinsically aesthetic in this photography, insofar as it aspired to be the sensory representation of an overarching reality that could not itself be made the subject of a presentation. The assemblage of all photographic images to which we can apply the label "photography of the revolution" is united by a common desire to state (in purely imaginary terms) *this* is a revolution. Such is the subtext that runs beneath the whole photographic register and determines, to different degrees, the act of composition. While this determination is subjective in nature, all photography was implicated in this task by virtue of the technical determination that the art received from its character as medium.

Edward Weston and John Reed in Mexico

After the revolution Mexico became home to two of the most important names in twentieth-century photography, Edward Weston and Paul Strand. Weston arrived in Mexico in 1923, along with Tina Modotti, drawn among other things by the stories of revolutionary life retold by Ricardo Gómez Robelo during the bohemian nights of a Los Angeles–based group of artists and intellectuals. Biographical facts are not beside the point, for Weston never dissociated his art from the avatars of his worldly life. He felt a serene repulsion for everything that bespoke falsity or error. Weston's truth was, however, circumspect. Because of its necessarily redundant character, he despised the imaginary capture of the world and preferred, instead, to bet on the symbolization of the real. Weston's real was nature (or objects) deprived of its teleological moorings: the trunk of a palm without its crowning, a chimney without its industrial surroundings. Since he believed that the natural world was too lavish to be photographed, Weston proceeded to isolate forms with almost surgical precision. In consequence, problems of scale or background-figure contrast rarely emerge in his photos. Although he went to Mexico attracted by its social atmosphere, once there he ignored politics, despite his immersion in a group of people (Diego Rivera, Xavier Guerrero, Carl Bates, Dr. Atl, the senator Manuel Galván) through whom revolutionary passions raged with the force of a storm.

In Mexico earthly things bewitched his eyes: small dolls made of clay and adorned with straw and loose pieces of cloth; birds carved out of the carcass of a pumpkin. While the Mexican avant-garde reacted cautiously to his interest in the popular, the most refined commentator of the period found it both amusing and understandable.[8] Weston found popular art valuable not because the canon of modern art vindicated it, but because it existed in a primordial relationship to the world. These objects were realistic beyond any principle of mimesis. Their realism lay in being an inalienable part of reality itself. In them a whole world made itself manifest. A similar canon applies to his photography. The camera clears the debris of the world. His visit to the convent of Churubusco, recorded in his *Daybooks,* is instructive in this regard: "The convent . . . is a gem. The rest of the party made photographs. . . . I did not, for the churches in Mexico are an end in themselves, needing no further interpretation. I stand before them mute—nothing that I might record could add to their beauty."[9] The selectivity to which Weston endowed his lenses was precisely what the photography of the revolution could not afford—not as a question of strategy, but as a matter of principle. The goal of establishing the singularity of the shot was constantly threatened by the need to show the unexpected arrangements, the uncalled-for arrivals, the torsion and new configurations of an imaginary finally released from the constraints of the proper and the authorized. As John Mraz observes, "The Mexican Revolution changed the face of the country. Suddenly, ordinary people were appearing in photographs, newspapers, illustrated magazines, and documentary films; the underdogs projected a force that overflowed the constrictions of the 'popular type' model within which they have been shoehorned."[10]

Paul Leduc may have had the exceptionally problematic nature of photographing the revolution in mind when, in one of the opening scenes of *Reed: México insurgente* (1973), he inserted a memorable shot in which the character John Reed (Claudio Obregón) takes a picture of Gen. Tomás Urbina.[11] The improvised general sits on a chair surrounded by some soldiers, his mother (or, less likely, his wife), and a couple of dogs against the background of a battered wall. The effect of the photo, isolated in a still of several seconds, is simultaneously ironic and affirmative. The general is in uniform. He pretends to be someone important, but myriad small details—the crooked chair, the scant number of followers, the dwarf soldier holding a banner—belie his intention.[12] Even the genre of the photo is uncertain: while the presence of the mother and the dogs points towards a family portrait, the defiant posture of the soldiers speaks of a "professional" photograph in the style of the revolutionary postcard. If this is not a true general, what is the truth of this representation? We cannot deny that the person photographed is a general, but the semiotic incongruities in the photo may lead us to state our reservation under the form of a delay: the photo shows a distance between concept and instance, or this general is not yet a general. Indeed, the photographic archive of the revolution abounds in images before which we exclaim, this is not yet a people, a governing body, or a president. Often the lag between concept and image is the very meaning of the photograph. (Villa in the presidential chair comes readily to mind.) In the photography (as well as in the films) of the revolution, the most visible is still elusive and conceptually "out of focus." In the time lag, the revolutionary body occupies the scene, but it is subjected to a regime of representation that claims that it is either too early or too late for it to come into the scene.

This asynchrony contradicts the vocation of photography while simultaneously providing photography with its implicit utopia by suturing the distance it exposes. What photography really wants is to make the subjects of the revolution contemporaneous with themselves. The temporal aspect only emerges as a problem because the photography of the revolution is narrative in nature. The revolution introduced a vast upheaval in the order of the world, and it was this upheaval that photography had to portray. However, photographing disorder runs against the canon of photographic art. It is, to a large extent, what photography cannot do. If photography were to follow the chaos of the world too closely, it would end up being an example of that chaos rather than its representation. On the other hand, if photography injects too much order into the perception of reality, it risks falsifying reality altogether. Photography has to claim that reality is stable enough to be photographed even while contributing to its stabilization. In this situation photography acquires an ontological function. For the photography of the Mexican Revolution, what was at stake was the existent itself.[13]

Captions

In informative photography, captions are always redundant to some extent. They complete or confirm whatever the visual register insinuates or plainly states. The demand to photograph something that does not show itself—like a revolution—puts considerable stress on captions. Often these captions do not anchor the meaning of the image but rather state the form of the world that, to some extent, the photo failed to elicit. In *Photographing the Mexican Revolution,* John Mraz reproduces an image that shows, according to the caption, the entrance of Madero into Mexico City after the triumph of the revolution. The caption that the photographer handwrote on the negative reads, "Francisco Madero enters Mexico City. View of Charles IV's statue." Madero is not in the photo and the statue of Charles IV is scarcely more present. Instead we see a wagon on top of which men, women, and their servants look expectantly towards the horizon. The statue itself is barely visible beneath the number of people mounted on top of the figure or hanging political signs from the horse. Although Madero is not in the photo, the caption is justified since it shows how social mobilization is what turned Madero's entrance into the capital into a political event. Still, we can hardly ignore the fact that while the caption organizes the world along the recognizable lines of liberal politics—in which a subject, Madero, is the cause of a mass movement—the photograph portrays the social excess that spills over the city and its (no longer) recognizable landmarks.

This image was taken in 1911. At that point the revolution was not yet a social revolution. The world the photo portrays was still firmly attached to the emblems of a past organization of politics that Madero's revolution sought to correct but not really challenge. Things will be different after 1913, when the insinuations of 1911 become a full assault on the normative of the visible. However, an element connects this photo taken during the institutional phase of the revolution to other photos that, after 1913, testify to a more socially minded understanding of the political process. This element is the human body, whose hermeneutics, insinuation, and domestication become the foremost objects of the photographic register once the revolution breaks the lethargic life of images that, according to Monsiváis, characterized Mexican photography in the nineteenth century.

The popular body gives to the photography of the revolution its exact, aesthetic density. The unscripted nature of the real fascinated the photographic eye, but it also represented the unique challenge to reproduce the seismic changes in codes that arose in so many different areas of society, from gender relationships to the surge of newly validated social identities; from the crisis of patriarchal authority to questions of mobility and social uprooting. The revolution, writes Mexican historian Claudia Canales, "irreversibly changed the ethnic and social landscape of Mexico by placing peasants and Indians of different regions" at its center; photography had to portray them not as "anthropological types" but as subjects in their own right.[14] The revolution did not unearth the popular itself. But it did bring with it a sense of out-of-placeness that was sometimes ironic—as with Villa in the presidential chair—but that also could be challenging and dramatic. Canales uses the oxymoronic expression "Juanes sin nombre" [nameless Juans] to denote this conceptual twilight by which a body emerged as simultaneously bound and disinvested, individualized and subtracted from all forms of adscription.

> A woman or an anonymous man: one of the so many Juanes without name or tomb, but one who emerges from the indistinct crowd with all the authority of his humanity, with all the overwhelming force of his singularity. Beyond the rules of representation, syntax, discourse, or style that we can infer from these images, it will be always impossible to ignore that force.[15]

The quote speaks of a certain irrefutability that the human figure acquired in the context of the revolution. This was the irrefutability of the any-body. Irrefutability names here a form of presencing, which did not depend on any qualification for its appearance and yet did not relapse into the nakedness of life. This irrefutability of the revolutionary body is not a retrospective illusion founded in contemporary theories of the ethical grounding of the social. It belongs to the historical moment itself. Now, this intrinsically utopian feature of revolutionary photography, by which it brings forward a figure that is both threatening and enigmatic, is also a conservative act of appeasing. There is a sense in which this photography seeks to soothe the anxieties of the gaze. This intention colors the photographic act with disciplinary tonality. One common strategy to conjure up the motley nature of revolutionary mobilization was the mass reproduction of a postcard style in which soldiers lined up for the lenses in full *paisano* gear, their rifles cocked in a simulacrum of aiming. This kind of photo was by far the most popular material in Mexican publications such as *El Mundo Ilustrado, Novedades,* or *La Ilustración Semanal,* which informed their readership on the course of the revolutionary fight.[16] The images presented the revolution as an organizable (if not organized) spectacle. Often the background of these photos was carefully selected to avoid any direct reference to chaos and destruction. In many cases the war postcard attempted to make the background entirely irrelevant and, in so doing, invited us to forget that the scandal of the revolutionary body does not pertain to the body itself but rather to its appearance in an unforeseeable context. In the fictional photo staged by Leduc in *Reed: México insurgente,* the element that puts in doubt the truth value of the representation is not the general himself but his surroundings. It is not so much that he fails to blend with the stage as that the stage fails to confirm his status.[17] One of the most persistent and significant rhetorical problems in the post-revolutionary imaginary consisted of negotiating between the irrefutability of the any-body and the nullifying effect of context upon the person. This tension provided a discursive dimension to this photography. The photojournalism of the revolution is never the presentation of a decisive instant, à la Henri Cartier-Bresson, but the unfolding of a story. This discursive trait compounded with the often incongruous relationship between figure and background invites a peculiar way of looking at these photos that I cipher in the term *relatedness.*

Relatedness

To some extent relatedness is a characteristic of all photography. Scanning a photo allows the viewer to notice spatial relations that are usually lost in direct experience. Of course, totality cannot be seen, even in a photo. A photo is a gateway for the utter subjectification of the world. This utter subjectification is never possible in its entirety. I cannot be, simultaneously, a subject vis-à-vis all the objects that confront me in a given situation. The photographer may strive to control all the elements in a composition, but undesirable figures or objects will fatally crop into his work. (Roland Barthes call these areas of failed subjectification "punctum.")[18] Even in artistic photography the different ways in which all the elements of the photo relate to each other provide photography with a modicum of narrative. There is, however, something inimical to narration built into the photographic act itself. Taking a photograph implies a preemptive cropping out of the undesirable elements that will ruin the simplicity with which the photographic eye is so acquainted. Yet, the textual construction of reality, the necessary togetherness implied by social existence as created by the revolution, means that photog-

Hugo Brehme, Zeltlager der revolutionären Truppen auf den Dächern von Eisenbahn Wagon in México *(ca. 1914). Getty Research Institute, Los Angeles (98.R.5).*

raphy cannot achieve its goal through a cropping so severe that art is no longer a witness to life.[19] The situation stretched photographic art to its limits. Let us refer the problem to a photo taken by none other than Hugo Brehme: *Zeltlager der revolutionären Truppen auf den Dächern von Eisenbahn Wagon in México* (ca. 1914).

Brehme composes his photo around the tension between the line of flight suggested by the angle of the train and its proximity to an encampment of *soldaderas,* whose motley arrangement takes up more than half of the image. Thus, while the perspective of the photo suggests that the world that the *soldaderas* has instantiated atop the train represents a fleeting moment, the massed confusion of clothes and utensils in the lower right corner asserts a more permanent and disturbing state of things. This is not the only tension in the photo. Thematically, Brehme stresses the heterogeneous nature of the present by juxtaposing signs of the modern and the traditional. While the *soldaderas* at the forefront of the photo represent a rural world that has changed little in centuries, a technological horizon looms behind the precarious encampment: telegraph posts and the chimneys and rooftops of industrial facilities. In a more connotative register, yet another tension arises in the play between a precarious sense of home—represented by the encampment—

and the transient nature of popular mobilization. The tension between the homely and the nomadic suggests that while the mobility associated with modernity is still alien—this is why these women make an "improper" use of it—the social and symbolic immobility tied to the notion of home has lost the character of the unavoidable.

But Brehme is at his boldest with the subjective element in the photo. The image does not present the encounter between the modern and the traditional as a result of mere chance but rather as a purposeful intervention in space by women of rural origin. (There are men in the photo but we hardly notice them.) Of all the unsettling signs in this photo, none is more profoundly unsettled than that of *soldadera*. It is a sign that has been carefully constructed and stabilized by tradition. Whether in Elena Poniatowska's critical recollection of the *soldadera*, or in the careful manipulation of her image in the Casasola collection, or even in the quiet eulogy to her figure in Fernando de Fuentes's *¡Vámonos con Pancho Villa!* (I touch on this later), the *soldadera* emerges as a figure of self-effacement. Defiant or submissive, she occupies a small corner of the world where she reproduces the strictures of gender by replicating a place that she seems to have never abandoned. Her function seems at best nostalgic. The *soldadera*—to say it with Heidegger—does not world. But in this photo by Brehme, the *soldadera* interrupts the worlding of the world and instantiates another order that photography captures, although it is reluctant to stamp it with the seal of the definitive.[20]

The photo tells an origin story that starts in the unknown and uprooted universe of popular mobilization as it appropriates the symbols of modernity. The ontological function declares, despite all misgivings, the essential relatedness between the *soldadera* and the world of technology. This relatedness rescues the situation from the ridicule that permeates the photo of Urbina in Leduc's film and offers us instead the irrefutability of the revolutionary body insofar as it acts, insofar as it presents itself in relationship to the complex semiosis unleashed by the emergence of the masses into the optical consciousness of the time. Brehme himself is not caught in the frenzy of this semiosis. His distance from the scene is embodied in the ominous vertical abyss that occupies the front of the photo, where the surface of the train stops, an abyss whose depth is left up to the imagination of the viewer rather than asserted by the photographer. A Barthesian reading of the photo could perhaps identify this void with the location of the punctum. I believe that it would be equally correct to see in it a sort of metaphotographic comment on the predicament of photography. The abyss marks the void about which photography needs to simultaneously testify and ward off in order for the visible—even when it is such a confusing visible—to come into existence.

One, Two, Three

Photography's ontological function is at the root of the oft-repeated idea that the snapshot is a clue to or revelation of an entire social or epochal structure. Obviously, such an ideology of photography—quite extended throughout the nineteenth century, as Pierre Sorlin informs us—has enormous uses in a context like the one prevailing in Mexico after the revolution.[21] Weston himself aspired to produce photographs that were more real than reality. Yet, although the materialist and revelatory drives were integral to Weston's photography, he would never have suggested that his photography could unveil a complex sociopolitical or historical configuration. Diego Rivera, however, made such a claim about one of Weston's photographs. Of the photo that Weston took of Senator Manuel Galván in 1924 (one in his series of "heroic heads"), Rivera enthusiastically asserted that the photo was "Mexico itself."[22] I am less interested in the question of whether or not this judgment is correct than in what made Rivera's assertion possible. The photo shows Galván with a scarf around his neck. As with most headshots of this period, Galván's eyes are directed to the left of the portrait. The eyes squint in the sunlight. (Or is he aiming?) The photo, after all, is titled *Galván Shooting*, although no gun or target is in view. A strand of his hair seems to ripple in the wind, which, combined with the squinting eyes, suggests that he may be facing a strong wind. He is neither advancing nor retreating but holding his ground with a sense of cautious awe. I cannot think of any equivalent to this image in Rivera's own murals.

This man (or rather this photo, but how to separate them?) is Mexico, Rivera said. But where is Mexico in the photo? Questions of relatedness do not even arise here—as they do not in Weston's photos in general. Likewise, there are no issues of scale or context. The camera liberates its object from any worldly restriction. In most of Weston's portraits the models have closed eyes so they cannot escape the secure containment of the photograph, even in intention. But if Galván's head is Mexico (and Weston was certainly flattered by the judgment), it is because, to Rivera's eye, Weston had managed to portray the definitive implication of world and subject. For Galván to be Mexico, he had to be receptive to Mexico. He had to live in a state of abandonment or openness to the revolution that I described at some length in chapter 4. Instead of the plotted life he was supposed to live, Galván needed to welcome the blows of destiny, bearing the marks of these blows on his face. Does not his pose, facing the assumed or simulated wind, attest to this disposition? Is not Galván the tragic hero giving himself up to his destiny (a destiny he certainly did not escape)? But again, what can we say about the world in minimalist photography? What world are we talking about? It is the world as intended by the organizing and desiring gaze of the human subject, the ontological world that photography is fated to reveal. All of this is implied in Rivera's judgment. Because, after all, if Galván is holding his ground, if he is not blown over by the force of reality, what is sustaining him in his obstinacy? The answer is simple: whatever he sees, whatever his gaze intends. Unlike most of his other portraits, Weston allows or invites Galván to see. (As Monsiváis points out, this portrait is both characteristic of Weston's production and atypical.)[23] Galván's eyes are fixed upon the same point that Rivera's eyes were fixed upon when he said: this portrait is Mexico.

At this point it is instructive to compare *Galván Shooting* to another photo with which Rivera was quite familiar but in which he never saw "Mexico itself" represented—the one of Emiliano Zapata that Rivera reportedly used as a model for his murals and Guadalupe Posada reproduced in a famous engraving. For many years the photo was attributed to Hugo Brehme, who is known to have spent some time with the Zapatistas. This attribution is today in dispute, although the exceptional quality of the image evokes some of the distinctive features often attributed to the German photographer.[24] Although the figure of Brehme is currently being reassessed by critics, the view of Brehme as a romantic pictorialist is based mostly on his 1923 book *México pintoresco*, composed of landscapes and popular types.[25] What makes Brehme's romantic photos an uneasy companion to the photography of the revolution is the self-possession of these images. If, as Vasconcelos once said, Zapata is a mystery, the pseudo-Brehme does not even bring the question of mystery into consideration. The out-of-jointness of the world is not revealed by the photo. Zapata is simply standing there right in front of the camera. The questions the photo elicits are all banal: Was that what he was really like? How could this gentle *charro* be mistaken for a wild Attila? Is this composure a pose or an actual reflection of a revolutionary persona? Like the convent of Churubusco that Weston preferred not to photograph, the pseudo-Brehme cannot add anything to Zapata. Weston's photo of Galván avoids this unearthly feeling by constituting its subject as one of lack. Here one can appreciate the subtlety of Weston's composition. What is Galván looking at? He looks at the punctum, which, in an audacious gesture, is located outside the frame. The displacement of the photographic punctum is what makes Rivera's judgment believable. We can read Galván's head as an expression of Mexico for the simple reason that its implicit unspoken utopia is a reminder of all the dreams that will not come true even when the subject opens and abandons itself to the winds of a revolutionary era. Galván's photo is Mexico because at the time it was taken, Mexico was impossible to portray—it

Anonymous, Venustiano Carranza Arriving at Cuernavaca with His Comitiva. *Centro de Estudios de Historia de México (CEHM).*

did not yet exist. It was located in a future towards which Galván's gaze is attracted (rather than directed), to an ethical instance to which he responds ahead of time.

There is, beyond the technical aspects of the photograph itself, another underlying element that grants credibility to Rivera's judgment that "this photo is Mexico": *Galván Shooting* is a portrait. We cannot insist enough on the fact that photography is part and parcel of the rise of bourgeois individualism.[26] Rivera's judgment is disputable in that it reinstates the individual as the hero and container of the historical process but omits too quickly what is, after all, the essential problem in his own painting. Weston's photography gives us the haunting but subtracts the haunters. It keeps the dynamic and creative force of the masses in that subterranean place from which Rivera himself said they were pushing and molding the form of the real. After all, is not the action of the masses what is ruining any tautological judgment, such as *this is Mexico*? And from that point of view, should not a photo like *Venustiano Carranza Arriving at Cuernavaca with His Comitiva* be a more appropriate rendering of the revolutionary moment? But the photograph itself is disappointing. There is nothing in this photo, aside from the caption, that allows us to connect this picture with Carranza or even with a political demonstration. Disappointment—another name for the asynchronic—is of course a literal, perhaps even too literal, presentation of reality. Left to its objective vocation, photography becomes a document of the centripetal forces of mass dissolution. In a certain sense, *Carranza Arriving at Cuernavaca* represents the revolution better than any other photograph, and yet, as I will discuss apropos Modotti's photography, there is a sense in which the redistribution of the sensible without the guiding concept of revolution—blurry as that concept was for the historical actors of the time—represents an always incomplete formulation of the historical moment.[27]

We are left in an untenable position. Reducing the revolt to the figure of the one is a form of deception, but the representation of the many is chaotic in terms of representation, or falsified in terms of testimony. In retrospect, one can see what an achievement it was for Brehme to produce his photo of the *soldaderas* on top of a train. But the photography of the revolution had at its disposal other solutions as well that I have not yet touched upon and to which I now turn.

Dialogical Images

Between the one and the many, and working with the conceptual knots of the visible, dialogical images were perhaps the proper photographic answer to the interpretive crisis posed by the revolution in the realm of the visible. Dialogical images should not be confused with Walter Benjamin's dialectical images, since what is at stake in this period of Mexican expression is space rather than time. In dialogical images the ontological function secures a space for the photograph to unfold, but it cannot cancel the indecision that is proper to the presentation of the revolution as a system of possibilities. Dialogical images openly acknowledge the textual nature of reality; they are an exact imaginary transcription of the clash of lifestyles and points of view that were characteristic of the revolutionary period. In dialogical images the uncertainty about the value of the present is referred to a play of gazes that makes photography itself the laboratory in which the question of the stability of reality is investigated. Although they were intrinsically connected to the revolutionary movement, dialogical photos were not the most common photos of the revolt. In fact, they were rare.

My example of dialogical photography sends us back to the figure of Zapata, who appears with an emissary of the U.S. state department, George Carothers, in a photograph taken in December 1914, shortly before Zapata's encounter with Villa in Xochimilco, a meeting that Carothers himself was said to have facilitated. The fact that both men are well dressed and self-composed produces an even more obvious visual clash of worldviews and lifestyles. The only element connecting Zapata and Carothers is the cigars they both hold with a certain familiarity in their hands. The cigars stand for

Anonymous, Zapata and Mr. Carothers *(1914). INAH. Fototeca Nacional México.*

the lack of direct dialogue or interaction between both men. Zapata does not seem to be particularly aware of the camera, although by now we recognize the quintessential Zapatista *pose* in his gaze. Mr. Carothers's position is even more enigmatic. He contemplates Zapata as if he himself were not in the photo or as if the figure of Zapata were already photographic. (The photo inside the photo takes on a new meaning here.) The fact that this photo is about a photo—about the act of photographing—is further accentuated by the blurred figures in the background who seem to be the only ones who register the photographic moment. Their looks and attire do not approximate those of either Carothers or Zapata, which intensifies the uniqueness of the two men in the foreground. Their presence, however, disturbs the strong idealization of Zapata and his American companion, who could otherwise pass for recent gods of a new Olympus. At least three conflicting gazes constitute this photo and attest to the crisis in the normalcy that the photo wants, nonetheless, to establish.

The haphazard, chancelike nature of the revolutionary encounter is even more manifest in one of the most emblematic photos of the revolutionary period: *Zapatistas in Sanborns* (1914, anonymous). Although the women serving the rebels squeezing in at the counter do not belong to the upper class—a parody that Best Maugard put into practice in his *noche mexicana* in Chapultepec—it is clear that the waitresses are uncertain about these men. As the soldiers rest their arms on the counter, leaning forward towards the "interior" of the commercial establishment, the women put some distance between their bodies and the counter. Very likely they would prefer to serve more dignified customers. Perhaps these waitresses entertain some sympathies for the Zapatista soldiers, but the crushing of the previous distribution

Anonymous, Zapatistas in Sanborns *(1914). INAH. Fototeca Nacional México.*

of the sensible is too visually violent to be ignored. After all, customers do not show up at Sanborns armed to their teeth every day. The Zapatista soldiers themselves are not any more at ease. Those in the back are neither resting nor moving but in a state of indecision about their role. The two men occupying the center of the photo seem oblivious to the situation, focused perhaps on the rite of passage that their rifles have bought them. The two closer to the camera are taken in by the photographic moment, creating a triangular exchange of gazes that accentuates the out-of-sync character of the situation. The multilayered and confused nature of the revolution takes on a new sense here, a sense that we can even call democratic insofar as it acknowledges the relationships of different historical agents on a common stage; the stage itself, however, is provided by the photograph in its ontological dimension.

Self-Fashioning and the Ideal

The revolution, as I noted before, provided some members of the middle classes with the chance to refashion their lives and identities; Frida Kahlo is the most successful example of this process of reinvention. The photographic register of her figure confirms the point. Lola Álvarez Bravo produced several pictures of Kahlo. These pictures have, of course, little in common with the series we have been discussing so far. We do not face here the unhinging of norms that characterizes the figure of the *soldadera*; the self-sufficient remoteness of Zapata's image; the incoherence of Villa in the presidential chair; the disciplining of the body in the model of the postcard; the male revolutionary gaze scouting the horizon; or the dialogical involvement of different subjects under a single illuminating framework. There is no need for a photo to synchronize the figure of Kahlo to our image of the times.

While Kahlo could exercise the activity of self-fashioning that was integral to the emergence of new forms of crafting a life, Tina Modotti often chose as her subjects situations and individuals in which this act of self-invention was more restricted and problematic. Let us take, for instance, her famous 1928 photo *Woman with Flag*. This picture has been left relatively untouched by the wave of scholarly work on Modotti that has exploded in the last twenty years, in which critics have paid enormous attention to form.[28] One reason, I believe, is that this photo is difficult to accommodate within any of the ideologies of the photographic act that surround the interpretation of the postrevolutionary canon. It has even been "misread" as a snapshot of an actual parade (in part, perhaps, because the communist leader Benita Galeana claimed to be the person in the photograph).[29]

In the photo a dark-skinned woman walks, carrying what may be a red flag. She is dressed in traditional clothes, and yet her shoes are modern and

Tina Modotti, Woman with Flag *(1928). INAH. Fototeca Nacional México.*

slightly incongruous with the rest of the elements in the photo. The photo itself smacks of propaganda. But is it no less propagandistic than *Hut, Hammer, and Sickle* and slightly more so than *Mella's Typewriter.* What complicates things here is the human figure. Propaganda in still life is bearable, but when the object is a person it becomes an ethical issue similar to the one that emerged in early modernity with the representation of saints or the Virgin Mary in itinerant theaters. The photo has obviously been staged. The staging itself throws a shadow of doubt on the actual commitment of the model to the idea portrayed in the picture. The whole notion of photography as revelation is put into question by a photo that aligns photography not with truth but with pretense. The fact that Modotti was a committed photographer dissipates any possibility of parody, which, in any case, is absent in the formal traits of the image.

A year after this photo was made, in her text-manifesto *On Photography*, Modotti states her rather complex photographic credo in ways that identify her photographs as realistic and testimonial only on the surface. She starts by declaring, "I try to produce not art, but rather, honorable photographs—without any tricks or manipulations." Making honorable photography, Modotti explains, is an act in which the photographer "values what photography has to offer of its very own."[30] What is, then, offered in a photo of a woman marching and embracing the emancipatory politics of Marxism through a model? In his masterful analysis of Modotti's *Workers' Parade*, Leonard Folgarait convincingly argues that the truth Modotti was aiming at could only be said through a falsification of the immediate, objective traits of reality.[31]

I would make a similar argument in regards to *Woman with Flag*. For Modotti, this staged photo was not just propaganda—in the sense of showing a state of the world through a fantasy—but rather the only way to reveal a real trait of the present, which would not otherwise come to light. Modotti did not photograph the emerging shape of things to come but the ideal itself. This ideal status of the image is further underlined by the lack of sites of identification in the photo: the flag, for instance, may or may not be a communist flag. This indeterminacy of the flag (Modotti was an outspoken communist militant) is itself revelatory. The ideal is not the absent but the half-seen. For Modotti revolutionary positions in Mexico were real. But they did not coalesce around a single focal point. The indeterminacy of the flag points to this unity in diversity. Likewise, the figure of the woman partakes of the same indetermination. We do not see her gaze or whatever she is looking at; it does not invite an identification with our own gazes, much less a dialogue. All of this does not mean that the photograph is a fiction in the derogatory sense of the word. We should count as real her standing in the world, the irrefutability of her presence. The certainty of her march and that ideal of which she is a bearer—or that she uses as a support for her own visibility—also belongs to the effective realm of the historical.

Opposing the stark idealism of a woman with a flag, we find the naked realism of Modotti's *Children of Colonia La Bolsa*. The same title applies to several photos taken by Modotti in the popular neighborhood of Mexico City. The one that I refer to here—and which restrictions on the cropping of copyrighted material make impossible to reproduce—is, as a matter of fact, a cropping of a larger image. It appears on page 196 of Mariana Figarella's *Ed-*

ward Weston y Tina Modotti en México. The photo shows the embrace of two impoverished children whose gazes, neither expressive nor hopeful, point to the opposite edges of the photo. The testimonial emphasis of this photo is underscored by the precision of the title. Like *Woman with Flag*, the photo is dated 1928, when Weston had departed for California and Modotti was at the height of her involvement with the Mexican Communist Party. Relatedness itself is minimal, as this photo could have been taken anywhere in the world. However, the dialogical play of gazes is totally incorporated into the photo even when it does not reveal anything about the situation. The drama that Modotti imprints in the photo is not easily reconcilable with most of her previous photographs. The realm of emotions, methodically suppressed in her most formalist work, finds voice here. But I do not think that the history of this photo should be read as a testimony of Modotti's struggle with expression and form, but rather as a testimony of a photographic history. In a sense, this photo is the reversal of *Woman with Flag*: a declaration that no ideal is in sight and that hope itself is a political trap.

We do not possess many photos of children in which they appear endowed with historical authority. Whatever these children are looking at, it is not the type of image that directs the gaze of Galván in Weston's photograph or the straight line that sustains the march of the woman with a flag. The eyes of the children reflect confusion and even disbelief. Something seems certain: they do not see what Galván or the marching woman sees. Perhaps they lack enough confidence, maturity, or education to see an object that is able to elicit hope or optimism. Their figures, however, are not representative of naked life. Insofar as they are looking, insofar as their eyes reveal what is at stake in this photo, the ideal is never far behind. The children may even be looking at the woman with the flag. They may be wondering what kind of world her march announces. Or they may find the image too complex altogether to be paid attention to, so that they relapse into a mute wondering. The two images can be considered dialogical after all, although in a supplementary sense. It is as if Modotti photographed two end-stages of possibilities in the postrevolutionary world: the irrefutability of the revolutionary body cornered in its historical limits, and the hovering presence of revolutionary ideals to which no precise configuration corresponds.

PART TWO: FILM—THE STRUGGLE FOR A UNIFIED MESSAGE

No artistic production did more than film to consolidate an image of Mexico in the national and even international imagination. And yet, this image has often been accused of falsifying the paths through which postrevolutionary Mexico developed. Carl Mora bitterly remarks that Fernando de Fuentes's *¡Vámonos con Pancho Villa!* was "the last Mexican movie to deal honestly with the recent historical past."[32] Undoubtedly the reign of industrial cinema marked a "flight into fiction" for Mexican film, but this escape into melodrama and stereotypes could not detach itself completely from the social conditions born of the revolution. Mexican film could not but constantly bespeak its troubling relationship to the country bequeathed by the revolution. The problem of synchronicity here takes the form of a search for an ever-elusive imaginary stabilization of the real. The proverbial lack of synchrony between image and expression that photography so forcefully revealed emerges now as an impossible narrative suture, as the expression of a series of breaks through which an unaccounted portion of the revolution shines through. Often, movies lapse into a pedagogical tone as a form of obscuring this pervasive sense of division that appears in either formal or narrative terms. As we will see later, the constant pedagogical cues offered to the audience acknowledge also the heterogeneous nature of the masses of moviegoers.[33]

But the establishment of industrial cinema in Mexico in the mid-1930s is predated by two decades of cinematic experience, decades that even more significantly coincided with the unfolding of the revolution itself. The Lumière company premiered *Arrival of a Train at La Ciotat* in Mexico City in August 1896. Cinema was heralded as an event entirely in line with the objective, progressive, and apolitical goals of the positivist era.[34] Perhaps one reason why cinematographers elicited so much approval in the close-knit socius of Porfirist Mexico was the ease with which they fit into a particular economy in which it was the lot of the image to reproduce a sanctioned existence.[35] In the beginning, Mexican film concentrated on two areas of movement and visibility: the rituals of power and the ceremonial display of the bourgeois body in the contained spaces of the religious procession or the chariot ride. Although realism was the dominant aesthetic, the cameraman was also guided by an aesthetic of bourgeois decorum. The Alva brothers' short film *Fiestas patrias en Morelia en el año 1908* can be read in terms of the discomfort that the image of the masses forced upon the arts of representation. A slightly elevated camera captures a civil and military parade just two years before the start of the Maderista revolution. The parade flows through the well-contained space of the city dispositive. The frame, however, is unstable. Children and curious people anxious to be captured on film irrupt onto the frame while assistants to the brothers push them to the sides.

Aurelio de los Reyes observes that, at this stage, Mexican filmmakers lacked consistent generic models for the development of their productions.

This lack, argues de los Reyes, was a blessing in disguise. The way the Alva brothers shot the Taft-Díaz encounter at the border gave rise to a film style—the chronicle of punctilious realism and strict observance to the sequence of events—that would become characteristic of the period and that, for de los Reyes, represents Mexico's genuine and most important contribution to world cinema.[36] The relationship between the public "and the topics addressed by the films was harmonious. The cameramen filmed the activities and lives of everyday people, and these same people went to the movies to see themselves or to admire their favorite political leaders."[37] We recognize in this style of filmmaking a forerunner of extension. However, the filmmakers' coverage of the country was still firmly aligned with the activities of state functionaries. The organicism eulogized by de los Reyes was severely called into question by the revolution, when values and expectations became less and less a shared certainty. So when in 1922 the Alva brothers return to Morelia to document the celebration of 112 years of Mexican independence, the difference from the 1908 footage is striking. The capital of Michoacán proved to be one of the most defiant cities for the revolutionaries, with its *gente decente* putting up a stern fight to preserve a slowly changing status quo. As in 1908 the center of the image is occupied by the parade. The parade itself is civil in nature, and the camera remains glued to the recognizable faces of the *gente decente*. But the number of people dressing in traditional peasant clothing multiplies at the borders of the image. At the film's beginning there are some feeble attempts to keep them out of sight, but the new social reality is impossible to hide. Popular bodies, represented as an unorganized mass rather than the disciplined apparatus of the civil parade, slowly occupy the entire screen and, in the end, look with confidence into the lenses.

Footage taken from the informative newsreels done in the style of the Alva brothers was used to produce the first visual historical narratives of the revolution. One of the most ambitious projects was Salvador Toscano's *Historia completa de la Revolución mexicana* (1927), a three-hour documentary covering the years from 1910 to 1915.[38] Toscano's film submitted the spontaneity of the newsreel to cuts, montages, and chronological rearrangements that displayed the new maturity of the medium. As in the case of photography, the authorship of this footage was seldom respected or recognized. The overall coherency of the film, however, attests to the visual sedimentation of the informative style underlined by de los Reyes. That this documentary genre encompassed the first Mexican productions to be the objects of individual showings—that is, unaccompanied by European or American short productions or feature films— indicates the importance that the political mapping of contemporary events acquired in Mexico in the first years of revolutionary agitation. Movies like *Viaje del señor Madero a los estados del sur* by the

Alva brothers (1912) were small blockbusters, in part because they gave Mexico City audiences the opportunity to see the feared Zapatistas interacting with the president. For de los Reyes, the appeal and success of the Mexican organic documentary retarded the emergence of narrative film. However if this was true on the side of production, it was far from true on the side of consumption. While Mexican film production centered above all on the model of the newsreel, Mexicans were avid consumers of European films. Spain and the United States were the points of origin for the vast majority of movies exhibited in Mexico City in the 1920s, but residents of the city also had the chance to attend premieres of German expressionist films, the new wave of Soviet films, and even Danish experimental film productions.

When by the end of the second decade of the twentieth century narrative films finally became established, they showed remarkable debts to theatrical forms. *Tepeyac* (1917) opens with the actors saluting the public as if they were performing a theatrical piece. The reported popularity of Salvador Toscano's *Don Juan Tenorio* (1898) rested in part on the popularity of the play itself. Sometimes the interaction with theater lent itself to playful and imaginative productions. In *Un espectador impertinente* (1932), Arcady Boytler and Raphael Sevilla make fun of the confusion between theater and film through an ingenious movie-performance that only survives on paper. An actor (Boytler himself) hidden in the audience starts harassing an actress on the screen who reacts indignantly to the spectator's comments. (Boytler, a Russian, was very likely aware of the avant-garde film *Factory of the Eccentric Actor*—produced by Sergei Yutkevich, Grigori Kozintsev, and Leonid Trauberg in the 1920s—which presented a similar structure.) Eventually the unruly spectator is escorted out of the theater only to reappear inside the film, where he eventually begins a romance with the same actress that he had previously been nagging. Released in 1932, when Mexican film began its independent industrial life, *Un espectador impertinente* is an oblique reminder of the weaving of reality and fiction that had presided over the launching of the arts of mechanical reproduction and that tempted film narrative from its very beginning. The film was even premonitory of the way in which dramatic cinema would end up engulfing and annulling the strong realistic vocation that many assumed to be the logical destiny of cinema in Mexico.

The advent of sound and the consequent creation of linguistic barriers for film distribution contributed to the establishment of industrial cinema in Mexico. The bulk of my analysis concerns the five years that elapsed between Sergei Eisenstein's arrival in Mexico in December 1930 and the premiere of *Allá en el Rancho Grande* in 1936. In these five years we find the famous revolutionary film trilogy of Fernando de Fuentes, Arcady Boytler's *La mujer del puerto* (1933), and the exceptional visual experiment undertaken by

Fred Zinnemann and Emilio Gómez Muriel (with the impeccable cinematography of Paul Strand) in *Redes* (1936). This period also saw productions that are now lost, such as the by all accounts dazzling visual experiment of Juan Bustillo Oro's *Dos monjes* (1934) and some shorter films by avant-garde filmmaker and photographer Antonio Amero.[39]

Five Years

The arrival of Eisenstein in Mexico almost coincided with the arrival of sound in cinema. The "talkies" revolutionized film production and represented unique challenges for the dominant American industry, especially in terms of its foreign markets. Conversely, the arrival of sound reactivated some Arielista motifs that were deeply ingrained in Mexican society. With the arrival of sound, newspapers like *El Universal* proposed a massive boycott of American productions.[40] Linguistic sensibility rather than illiteracy—which made subtitles unviable—was one of the most formidable obstacles that sound synchronization posed to Hollywood dominance of the Latin American market. Hollywood attempted to address this problem by producing Hispanic versions of its films with casts of Hispanic actors. The confusion of different styles and varieties of Spanish, along with different schools of dramatic interpretation, turned the attempt into a near disaster. In addition, crews of mostly unknown Hispanic actors doubling the big Hollywood hits subtracted Hollywood's fundamental commercial weapon: the star system. The temporary crisis in the hegemony of U.S. cinema over Latin American audiences opened a window through which national cinemas started to develop.

Mexico, like most Latin American countries with a sizable local market, was not necessarily at a disadvantage in terms of technical equipment. Film was a booming business, not a state secret, and companies promoting different technologies like the synchronization of image and sound were eager to sell their products to entrepreneurs of relative financial stability. In addition the 1910s and '20s had been years of great geographical mobility. Literally dozens of Latin American technicians, directors, and actors were trained in both Hollywood and Europe. Unlike other Latin American film industries, the Mexican film industry's development was not directly dependent on state funding for its productions. President Calles, whose social views were often based on the emulation of American entrepreneurism, conceived of film as essentially a private enterprise. Of course, Mexicans did not expect to beat Hollywood at its own game. The essential ingredient for the development of Mexican cinema was the search for a film language that was simultaneously Mexican and international. As with so many other icons of Mexican authenticity, a good deal of that language is rooted—via Eisenstein—in the ideas and projects of the cosmopolitan, plastic avant-garde of the 1920s.

Although Eisenstein's *¡Que viva México!* (filmed between 1930 and 1931) would not be released until 1978, some of its images were available through American movies that had cannibalized parts of the original footage. These sparse images are often credited with creating a visual language that Mexican film would exploit in its years of consolidation, especially in the productions of Emilio "el Indio" Fernández.[41] Gabriel Figueroa, who was responsible for the cinematography of Fernández's movies, was quite taken by the visual iconography made available by Eisenstein in *¡Qué viva México!* This iconography would include compositional elements such as the low-angle cameras that allowed generous views of Mexico's dramatic, clouded skies (a repeated subject in Weston's reflections of his photographic activity in Mexico), the identification of natural elements such as the maguey as iconic of the Mexican landscape, and a dramatic and expressionist style of acting that relied heavily on the presence of indigenous and nonprofessional actors.[42] As we know from Eisenstein himself, none of these motifs were invented by the Russian director. Instead, they were the result of his interactions with artists like Rivera, Orozco, Atl, Montenegro, and Best Maugard. This set of influences was facilitated when Eisenstein arrived in Mexico and state representatives did not know what to do with him. In the space of only three days, he was accused of being a communist spy, incarcerated, and then liberated and declared a guest of honor of the Mexican nation. As a compromise the Mexican state resorted, as usual, to one of "its" intellectuals. Adolfo Best Maugard was appointed as a guide and guard to the Russian filmmaker. It was through Best Maugard (who was hardly a political commissar) that Eisenstein came into contact with the modernizing avant-garde of the 1920s. The multifaceted Best Maugard would eventually direct his own dazzling and polemical film.[43]

But Eisenstein's *¡Que viva México!* did more than provide a visual vocabulary to illuminate Mexico at a time when Hollywood's xenophobic exoticism was one of the few languages articulating a cinematic discourse on the country. The film is unique even within Eisenstein's canon. He conceived of the movie as a vast tapestry: he referred to it as a serape. The main idea was that Mexico was a wild superimposition of temporalities and cultural modalities that could not possibly be articulated into an integrated cinematic view. This heterogeneity of subject matter led Eisenstein to a heterogeneous formal construction of the (planned) narrative. Each chapter of the movie was to be dedicated to a Mexican painter, and the visual style was to be evocative of Eisenstein's interpretation of the arts of the Mexican masters.[44] Gregory Alexandrov, who put the film together in 1978, attempted to remain loyal to the symphonic effect that Eisenstein intended. In the end, what is striking about the movie is the superimposition of different narrative modalities that may justify seeing in it one of the most accomplished examples of extension as a trope of revolutionary self-understanding. Equally significant is Eisenstein's use of revolutionary nationalism to construct a thoroughly politicized view of the historical process. While most Mexican cinematic productions approached the revolution as a finished affair upon which it was now time to pass judgment, the Russian crew and its local advisors painted a dynamic portrait that aspired to make the people themselves—in all their indeterminacy—the subject of the historical narrative.[45] As a result the properly political moment in the movie—the moment in which *¡Que viva México!* conjures up a people by addressing them—could easily speak to contemporary audiences with the same force that it might have voiced (if its destiny had been other) to its intended audiences of the 1930s. Simultaneously a fantasy of politics and a politics of fantasy, the movie explicitly underlines the struggle for the meaning of the present as the proper inheritance of the revolutionary model. This lesson is beautifully incarnated in the closing scene of the film, with its play of masques and faces.

Unlike Eisenstein's production, Mexican film would be plagued by the inability to present a portrait of the country in which aesthetic representation could fuse harmoniously with interrogations of its political present and future. Instead, we find a sort of aesthetic double consciousness in which a disavowed lack of unity is reinscribed into a totalizing (national) discourse. That trend, we are told, began with the somewhat truncated aesthetic critical project of Fernando de Fuentes.

Fernando de Fuentes's Revolutionary Trilogy

Considered the most significant Mexican director of the early sound period, Fernando de Fuentes composed his trilogy in the brief span of three years: *El prisionero 13* was released in 1933; *El compadre Mendoza* in 1934; and *¡Vámonos con Pancho Villa!* in 1936. All films of great technical and visual maturity, the trilogy seemed to indicate a realist and critical direction for Mexican film. Such a destiny would not come to fruition, however, in part because in 1936 de Fuentes himself would put Mexican cinema onto a different path with the release of *Allá en el Rancho Grande*.

Despite their enormous importance in the history of Mexican film and their extraordinary cinematographic quality, the revolutionary trilogy was a commercial failure.[46] Not many people saw those films and even fewer people discussed them. In fact, we owe the recovery and revaluation of de Fuentes's original trilogy, and especially of *El compadre Mendoza*, to the work of

French critic Georges Sadoul. Recent studies of the trilogy have interpreted the movies as sustained criticisms of the postrevolutionary period. For Carl Mora, a film like *El compadre Mendoza* expresses a feeling of disillusionment at the corrupted ideals of the revolution.[47] John Mraz notes that the film "exudes disenchantment with the revolution's shortcomings instead of celebrating its achievements."[48] Andrea Noble writes that the three films represent

> recent conflict in a specific idiom. Each focuses on some form of human relationship that culminates in betrayal. The human relationships dramatized in each movie clearly function as metaphors for the revolution at large and all can be read as denouncing the ultimate betrayal of its more radical, utopian ideals.[49]

At least two of these films suffered some form of censorship, which reinforces the interpretation of de Fuentes's productions as critical of the revolutionary status quo. Verifiable as de Fuentes's critical attitude is, most judgments of his work fail to acknowledge the constant endorsement of nationalist values—and even of the postrevolutionary order—that is also a prominent feature of his productions. As a matter of fact, de Fuentes received important logistical and financial contributions from a state that does not seem to have cared too much about the critical edge of these movies. A more balanced look at de Fuentes's productions will easily disclose a marked ambivalence in each film. These films are not just critical of a social configuration that we can sum up under the expression "postrevolutionary state," an option that would too easily alleviate the problem of intellectual or even popular responsibility for the fall of revolutionary ideals. The emphasis on de Fuentes's "critical attitude" towards the revolution has flattened the enormous complexity of each film. Responsibility is too easily adjudicated at the level of the individual. In chapter 4, "Life," I criticized the use of an ethics of individuality that clouds our understanding and valorization of individual decisions. A similar argument can be mounted in the case of de Fuentes. I would contend that the whole trilogy could fit squarely under the rubric *life*, since what is at stake in all the movies is the individual failure to unify what was indeed a vastly disaggregated subjective experience.[50]

De Fuentes worked on the three movies almost simultaneously, and the movies themselves can be seen as a vast tapestry of revolutionary Mexico. The films distribute their focus among the three main fronts that characterized the most violent years of the revolutionary struggle: *El compadre Mendoza* deals with the Zapatista front in the south of Mexico; *Vámonos* with the Villista north; and *El prisionero 13* with the tribulations of the Mexican middle class at the time of Huertismo. The three movies are set in the years 1913-

1914. Tellingly, Obregonism (or Sonorism)—the faction in power at the moment of production—is mostly absent from representation. *Allá en el Rancho Grande,* on the other hand, takes place entirely in the time frame of Sonorism.

Each movie in the trilogy presents the familiar revolutionary treatment of life as fate, as a symbolic maze where intentions are no match for the overwhelming forces of historical necessity. The forces faced by the characters are not just too large to be confronted, they defy understanding. De Fuentes's treatment of this problem is not epic but personal and almost existential. As a result, what is actually staged once and again in the trilogy is the crisis of subjective autonomy and its impossible rearticulation within the larger sphere of social or historical meaning. Of course, de Fuentes does not take this crisis to its final consequences as Tomás Gutiérrez Alea will do in *Memorias del subdesarrollo,* for instance. In each movie there is a moral element that rescues the narrative from a fall into the existential absurdity to which it seems condemned: the mute as the voice of consciousness in *El compadre;* alcoholism in *El prisionero;* and *machista* atavism in *Vámonos.*

The first movie in the series, *El prisionero 13,* stars Alfredo del Diestro as Carrasco, a colonel in the federal army, whose drunkenness is no longer tolerated by his wife, Marta (Adela Sequeyro). After Carrasco makes an attempt on her life, Marta flees the house along with her infant son, Juan. Almost twenty years go by in which Colonel Carrasco never gives up on the possibility of finding his son. When Carrasco arrests some revolutionaries and is ordered to shoot them, his friend Zertuche (Luis Barreiro) introduces the colonel to the relatives of one of the prisoners, who offer thirteen thousand pesos for his release. Since Carrasco captured thirteen prisoners and needs to shoot thirteen, he sends out soldiers to arbitrarily pick up any young man to be killed instead of the released prisoner. Unknowingly, they pick up his own son, Juan, who is shot to Carrasco's utter despair shortly after he realizes the truth of the situation. Filmed in a visually stunning expressionist style, the shooting of the prisoners is an extraordinary indictment of the absurd essence of militarism. According to some authors the army objected to the plot, so de Fuentes had to frame the whole sequence with two scenes that indicated that the whole affair was the product of a dream.[51]

With *El compadre Mendoza,* the most celebrated film of the trilogy, de Fuentes goes deeper into the exploration of the tensions between individual designs and the historical forces shaping Mexico at the time. The movie also stars Alfredo del Diestro, this time as the rich landowner Rosalío Mendoza, who ambivalently supports both Huerta and the Zapatistas and arranges for special welcomes each time any of the two groups visits his hacienda. Mendoza's demeanor is one of mastery over the situation, a mastery Mendoza is fond of punctuating with the repetition of the same adage: "I am an enemy of romanticism and sighs. What is to be done has to be done well and quickly." On the night of his marriage to Dolores (Carmen Guerrero) the hacienda is attacked by the troops of Eufemio Zapata, who orders the execution of Mendoza when he finds a Huertista general among the guests. The timely arrival of Zapatista general Felipe Nieto (Antonio Frausto) avoids Mendoza's death. That night, Nieto is introduced to Dolores, the bride, with whom he falls in love. Eventually Nieto becomes the godfather of Mendoza's child, named Felipe after the general.

Time passes, and now the enemy of the Zapatistas is the Carrancistas, in particular the implacable General Bernáldez (Joaquín Busquets). As political turmoil increases, Mendoza's position becomes less stable. His befriending of the Zapatistas poses a contradiction to his class status, something he becomes painfully aware of when the Zapatistas blow up a train containing all the year's crops, leaving Mendoza bankrupt. Bernáldez comes to his aid, offering Mendoza good payment in exchange for facilitating an ambush of his *compadre* Felipe Nieto. Troubled and uncomfortable with the proposal, Mendoza accepts it nonetheless and betrays Nieto, whose cadaver is hung from the arcade of the hacienda while a horrible storm rages over the ranch.

More than any of de Fuentes's other movies, *El compadre Mendoza* relies on the dramatic interpretation of its actors. Each character represents a different worldview, which collide at Mendoza's ranch, a space that figures a point of material sustainability in a crumbling world.[52] In this world the decisions made by all characters are constantly twisted and thwarted to the point of impotence and despair. This is especially true of Mendoza, whose delusion that he could ride the revolutionary wave in a state of personal command comes to ruin in the automatic, drunklike, and faltering voice with which he intonates his favorite lines after betraying his friend to a death sentence: "I am an enemy of romanticism and sighs. Things have to be done correctly and quickly." Yet it is clear that even if the thing "has to be done," Mendoza cannot find his action "correct." This split between what has to be done and what is correct represents the moral dilemma at the end of the movie. Mendoza may be paying for his miscalculation. He misrecognizes Felipe Nieto as a possible friend when he was his objective enemy. But Nieto himself is also guilty of this misrecognition since, smitten with Dolores, he does not look or act like a Zapatista at all. Mendoza, I argue, cuts a more tragic figure than the postrevisionist criticism on the movie has so far proposed. (Tellingly, the *New York Times* review of the premiere of *El compadre* in 1936 was titled "A Mexican Tragedy.")

¡Vámonos con Pancho Villa!, the most ambitious title of the series, is based on the homonymous novel by Rafael Muñoz, who stars in the film as one of the Lions of San Pablo. Led by Tiburcio Maya, six friends join the Vi-

llista army, where they will die one by one. At the end only Tiburcio and the youngest, Becerrillo, are left. Their prowess in battle wins the Lions a place among Villa's *dorados*. However, on the eve of a battle an outbreak of smallpox claims Becerrillo as one of its victims. Villa orders Tiburcio to sacrifice Becerrillo and cremate the body. Tiburcio is shocked by the order and asks if this is how a revolutionary army repays the valor of its men. In the end, he follows the order and then reports to Villa, who, afraid of a possible contagion, dismisses him from his army. A disillusioned Tiburcio walks away while in the background a sentinel plays a martial tune. The film's depiction of Villa's act of cowardice concerning Becerrillo and the presumed censorship the movie endured (the film had two alternate endings, the shocking one only released on television in the 1980s) are central to the consideration of this movie as critical of the postrevolutionary regime.

Much has been made of *Vámonos*'s two endings and of the possible intervention of Cárdenas himself as censor. If one takes into consideration that de Fuentes was already working on an enormously conformist movie such as *Allá en el Rancho Grande,* it is possible to think that the alternate ending of *Vámonos,* in which Villa kills Tiburcio's wife and daughter as a means of relieving Tiburcio from his responsibilities, was already gruesome by the middle-class standards that de Fuentes was eager to accommodate.[53] Although the alternate ending would have cast Villa in a very negative light, it is not altogether clear that such a portrayal would have disgusted the postrevolutionary establishment of 1934.

To complicate things further, by the time of the movie's production Villa was far from being a one-dimensional figure, especially when it came to cinema.[54] Whatever light de Fuentes could cast upon Villa's figure, he could not ignore the dense web of references and allusions that had already been woven around the revolutionary from Chihuahua. Villa had elicited tremendous media attention since the time of his contract with the Mutual Film Corporation. Several Mexican and American cameramen followed his army and documented his movements. The U.S. press published dozens of articles on him on a weekly basis. Villa's often brilliant military campaigns were sometimes difficult to accommodate into the narrative of him as a road bandit turned revolutionary. At least one American journalist found the solution to the enigma by postulating that Villa was, in fact, an American who participated in the Spanish-American War as part of the Rough Riders before going to the Philippines and San Francisco as a member of the American army.[55]

After the attack on Columbus, New Mexico, in 1916, American perception of Villa changed dramatically. He was vilified in a series of cheap productions that did not care much about differentiating the murderous Villa from Mexicans in general. As de Fuentes did not ignore, portraying Villa as an unreliable and bloodthirsty criminal turned revolutionary was the easiest way for some American interests to assert the impossibility that the mobilized poor of Mexico could play a leading role in the revolution once the guns were laid down. De Fuentes, who was for all practical purposes a cultural nationalist and a genuine product of the revolution he criticized, displaced or split the question of Villismo. Such a split is revealed in the opening scene of the movie, in which a sign written in tortuous Spanish announces a no less tortuous message: "This film is a homage to the loyalty and bravery that Francisco Villa—the disconcerting Mexican rebel—was able to infuse in all the men (*guerrilleros*) who followed him." Calling the film a homage reveals the high political stakes of the production.

Of Villa himself we are told three things: he is disconcerting (something the movie surely emphasizes); he is a Mexican (a point that was less obvious then than now); and he lies at the origin of an enigmatic power that endows his followers with loyalty and bravery. The film itself is not a homage to Villa or to his followers but to these abstract qualities. Indeed, *Vámonos* is an attempt to wrestle these qualities from Villa in order to transfer them to the sphere of state representation. Loyalty and bravery—the bravery that Villa lacks because he is too human to live up to the exorbitant demands of nationalism—are the final subjects of *Vámonos*. This means, among other things, that—in contraposition to *El compadre Mendoza*—personal profiles will have to be sacrificed in favor of ideals. While *El compadre* is the story of a personal dissolution, *Vámonos* is the story of the increasingly relentless construction of a firm nationalist identity.

The model for this individual consolidation is obviously Tiburcio Maya, who, through his identification with the military apparatus, is able to transfer his allegiance from Villa to the nation. This capture of Tiburcio in the net of state representation is already announced by the—initially incipient and then manifest—costuming of his figure along the lines of a traditional *charro*.[56] The apparatus of capture is the army, a renegade army that Tiburcio fantasizes as a national one. It is in Tiburcio rather than in Villa that the superegoistic nature of the institution is fully endorsed. When Tiburcio and the Lions first encounter Villa, they hold their hats in their hands as a sign of respect for the general. But Villa exhorts them to avoid such displays of respect: "*Muchachos*, put your hats on; what did you buy them for?" In contraposition to this informal style of command, and as the movie progresses, Tiburcio's behavior becomes almost totally determined by the rules of the military structure. He salutes in martial fashion every superior he finds in his way, although he is not met with corresponding gestures. Even the fierce and ill-famed Rodolfo Fierro (the press had cast a large shadow over this figure, and Martín Luis Guzmán demolished him in *The Eagle and the Serpent*) elicits nothing but the utmost martial respect from Tiburcio.

In the end, Tiburcio is ready to sacrifice everything for army and nation, asking nothing in return. Even his emotional reaction to the death of Becerrillo is mediated and subsumed by the disciplinary effects of a nationalist discourse upon the revolutionary body. After shooting Becerrillo and setting his corpse on fire, he salutes the youngster by standing at attention. Shortly afterwards the first notes of a martial tune halt him in his tracks and elicit another salute that the camera emphasizes by taking his figure from a low angle: What is Tiburcio saluting if not the ideal subsumption of revolutionary force into a nationalist discipline that Villa fails to incarnate? At the end, Tiburcio walks away, alone, leaving the Villista camp behind. However, even if Pancho Villa loses a fighter, the nation has gained a soldier. The closing scene makes good the desideratum of the opening disclaimer.

The Question of Women

In the three de Fuentes films discussed above, the element of division—narrative or technical—that I argue is characteristic of all postrevolutionary cinema is brought about by women. The function of the female figure as the point of fracture of a would-be social imaginary is a tremendously overdetermined question in the film and culture of the postrevolutionary period. In other words, it is a question that does not appear under the same guise or is not formulated in the same terms in different cultural productions. It seems to me that de Fuentes is less concerned with the emerging question of women (or with women as the cipher of the code of the emergent) than he is with the steady decline of the patriarchal paradigm. Because the historical father (none other than Porfirio Díaz himself) has failed or died, the whole weight of the symbolic is shifted towards other more abstract and reliable figures like the state or like a national army, as in *Vámonos*.

The revolution was unable to conjure a paternal figure able to suture the enormous rift in reality caused by the revolution. Clearly de Fuentes could not accept that a character like Villa was "the man," as the revolutionary from Chihuahua was sometimes referred to. Villa epitomized the crisis of the paternal figure insofar as it was tied to an atavism of sacrifice. In this sense, the recurring anomie that traverses the three movies is closely related to the futility of any sacrifice, insofar as all sacrifices are offerings to false idols from whom no actual redemption can be expected. Felipe Nieto, in *El compadre Mendoza*, is sacrificed to the anachronism of a social relationship; Becerrillo, in *Vámonos*, to a loyalty to which the figure of Villa is unable to correspond;

and Juan, in *El prisionero 13*, to the ambitions of a father who seeks in money the symbolic equivalent of a lost paternal law. (This absent paternal law is obliquely evoked by the ever-present portrait of Huerta hanging in Colonel Carrasco's office.) But Huerta, as we know, was already a deficient simulacrum of Díaz as father of Mexico. What menaces the fathers is not just their inability to contain social dynamics—if that were the case, the criticism of paternalism would be one with the criticism of political *caudillismo*—but also the existence of a new set of social relationships that, although largely associated with modernity, finds in women its index of presentation.

Two uncontestable threads of impending modernity, women and money, form a persistent knot in the trilogy. Episodes of subtle or open economic extortion are depicted in *El prisionero 13*. Margarita Ramos and Adela, mother and sister of the imprisoned Fernando, are twice financially abused: first by Colonel Carrasco when he asks them for thirteen thousand pesos to liberate Fernando, and later by an accountant named Ordóñez when they need to sell their ranch. Economic extortion often appears alongside erotic interests. In *El prisionero 13*, Adela shows her knees to a lawyer to encourage him to mediate with Colonel Carrasco on behalf of her brother. When the mother reprimands her by pulling her skirt down, she raises the skirt again in a complex visual commentary of the film's hesitation between championing the narrow morality of its middle-class public and promoting a visual liberalization of the erotic realm that was long overdue.[57] In *El compadre Mendoza*, Don Rosalío first meets Dolores when she is with her father at an office paying a loan, suggesting that Dolores is forced to marry Rosalío Mendoza because of her family's financial weakness.[58]

In *¡Vámonos con Pancho Villa!*, in which the plot of the movie is partially foreign to the middle-class ethics that prevail in the other two, a certain alignment of the movie with the plights of women takes place in its brief but significant depiction of *soldaderas*. The whole episode in which the Lions of San Pablo join Villa's army is framed by a spectacular cinematographic rendering of the Villista camp. As the Lions approach the camp a group of soldiers play "La Adelita," the classic *corrido* eulogizing an unknown *soldadera*. However, the camera panning the camp reveals a reality at odds with the lyrics of the *corrido*. One *soldadera* barters with soldiers with a dog by her side. A series of cuts, especially one in which the dog looks up at the *soldadera* with sheepish eyes, suggests that she is to the soldiers as the dog is to her. This idea is reinforced in the next shot, where the position of the dog by her side makes it clear that the previous face-to-face interaction between dog and woman is impossible. Formally these critical traits will also appear in *Allá en el Rancho Grande*, but its treatment of sexual difference and oppression is completely dissimilar.

In contrast to the politically edgy and cinematographically venturesome traits of the trilogy, the inaugural *comedia ranchera* promoted the eulogy for patriarchal prerevolutionary society in conventional film language at the very moment that revolutionary radicalism was finding its way to power through the presidency of Lázaro Cárdenas. The movie's relentless promotion of hierarchical values, Carl Mora writes, "Struck a responsive chord in the Mexican middle class, which was fearful of the spread of communism under the leftist Cárdenas."[59] As in the trilogy, Fernando de Fuentes is careful to frame the action of the movie within strict temporal limits. These correspond to the period of governments from Sonora, with the first scene taking place in 1922, on the first anniversary of Obregón's government, and the last one in 1935, the last year of Calles's direct influence over the Mexican executive office. Although the movie has been described as a nostalgic display of Porfirista values, the postrevolutionary setting also speaks of a rewriting of Mexican history in which the violent class struggle that characterized the immediate past is rendered ethically unviable by the enlightenment of the new managerial class. The antirealist features of the movie are striking: no mention is made of politics, modernization, or media. The time of the action and the time of representation simply do not coincide. This is even more pronounced in terms of social relationships. The tensions and abuses depicted by Eisenstein in *¡Que viva México!* are replaced by the patronizing attitude of the owner of the great ranch.

In the opening scene, Don Rosendo (Manuel Noriega) admonishes his young son that they owe everything to these "honest people, who work so hard for us and whom we should swear to protect." Given that social tensions are banned from the movie, and desire, if not banned, is at least frowned upon, the only thing left is amorous misunderstandings. By 1935 Don Rosendo has died, and his son Felipe (René Cardona) hires José Francisco (Tito Guízar) as his foreman. José and Felipe have been friends since childhood, when Don Rosendo rescued the orphan Felipe and raised him. However, class distinctions are still strictly observed since this world is thoroughly hierarchical. When Felipe insists that José should not address him as *patrón* (boss), José replies by addressing his lifelong friend as *don* instead. The displacement is revelatory, since *patrón* is a social relationship but *don* is the naturalization of the same social relationship.

The most famous scene of *Allá en el Rancho Grande,* the one in which Tito Guízar sings in the local cantina, is an exact visual rendering of the ideology that sustains the movie. In compositional terms, the figure that dominates is the circle: the circle of faces and bodies around Guízar. The circle itself is strengthened by the acting of those who surround the singer. De Fuentes seems to have exerted absolute control over every actor in this scene: not one deviates his or her devoted gaze from Guízar as he performs his song. The lighting responds to the need to underline every feature in the faces of the actors. Nobody casts a shadow. The rampant expressionism of the Mexican films of this period (for example, the subtle and contrasting illumination of Boytler's *La mujer del puerto*) is replaced here by the type of unanimity that only a full exposure of life to light can bring with it. The circle contains itself and detaches the space of the cantina from everything that surrounds it. No alien presence comes forward to trash the party as Eufemio did with Don Rosalío Mendoza's wedding. No ghost of an alternate world looms behind this scene like the one conjured by the ill-fated decisions of Colonel Carrasco in *El prisionero 13*. No atavistic attachment to death comes to rupture the circle from the inside as happens in *Vámonos* with its memorable scene of soldiers playing Russian roulette. Synchronicity does not seem to play any important role in *Allá en el Rancho Grande*, because the untimely itself has been removed from the frame.

Except, of course, for the figure of a woman. When Guízar finishes his song, he is confronted by the news that his sweetheart had spent the previous night at Rancho Grande with Felipe. Although the accusation is ultimately false—as Felipe manages to convince everybody when confronted by José—what emerges here is a strange recurrence of women to signal historically outdated and morally questionable patriarchal practices. In the end erotic tensions are resolved as practical misunderstandings. In the world of the film each person desires exactly what he or she should aspire to, while a gracious providence is happy to bestow on them their well-measured wishes. The movie ends with three simultaneous weddings—those of José, Felipe, and Florentino—in an open contrast to the anxiety-riddled endings of the trilogy and in light of which the following declaration of de Fuentes, uttered a mere year before the release of his blockbuster, is even more ironic: "We believe that our public is sufficiently cultured to stand reality's bitter cruelty. It would have been easy to make the story with a happy ending, as we are accustomed to see in American films; but we think that Mexican cinema should be a faithful reflection of our severe way of being . . . , not a poor imitation of Hollywood."[60]

Outside the Mainstream: Redes

In its struggle to create a stage upon which meaningful historical actions can take place, the almost mythical *Redes* (1936) stands as an apt representative of the question of fantasy in film. No commercial copy of the film was available until 2010.[61] The movie was commissioned by the SEP under the leadership of Narciso Bassols (its most radical period), and it brought together a group of Mexican and American artists who coexisted uneasily during and after the film's production. Ironically, a movie that was designed to foster unity among working people in the face of mounting antirevolutionary reaction was marked at the production level by endless quarrels and disagreements among those responsible for it.[62] Despite the fact that state economic support for *Redes* was less than modest, the movie attracted an astounding array of talents for its production. Ned Scott, in charge of documenting the making of the film, produced what many believe to be one of the best still photographs in the history of filmmaking. Paul Strand was an enormously prestigious photographer when he agreed to collaborate with the SEP on the project. Fred Zinnemann, who was hired to lend some cinematographic movement to the overly static composition favored by Strand, was Austrian-born but had trained in Hollywood, where he would later carry out an illustrious career. The musical score was entrusted to Silvestre Revueltas, who produced a breathtaking mixture of popular motifs and classical music. John Dos Passos prepared the subtitles for the American premiere with zeal and a good dose of creativity.

Although *Redes* stands practically alone in terms of a movie production sponsored, supervised, and financed by the state, there had been some attempts to use film as a means of state propaganda in the years immediately following the end of the armed struggle. In 1922 Manuel Gamio supervised the production of *La población del valle de Teotihuacán* with the assistance of the versatile Antonio Noriega Hope. This type of ethnographical film—others were produced although all of them are lost—enjoyed a certain popularity, especially since state sponsorship could guarantee production in a time of extreme economic uncertainty.[63] In the 1930s the extreme popularity of film tempted the SEP once again. Although it proved to be the only film of its type completed in this period, *Redes* itself was supposed to be part of a larger experiment to favor the political education of the popular classes. In the end, budgetary problems and the realization that the increasingly conformist ideology of the Mexican state was well served by independent industrial productions made these attempts at state-sponsored film rare.[64]

Much of the beauty of the individual scenes in *Redes* comes from Strand's careful framing. But the photographic quality of the film sometimes risks freezing the cinematographic dynamic and putting its propagandistic aims in jeopardy.[65] Still, the acting was slow and deliberate. Most of *Redes*'s actors were amateurs recruited in Alvarado, the fishing village where the movie was shot on the coast of Veracruz. The plot of the film was zealously guarded during the shooting. Even the actors were not informed of the words that comprised the incendiary speech with which Miro invites the fishermen to unite and go on a strike. These were some of the costs associated with producing a radical film in what was a largely conservative social milieu. But they were not only the ones.

At least three emphases vie for the control of the movie: an aesthetic impulse ciphered in its careful photography; a political content that is supposed to fold easily into its aesthetic counterpart; and finally a pedagogical discourse whose clumsiness comes from the ineluctable distance that separates the message from the public imagined by the movie. The avowed goal of the film was to promote social and class consciousness among rural populations. The original documents drafted to justify the production called for the use of new technologies as a way to show "in an objective way the production of wealth within the current social regime."[66] Paul Strand, who authored the script, was completely in sync with the SEP on this ideological aspect and even pushed to give more room to classist statements.

Redes did not enjoy popular success, although it was well received in intellectual and artistic circles in Mexico, the United States, and France. American reviews of the movie heralded Strand and Zinnemann (the actual titles credit Emilio Gómez Muriel as director, but his influence on the film was minimal) as creators of a new visual language and singled out the movie as the first truly Mexican cinematographic expression.

Watching *Redes* today is a remarkable aesthetic experience. The plot, however, and the many torsions needed to make it believable are too simplistic to the contemporary eye trained in decades of film consumption. The fact that a movie destined for rural or even indigenous people was produced following an avant-garde aesthetic seems not to have troubled the producers. Nor, does it seem, did anyone raise the question of how rural and indigenous folk were supposed to decode a message that was often dexterously encrypted—as in the few, poignant uses of Eisenstenian montage, the use of the background as a cue to the nature of some characters, the allegorical visual equivalence between fishermen and fish, or the complex association and dissociation of sound and image at some of the most didactic points in the film.

In opposition to these formal features, the plot of *Redes* is straightforward. In a small village, local fishermen are completely at the mercy of a local industrial boss (an *acaparador* in the language of the movie), who commercializes the market for the fish and makes a fortune through his exploitative relationship with the fishermen. In one of the opening scenes of the movie, Miro (Silvio Hernández) asks the *acaparador* for a small loan to take his ill son to a hospital in a nearby city. The rich man of the town excuses himself by saying that there are no fish and he has no money at this point. Miro's child dies and a beautifully filmed funeral procession ensues. Before the tomb of his recently deceased son, Miro produces his first speech to the camera. The narrative frame is that of melodrama, but a melodrama traversed by at least two discordant discourses. The camera portrays the whole burial in terms of social relationships rather than in terms of Miro's pain. That is, we stand opposite de Fuentes's revolutionary trilogy, in which social conflicts are depicted as individual dramas. Miro's only concession to his fatherly grief comes when he asks for a spade and begins to throw dirt onto the open grave. Immediately, Miro's speech follows. So far Miro has been a person absorbed in the immediacy of his needs. But now he speaks in the universalizing language of the political. As he speaks he looks beyond the camera, a look that in a melodramatic framing would suggest a connection with the spiritual and ultimately with God. But Miro's beyond is unmistakably a figure of this world. Such is the first attempt at a reversal. It is the first antitheological gesture in a movie full of antitheological gestures, a movie that frames *tradition* (of which religion is just one form) as its main dialectical enemy.

Let us take a closer look at his speech, a speech that was not uttered at the moment of filming because of fear of the reaction of local authorities and was then added in secrecy during postproduction. Miro says: *Where is justice when a child dies because a father did not have money to cure him*? Political universalization always comes at the cost of some abstraction: not *my* child but *a* child, not *I* but *a father*, any father. The political itself receives a new and ancient name, encrypted in just one word: justice. From this point on, the whole movie will track between two modalities: what is known, customary, and to some extent fatal; and reinscription into another discourse that names these traditional grievances—calling them injustices—and that invites spiritual and political insubordination in its place. Once Miro utters the word *justice*, the movie opens itself to a dialectic that confronts a world that is known to everybody and that can be registered and shown—that is, moreover, beautifully registered and shown—with another world that only Miro seems to have glimpsed: the promised land of equality. This dialectic between seen and unseen marks the development of *Redes* and enters into a significant tension with the aesthetic wager that so deeply marks the film. When a few days after the funeral Miro goes along with the rest of the fishermen to deliver the product of their labor to the *acaparador*, the local politician, who will eventually kill Miro in an ambush, states that the fishermen look happy.

> "Happy?" Miro replies. "Have you ever lost a son because you did not have money to cure him?"
>
> "No comrade," the politician replies. "Such a disgrace has not visited me."
>
> "You call it disgrace. I call it injustice."

The melodramatic scene of the funeral is reinscribed here in the realm of social exchanges, revealing a push for an increasing politicization of everyday experience. One of the reasons why *Redes* is so slow in cinematographic terms may have to do not so much with Strand's attachment to still photography as with the fact that a good deal of the movie concerns a quarrel about words: old meanings are exhibited, shown to be false, and then replaced by new ones. Miro's interventions are constantly punctuated by the need to translate a prevalent linguistic universe of marked resignation into a political language of mobilization. Miro's speeches attempt to foreground a possible national alliance of the underdogs, although clearly Miro's *ideal* audience lacks even the means to imagine such a shared national community. In his didacticism, Miro constantly risks falling into disappointment. This is the dialectic of disappointment that de Fuentes preempts in *Allá en el Rancho Grande* by erecting an isolated universe of relationships that radically excludes any register of the actual antinomies that populated the country.

The SEP did not trust the movie's political efficacy to its producers alone. Since the 1920s the SEP had prepackaged dozens of theatrical scripts to be rehearsed before peasant audiences. The teachers' instructions contained precise guidelines to foster discussions that would allow the public to read the intended message of the plays. This modality was continued when live theater was replaced by movies—to the relief of the many peasants who found the plays' diction and pedagogical tones unbearable. *Redes* was designed for similar use. This fact explains the open nature of the film's ending. Two groups of fishermen get into a brawl about their right to sell fish to the *acaparador.* The local politician makes use of the confusion to kill Miro. Defeated, Miro's group take his body back to the village. Later in the day the other group shows up, but this time to join the fight against the *acaparador.* Now united, all the fishermen decided to row to the village to share their discontent with the townspeople. The film itself, however, does not return to words as its main vehicle but instead aligns its ideological statement and its visual forcefulness in a last shot that shows the fishermen rowing towards the town with decided and defiant faces.

Many viewers perceived as an irony the fact that a state would fund the production of a movie that describes politicians, police, and communal authorities as enemies of the people. Beyond the screen, irony was turning into tragedy. In 1934, while *Redes* was being filmed, a workers' strike in Oaxaca ended in brutal repression. One of the workers who died that day is the subject of Manuel Álvarez Bravo's famous photograph, *Obrero en huelga asesinado.* Alfonso Morales comments, "The plight of Miro, who in the cinematic world of *Redes* makes his comrades understand the need to unite against the corrupt and greedy fish-buyer, echoed the harsh realities of the day. Manuel

Álvarez Bravo's harrowing 1934 photo . . . provides an all-too-clear example of what the workers were up against."[67] Álvarez Bravo, an avant-garde photographer by training and conviction, renewed with this photo a trend of daring photojournalism that continues in Mexico to this day. The makers of *Redes*, on the other hand, stand in solitude. After *Redes*, or after the time of *Redes*, Mexican film is said to have taken flight into fantasy—in terms of this book, an ungrounded fantasy. However, as much as Mexican film wished to forget reality, reality was not willing to forget film.

Ahí está el detalle: *The Utopian Flight*

Ahí está el detalle (1940), directed by Juan Bustillo Oro and starring Mario Moreno—Cantinflas—is a classic comedy of errors not lacking in political significance. In fact, it contains one of the most subversive, utopian scenes in the history of Mexican filmmaking. A few years before his cinematographic debut, Bustillo Oro had, together with Mauricio Magdaleno, promoted the *teatro de ahora*, an attempt to open a conduit for a theater of high dramatic quality and political awareness in Mexico. The idea behind the *teatro de ahora* was to bridge the distance between the politically charged but mostly entertainment-oriented *revista* and the more formal but politically detached artistic theatre. Despite the youth of both authors—Bustillo Oro was twenty-eight in 1932 and Mauricio Magdaleno twenty-six—the *teatro de ahora* showed remarkable dramatic maturity. The duo completed four plays. One, on Emiliano Zapata, was an attempt to popularize the figure of the leader from Morelos among the still largely antirevolutionary Mexico City public. The other significant piece was Bustillo Oro's *Los que vuelven*, one of the first dramatic elaborations of the subject of Mexican migration to the United States. In this piece Bustillo Oro touches on the subject of forced deportation of Mexicans from the United States in the wake of the Great Depression and explores the reactions of both the returning people and their Mexican counterparts to their presence in Mexico.

The plot of *Ahí está el detalle* is quite straightforward. A well-dressed man stalks a woman in a middle-class neighborhood. He himself is being followed by someone bearing all the traits of the *pelado* (Cantinflas). Five minutes into the movie, we have Cantinflas at the kitchen courting the domestic employee, although he is clearly more interested in his free dinner than in the metaphysics of love. Meanwhile, in the living room a drama of a different order unfolds: Cayetano Lastre (Joaquín Pardavé) exhibits his jealousy to his young, beautiful wife, Dolores, while she tries to dissipate his doubts, although not without some irony. Each space—kitchen and living room—is the site of a small drama of division, although the real drama is played out in between both spaces. Meanwhile, Sara, the cook (Clotilde Regalado), promises to appease Cantinflas's hunger in exchange for a small favor: to kill a dog with rabies in her stead. The cook/maid goes from one space to the other, bridging but also revealing the fractured universe of postrevolutonary illusions. When she goes from the kitchen to the living room, she brings with her the remnants of an unutterable discourse of social confrontation and political antagonism. When she goes back to the kitchen, she transports with her a bourgeois and middle-class morality that will become more and more dominant in Mexican film production. While Cayetano is, to all indications, a successful businessman, Cantinflas incarnates neither work nor success. When confronted by his girlfriend about the virtues of work ("Only work elevates man," she repeats), Cantinflas replies with a sharp: "Listen, *mocita,* if work were so good, the rich, who have a tendency to accumulate all good things, would have all the work for themselves. Instead, they rarely work. So, work cannot be such a good thing." We have here an image of how social divisions stirred by the revolution—for instance through the massive migration of *pelados* to Mexico City—take on a figural form in the narrative of a film that has, supposedly, left all aspirations to realism behind.

If division is strong, the call for unity is not less so. Through another equivocation, Cantinflas is mistakenly identified as a relative of the lady of the house, despite his shabby clothing and his shockingly uncouth social behavior. The pedagogical message of the film is clear: Mexico is such a unified country that anybody can relate to anybody else. This ideal of equality—which is the most pervasive theme of the movie—produces quasisurrealist solutions to problems that are posed in realist style. Family being family, the situation seems to allow for dispensing with appearances, even in the register in which only appearances count. Eventually, Cantinflas is put on trial for the death of a man, a direct result of his pretense to be Leonardo (Dolores's cousin). It is against the background of this story, in a courtroom, that one of the most utopian scenes in the history of Latin American film takes place.

The selection of a courtroom to disentangle all the confusions that make up *Ahí está el detalle* is significant in a number of ways. The courtroom is deeply related to postrevolutionary history as one of the practical instances under which Mexico City experienced the revolution. In the first years of postrevolutionary rule popular tribunals were created, and the courtrooms often turned into full-fledged mass spectacles in which melodrama shared the stage with legal procedures. At that point, a group of lawyers emerged who had a remarkable ability to argue their cases to the enthralled judging audiences. The best-known among them was perhaps Amado Moeno, who specialized in defending women who had killed their husbands. Moeno not only presented impassioned defenses of his clients, he also carefully schooled them in behaviors, ways of dressing, and overall performance in order to more positively impact the decisions of the judges. Bustillo Oro was acquainted with Amado Moeno and owned a photograph that Agustín Casasola had taken of the lawyer in court. While the courtroom in which Cantinflas is judged is not a popular courtroom, the public in it and their reactions closely resemble the first juridical experiments of the early postrevolutionary regime. Simultaneously, the courtroom is the quintessential Hollywood and American topoi. It is the centerpiece of social fantasy insofar as it offers the proper hegemonic articulation of American political imagination. As such, the courtroom is the stage for the display of possessive individualism as the general ideology of the modern subject. In this imaginary, the courtroom appears simultaneously as the regulated but completely guaranteed site for the manifestation of a citizen who is constituted in his or her entirety by the intersection of truth (or technologies of truth) and accountability (or technologies of confession/self-representation). Of course, the courtroom does not declare this last point openly. The assumption is that such a subjectivity preexists its appearance in court: the court simply provides the fairest setting for its expression. But while the courtroom speech (often transformed and disguised by myriad other forms in Hollywood films) appears as a sort of filmic archetype in American movies, in *Ahí está el detalle* the same space emerges as the interruption of sanctioned representation by a disavowed reality, that of the migrant of peasant origin at the heart of the modern city.

Cantinflas incarnates to perfection the ghostly presence in the courtroom of another speech that is always, and by definition, another valuation of the world—or, even more unsettlingly, a refusal of valuation. Before his judges, Cantinflas speaks the entire time in a gibberish that leaves the public amused, the court dumbfounded, and his lawyer in perpetual despair. This discourse borrows its purchase not from what it wants to say but rather from its perseverance in saying. The *pelado* is not so much the one who cannot speak—although in a certain sense, the courtroom scene is a dramatization of Gayatri Spivak's famous argument—but rather the one who speaks despite the fact that he does not know, cannot know, how to speak. Cantinflas's case seems lost; he himself has defeated all the attempts at a defense by his lawyer. But when a sentence seems imminent, the real Leonardo comes forward, assuming responsibility for the murder and proving Cantinflas's innocence. At this point, the excess of justice over the law dresses itself in the garments of the *pelado*'s desire-to-express. This is the movie's utopian moment. The judge, the prosecutor, and the defending lawyer start mimicking Cantinflas's speech. They talk to each other in the same gibberish that Cantinflas had been using, to everybody's amusement. The dissolution of intention in language that characterizes the *pelado* discourse becomes the language of the law tout-court. In this verbal exchange nothing is exchanged. Language is literally desubstantiated—returned to a form of primary innocence. This is how *Ahí está el detalle* manifests its deep allegiance to the tradition of synchronization that is one of the founding pillars of mechanical reproduction. No shot of the audience, which has been prominent thus far, interrupts this flow of words, foregrounding the fact that the institution of the law itself—the incarnated universality of the state—is willfully transformed here and put into synchrony with the bodies and the desires that first stirred its tranquil waters more than three decades earlier.

Notes

CHAPTER 1. 1921

1. Folgarait, *Seeing Mexico Photographed*, 4. As early as 1978 David Bailey observed that a byproduct of increasing research on the revolution was that "there is less agreement today about the nature and meaning of the Mexican Revolution than at any other time since scholars first turned their attention to it more than fifty years ago." Bailey, "Revisionism and the Recent Historiography," 63.

2. For Barthes's notion of textuality, see "From Work to Text," in *Image, Music, Text*. Jorge Aguilar Mora's *Una muerte sencilla* provides a fine example of the pervasive nature of textuality in the exegesis of the revolution.

3. Mraz, *Looking for Mexico*, 5.

4. Charlot, *Mexican Mural Renaissance*, 29.

5. Novo, *La estatua de sal*, 55. All translations of text referenced in a language other than English are my own.

6. Žižek, *Plague of Fantasies*, 7.

7. That lack is the truth of historical subjectivity is a Hegelian insight that I consider most apt for rendering the type of subjectivity prompted and demanded by a revolution. On Lacan's Hegelianism see Mikkel Borch-Jacobsen, *Lacan*.

8. Vom Hau, "Unpacking the School."

9. Knight, *Mexican Revolution*, 2.

10. Weston, *Daybooks*, 26.

11. Quoted in Charlot, *Mexican Mural Renaissance*, 68. Of course, the battle for the survival of the postrevolutionary state—a battle whose triumph was at times uncertain—was fought on many different fronts, and the importance that cultural reconstruction held for the successive Mexican administrations has to be seen against the horizon of other challenges.

12. Benjamin, *La Revolución*, 6.

13. Ibid., 7.

14. Ibid., 11.

15. Luis Cabrera's first and lasting intervention on the concept of revolution took place as early as 1911, which shows that we are dealing with a charged word that was indeed the object of an extensive social treatment.

16. The point is made by Nicola Miller in *In the Shadow of the State*.

17. Scott, *Seeing Like a State*, 5.

18. That is, sovereignty—in its dual role of creating the conditions for the existence of the social through exceptionality and of guaranteeing the autonomy of the political sphere through social engineering—appears split between the function of the state and the function of cultural mediation.

19. See, for instance, Alan Knight, "Frank Tannenbaum and the Mexican Revolution."

20. Broadly speaking, we can distinguish four periods in the historiography of the revolution. The first, dominated by names like Ernest Gruening, Frank Tannenbaum, and Silva Herzog, produced books that depicted the revolution as a popular event and the resulting state as the rightful, if deficient, heir to the movement. Revisionism challenged that view. The first important revisionist work is Jean Mayer's *La cristiada* (1968), although its critical perspective of the revolution drew on work extending back to early 1950s by historians like Cosío Villegas. Pablo González Casanova's devastating critique of the postrevolutionary regime in *La democracia en México* (1965) also anticipates revisionism. For an overview of revisionism, see David C. Bailey, "Revisionism and the Recent Historiography." In the third stage, neopopulism, many historians perceived the state-centrism of revisionist analysis to be untenable. Authors such as Friedrich Katz, who authored a monumental book on Pancho Villa, and Alan Knight fall into this group. More recently a series of authors have comprised a fourth state, answering the call issued in *Everyday Forms of State Formation* (Joseph and Nugent, 1992) to deliver a cultural history of the revolution able to bring "the state back in without leaving the people out" (12). Contributing authors include Mary Kay Vaughan (who also wrote *Cultural Politics in Revolution* and coedited *Eagle and the Virgin* and *Sex in Revolution*).

21. Knight, *Interpreting the Mexican Revolution*, 5.

22. Vaughan, *Cultural Politics in Revolution*.

23. Max Parra makes a similar argument in the opening pages of *Writing Pancho Villa's Revolution*. See the section "Politics and Culture," 3–6.

24. As a matter of fact, several different photographers took slightly different snapshots almost simultaneously. According to John Mraz, two very well-established photographers of the time, Antonio Garduño and Manuel Ramos, took the two photos that appeared in the press. Mraz, *Photographing the Mexican Revolution*, 251–252.

25. Carlos Monsiváis describes the scene as "Zapata y Villa se acomodan inciertamente en la cercanía de la silla presidencial" (Zapata and Villa seated uncomfortably near the presidential chair). Monsiváis, "Soy porque me parezco," 197.

26. Aguilar Camín and Meyer, *In the Shadow of the Mexican Revolution*, 56.

27. Rancière, *Dissensus*, 43.

28. Williams, "Sovereign (In)hospitality," 104.

29. Roger Bartra notes, "National culture is identified with political power in

such a way that whoever wants to break the rules of authoritarianism will immediately be accused of renouncing—or, worse, of betraying—national culture." Quoted in Williams, *Mexican Exception*, 12.

30. Having a similar question in mind, Esther Gabara speaks of "critical nationalism" in *Errant Modernism*, 5. Thomas Benjamin notices with some surprise that "curiously, subsequent dissent and protest against the direction and policies of particular regimes often affirmed the Revolutionary Tradition, indeed used it symbolically against successive governments" (*La Revolución*, 158). David Lloyd delves into the ambivalent nature of nationalism in a significant essay, "Nationalism against the State."

31. The most ambitious discussion of nationalism in Mexico is Claudio Lomnitz's book *Exits from the Labyrinth*. In it, Lomnitz attempts a hermeneutics of nationalism that does not presuppose the categories of nationalism itself for its deployment.

32. Knight, *Mexican Revolution*, 2. Knight's statement agrees with a long line of Mexican self-interpretation that goes back to Andrés Molina Enríquez. In *Los grandes problemas nacionales* (1909), Molina Enríquez writes, "In Mexico there is no unified social ideal. We are a nation without a common origin, without a common religion, without a common racial type, language, or tradition. We lack a unified desire, a common purpose, everything that makes of the ideal the product of an unified will" (292).

33. Cosío Villegas, *Memorias*, 74. There were, however, several attacks against Chinese and Spanish immigrants in the 1913–1915 period.

34. "La pintura en Mexico," *El Universal*, 19 July 1923.

35. Thomas Benjamin establishes a correlation by which "the tempest of events was accompanied by a torrent of words." Benjamin, *La Revolución*, 3–4.

36. Aguilar Camín and Meyer, *In the Shadow of the Mexican Revolution*, x.

37. Azuela, *Arte y poder*, 16.

38. Quoted in Brading, *Octavio Paz y la poética*, 35.

39. Ignacio Sánchez Prado's *Naciones intelectuales* provides a keen discussion of the dialectic between state-backed nationalism and competing forms of cultural production in the period.

40. Scott, "Foreword," in *Everyday Forms of State Formation*, ix.

41. Knight, "Weapons and Arches," 27.

42. Actually this phrase is an interesting example of democratic textuality. As the same Cabrera informs us in a reprint of "La revolución es la revolución" (the revolution is the revolution), the original title of his intervention was "La revolución es revolución" (the revolution is revolution), but since the public persisted in misquoting his essay, Cabera ended up adopting the misquoted phrase. See Cabrera, "La revolución es (la) revolución," in Mayer, *Luis Cabrera*, 60–62.

43. Deleuze and Guattari, *What Is Philosophy?*, 177.

44. The Mexican Revolution—whose list of betrayals includes the charge of not being a revolution at all—occupies a distinctive position in this context. The moment of chaos and uncertainty, the not-yet-territorialized instance of pure action, extended its influence well beyond the end of the armed struggle. Even the arising

of different revolutionary programs did not suffice to suture its formidable force. Since revolutionary programs were rather vague and events kept reformulating them, there was no clear way to measure the distance between the revolution and its achievements. This weakness of the revolution proved to be its strength, one of the secrets of its astounding longevity. Abelardo Villegas argues, "Ideologues and politicians of a certain tendency thought that the Revolution betrayed them when the emphases fell on some questions that were not their favorite ones. This is why the revolutionary process was called sometimes socialism, sometimes capitalism, and sometimes just revolution. As a matter of fact, it was a case of critical liberalism, classical liberalism, all this spiced, corrected, or augmented by doses of positivism, realism, and later anarchism, Marxism, etc." Villegas, *Autognosis*, 23–24.

45. Furet, *Interpreting the French Revolution*, 7.

46. Florescano, *El nuevo pasado mexicano*, 104.

47. Hobsbawm, "Revolution," 7.

48. Krauze, *Mexico: Biography of Power*, 480.

49. Of course, a relationship still exists: the fantasy belongs to a given situation. However, the form itself of the fantasy is not traceable to a dominant or implicit form in the realm of potentialities. This argument can be seen as stating in the realm of the figural something similar to what Theda Skocpol has called "the non intentional analysis of revolutions" in her classic study *States and Social Revolutions*, 16–18.

50. Florescano, *El nuevo pasado mexicano*, 171. In *Interpreting the French Revolution*, François Furet writes, "No Frenchman living in the second half of the twentieth century can perceive the French Revolution from the outside" (10).

51. Even the supposed "Callista" manipulation of the executive after Obregón's death is to some extent a historical fabrication. Arnaldo Córdova calls attention to the absurdity of inferring an all-powerful grip on the political by Plutarco Elías Calles based on the constant changes of presidents during the Maximato. If anything, the need to find new replacements in the executive office proved the contested nature of the political situation: see Córdova, *La revolución en crisis*, 34.

52. Florescano, *El nuevo pasado mexicano*, 149.

53. *El Universal*, 25 September 1921, 5.

54. Williams, *Mexican Exception*, 17.

CHAPTER 2. EXTENSION

1. *In the Shadow of the Mexican Revolution*, 51. The passage also appears verbatim in Aguilar Camín's *La frontera nómada*.

2. The creation of the SEP entailed a constitutional amendment that required preapproval from the twenty-eight state legislatures.

3. Fell, *José Vasconcelos*, 243.

4. The other members of the retinue were Roberto Montenegro, Adolfo Best Maugard, Jaime Torres Bodet, Carlos Pellicer, and Pedro Henríquez Ureña.

5. R. Burton, quoted in Noble, *Mexican National Cinema*, 51.

6. López, *Lo más mexicano*, 26.

7. Florescano, *El nuevo pasado mexicano*, 103.

8. Principles, ideas, and manifestos were certainly not lacking, but they were powerless before the heterogeneous diversity of revolutionary actors and factions.

9. Parra, *Writing Pancho Villa's Revolution*, 45.

10. Azuela, *The Underdogs*, 98.

11. Parra, *Writing Pancho Villa's Revolution*, 27.

12. Gareth Williams synthetically describes this process: "In the official post-revolutionary discourse of Mexican modernity, then, popular will was deposited in the Constitution and from there passed into the state, thereby implying that the will of the state was and is the de facto will of the people." Williams, *The Mexican Exception*, 11.

13. Revueltas, *Obras completas*, 19: 85.

14. Reyes, *Obras completas*, 12: 96. It was not the regions themselves that were improbable but their relationship to their representatives. Pablo Prida Santacilia was a representative during the last years of Díaz's government. He was born and raised in Mexico City, but when he turned twenty-one, Díaz made him the representative for the state of Chihuahua, a region Prida had never even visited.

15. O'Gorman, *Reflexiones*, 5

16. Davis, *Urban Leviathan*, 75.

17. On the preparation for the celebration, see Beezley and Lorey, *Viva Mexico!*, 168.

18. Davis, "El rumbo de la esfera pública," 240.

19. Guedea, *Asedios a los centenarios*, 23.

20. Annick Lempérière writes, "For Porfirismo, history is not just an instrument of power useful for the constitution of nationality. Historical consciousness has a direct impact on the ways of thinking. It is the mode of consciousness par excellence. There is no thinking, intellectual production, or political inspiration which is not governed by topoi organized around a temporal consciousness." Lempérière, "Los dos centenarios," 325.

21. Ibid.

22. Guedea, *Asedios a los centenarios*, 19.

23. Knight, *Mexican Revolution*, 2.

24. Magdaleno, *Retórica de la Revolución*, 17.

25. Ramírez Plancarte, *La ciudad de México*, 173.

26. Ibid., 53.

27. Ibid., 63.

28. Carr, *El movimiento obrero*, 63. It was only in 1933 that a new labor union, created out of the remnants of the Confederación Regional Obrera Mexicana (CROM), actually included both urban and rural workers. But even through the 1930s and '40s, those intellectuals who deeply identified with a Marxist worldview actively sidelined the peasantry in a country that was still over 80 percent rural—as Diego Rivera and Gabriela Mistral never tired of arguing. Rivera's support of the autonomous *ligas agrarias* put him in conflict with the Partido Comunista de México (PCM). Mistral

championed the cause of peasant organization while in Mexico and denounced favoring a small working class at the expense of the large, mobilized peasant masses. See her 1928 essay, "Pasión agraria."

29. See Olsen, *Artifacts of Revolution*; see also Katzman, *La arquitectura contemporánea mexicana.*

30. See Olsen, "Revolution in the City Streets," 119–135.

31. Vasconcelos, *El desastre*, in *Obras completas*, 1: 1249.

32. In his *Apuntes autobiográficos*, Alberto Pani criticizes the Porfirian centennial as "a program of festivities that through the whole month of September caused a notorious popular irritation because of its pomp and because it was restricted to the official and social aristocracy" (75).

33. There are two official sources for the study of the celebration, the *Programa oficial de las fiestas del centenario de la consumación de la independencia de México* (n.a.), and Federico Graue, La *noche mexicana en los lagos del bosque de Chapultepec.* The rest of the information appears scattered among different periodicals.

34. Lacy, "1921 Centennial Celebration."

35. Quoted in Guedea, *Asedios a los centenarios*, 91.

36. "Entrevista con el Dr. Emiliano López Figueroa," *El Universal*, 6 September 1921.

37. It would be interesting to contrast memories of schooling written by people educated before and after the revolution. A possible series of texts would include Vasconcelos's *Ulises criollo*, Juan José Tablada's *La feria de la vida*, Salvador Novo's *La estatua de sal*, and Andrés Iduarte's *Un niño en la Revolución mexicana.*

38. Natalia Brizuela observes that the availability of photographic cameras introduced a strong interest in geography in a century—the late nineteenth century—"whose concerns are presumed to be temporal rather than spatial." Brizuela, *Fotografia e império*, 16.

39. Quoted in Charlot, *Mexican Mural Renaissance*, 68.

40. Fabian, *Time and the Other*, 58–62.

41. This principle is instituted by Kant in *Critique of Judgment*, where he argues that aesthetic judgments, which are always singular but phrased as universal, show "in action" the assumption of a common disposition of all human beings.

42. Morales, "Spanish for Your Mexican Visit," 240.

43. While my discussion of the contest is largely based on Rick López's presentation in *Crafting Mexico*, there are other scattered references to the festivities in the press and in some extended publications. Ricardo Pérez Montfort offers a brief analysis of the event in *Bajo el cielo de México.* See also Pérez Montfort, *Estampas de nacionalismo popular mexicano*, and de los Reyes, *Cine y sociedad en México.*

44. Loyo, "La lectura en México, 1920–1940."

45. Bazant, "Lecturas del Porfiriato," 219.

46. López, *Crafting Mexico*, 37–39.

47. Lacy, "1921 Centennial Celebration," 216.

48. The Porfirist celebration of 1910 entertained a similar idea. The organizing committee for the Centennial Celebration requested "if at all possible . . . twenty of

the prettiest Indian women from the state of San Luis de Potosí, to participate in the national parade." Quoted in Davis, "El rumbo de la esfera pública," 185.

49. Quoted in López, *Crafting Mexico*, 312.

50. Ibid., 44.

51. Article in *El Universal*, quoted in López, *Crafting Mexico*, 53.

52. "Exposición de arte aborigen en el mes de septiembre," *El Universal*, 25 June 1921, 3.

53. Most of the 1921 exposition traveled to Los Angeles in 1922 for an exhibition whose catalogue was written by Katherine Ann Porter.

54. It is interesting to note that towards 1921, there was no gallery of modern art in Mexico City. According to Xavier Villaurrutia, the first gallery to commercialize modern painting opened in Mexico in 1926. See Villaurrutia, "Una galería de arte moderno en México."

55. Quoted in López, *Crafting Mexico*, 81.

56. See in this respect the interesting remarks of Rick López on the vogue of "Mexican rooms" in middle-class neighborhoods in his *Crafting Mexico*.

57. Rick López writes in reference to the exposition, "There simply existed no person, group, or agency with the kind of knowledge needed to amass such a collection. Very little was known about the languages or cultures of rural Mexico, much less about the diversity of popular art." López, *Crafting Mexico*, 78.

58. Ibid., 93.

59. Kant writes, "We regard free art as . . . an occupation that is agreeable on its own account, mercenary art we regard as labor." Kant, *Critique of Judgment*, 171.

60. Atl, *Las artes populares*, 47.

61. Ibid., 49.

62. Atl mentions his work organizing indigenous cooperatives in his memoir, *Gentes profanas en el convento*, 216–223.

63. Morales, "Spanish for Your Mexican Visit," 255.

64. Atl, *Las artes populares*, 33.

65. López, *Crafting Mexico*, 16–17.

66. Atl, *Las artes populares*, 57.

67. López, *Crafting Mexico*, 17.

68. Ibid.

69. Atl stumbles here upon a major problem of modern aesthetics that occupied some of the best minds of the late eighteenth century. In the third Critique, Kant notices that one of art's fundamental roles lies in the presentation of an aesthetic idea. And he goes on to clarify that by aesthetic idea he means "a presentation of the imagination which prompts much thought, but to which no determinate thought . . . can be adequate, so that no language can express it completely" (*Critique of Judgment*, 182). This passage represents one of the most conclusive references that Kant makes to the radical indeterminacy to which the beautiful is a clue. But if the imagination is free to conjure any order whatsoever, what prevents it from bringing upon the present the most irrational of decisions under the pretense of the rational? Can we say that indeterminacy—which is the kernel of art as free activity—is necessarily tied

to an enlightened predisposition? The political potential of this indeterminacy (celebrated today in the work of Derrida under the heading of the quasimessianic) was held suspect by Edmund Burke in his *Reflections on the Revolution in France*, since it contained the possibility to "subject the present time . . . to immediate calamities in favour of the future and uncertain benefit of persons who only exists in idea." Letter quoted by Cruise O'Brien in the introduction to the *Reflections*, 23.

70. López, *Crafting Mexico*, 98.

71. Graue, "La noche Mexicana en los lagos," 1.

72. In "La noche mexicana en el Bosque de Chapultepec," *El Universal Ilustrado*, 29 September 1921, 26.

73. Gamboa, *Diario*, 35.

74. For a thorough reconstruction of *La noche mexicana*, see Rodríguez, "La 'noche mexicana.'"

75. Rick López indicts Best Maugard and the rest of the high modernists of the 1921 centennial on this account. Their activities, he points out, "recognized neither indigenous people nor artisans as agents possessed of their own volition." And shortly after, he adds, "Neither of these events acknowledged that the rural masses may possess their own thoughts about their art." López, *Crafting Mexico*, 94.

76. Davis, *Urban Leviathan*, 53.

77. Arguably Tina Modotti is the artist who put forward the question of the masses most consistently and lucidly. See Folgarait's discussion of Modotti in *Seeing Mexico Photographed*.

78. *Su majestad, el hambre* was written by Pablo Prida. *El país de los cartones* is a collaborative play authored by Carlos Ortega and Pablo Prida. These plays always worked under the limitations of the ever-changing political fortunes of the country. While the importance of the *tandas* began to peak during Huerta's government, the popular forms were often used to carry conservative propaganda as well. One of the first highly successful pieces of the *género chico* was José F. Elizondo's *El país de la metralla*, a rabidly anti-Carrancist piece that advocated for a return to a military rule. Elizondo was an educated poet with close ties to the entourage of Porfirio Díaz. Alfonso Morales's *El país de las tandas* contains valuable documentation on this period of Mexican theater.

79. The popularity of the *género chico* predates the revolution. In the opening years of the twentieth century, a Spanish piece entitled *El bateo* (Antonio Domínguez and Antonio Paso) was the center of attention for theatrical audiences in Spain. When the play was performed in Mexico City one year later, it caused an even greater uproar. The main plot of the story is the baptism of a child whose godfather (Wamba) happens to be a free-thinker of anarchist tendencies. Wamba refuses to enter the church for the baptism and asks that the newborn be baptized with a Phrygian cap while pressuring the parents to name the baby Robespierre—whom Wamba misinterprets as the father of anarchism. The play excuses Wamba's iconoclastic political ideas in the name of his ignorance and simplicity. However, the most virulent verses of the play became immensely popular in the low ranks of Mexican society. "They day I become president / if that day comes to pass / at least ten thou-

sand heads / will be cut. / We will erect a statue of Robespierre / all made only with human flesh." Quoted in Beezley, *Mexican National Identity*, 45.

80. Quoted in Bryan, "Teatro popular y sociedad," 193. For a solid attempt to balance the role of popular and learned theater in modern Mexican theater see Alejandro Ortíz Bullé Goyri, *Cultura y política en el drama mexicano posrevolucionario*.

81. Quoted in Bradú, *Antonieta*, 34.

82. Baca Barajas, "Prensa, quehacer cultural," 101.

83. Reyes, "La cultura en los años '20," 34.

84. Ramírez Plancarte, *La ciudad de México*, 127.

85. Part of this description is taken from Ageeth Sluis, "City of Spectacles."

CHAPTER 3. DEPTH

1. Lomnitz, *Death and the Idea of Mexico*, 32.

2. Quoted in Florescano, "Etnia, estado y nación," 382.

3. Cañizares-Esguerra, *How to Write the History of the New World*, 62.

4. Florescano, *El nuevo pasado mexicano*, 103.

5. There were, of course, attempts at an *indigenista* narrative in the 1920s. A particularly noticeable failure is *La tierra del faisán y del venado*, by Antonio Médiz Bolio, published originally in 1922.

6. Caso, *Métodos y resultados de la política indigenista*.

7. Sommers, *After the Storm*. In contrast, Sommers sees a properly *indigenista* movement emerging in the 1950s: see Sommers, "El ciclo de Chiapas."

8. An example of independent *indigenista* discourse is Frances Toor's journal *Mexican Folkways*, which was published between 1925 and 1937. Although financed by the Mexican state through the SEP, *Mexican Folkways* put much more emphasis on the immutability of the indigenous culture (under the guise of an indigenous identity) than on any potential for transformation, and this despite the leftist tendencies of most of its collaborators.

9. Like Vasconcelos, Manuel Gamio and Andrés Molina Enríquez were tenacious critics of the abstract and formal nature of Mexican liberalism. The three men supported the reconstitution of the *ejidos* whose banishment had deprived the Indians of their means of subsistence following the constitution of 1857.

10. See López Bárcenas, *Autonomía y derechos indígenas*, especially pages 30–36. See also Stavenhagen, *Derecho indígena y derechos humanos*.

11. Villoro, *Los grandes momentos del indigenismo*, 199.

12. The double valence of the indigenous as simultaneously an anchor to the land and a malleable foundation for the future clearly distinguishes its figure from *criollista* emblems of a relationship of depth, such as the *charro*. The use of *charrería* to cement popular nationalism took on special weight following 1921, and it often served to channel a reactionary nationalism. It is telling that in its moment of utmost triumph—which we can locate around the enormous success of the film *Allá en el Rancho Grande* (1936)—the *charro* could become an icon of Mexicanness to be ex-

ported but not a tool to imagine new social or political articulations. In its intrinsic docility, the *charro* fused its use value with its visual value.

13. Pérez Montfort, "Las invenciones del México indio."

14. The conferences are collected in Vasconcelos and Gamio, *Aspects of Mexican Civilization*.

15. Often commentators find in the sociological impasse represented by the notion of "mass" the authorization to construct the history of the period as a story of personal greed and corruption. The individual that emerges from the mass—the *soldadera* who ransacks a church, the revolutionary who appropriates a house for his own gain—are subjectified as fallen revolutionary identities. Through them the revolutionary process is presented as a social pathology rather than as a political confrontation.

16. For a review of state policies towards the indigenous see Urías Horcasitas, *Las historias secretas del racismo*.

17. González Gamio, *Manuel Gamio*, 56–57.

18. Florescano, *Memoria mexicana*, 355–363.

19. Vasconcelos's rejection of education in indigenous languages was driven above all by political reasons. He feared that a linguistic fragmentation in Mexico would weaken the country before the United States. On his linguistic policy, see Carbo, *Los indígenas debatidos y legislados*, 105–109.

20. Brading, *Octavio Paz y la poética*, 56.

21. The *teatro sintético* of Teotihuacán was partially funded by Vasconcelos's SEP. Gamio enrolled the help of painter Carlos González, musician Francisco Domínguez, and ethnographer and playwright Rafael Saavedra. The latter wrote the best-known production of this theater, *La cruza*. Rodolfo Usigli, who attended some presentations, saw this theater as modeled after avant-garde procedures akin to deautomatization (although he did not use this vocabulary). Manuel Palavicini, writing for *El Universal Ilustrado*, heralded the productions as the beginning of a true Mexican theater. These judgments, like others that appeared in the press and even in academic writings, do not stress what is in my opinion the most interesting aspect of the *teatro sintético*: its staging of everydayness as a spectacle that becomes interesting in itself. Most judgments on this superbly original form of production tend to emphasize its failed or successful connections to a larger history of a hypothetical tradition of "Mexican theater." See Usigli, *Mexico en el teatro*, 129; Manuel Palavicini, "El Teatro Regional de Teotihuacán," *El Universal Ilustrado*, 25 March 1922, 21–52. See also Claude Fell's excellent article, "Théâtre et société dans le Mexique post-révolutionnaire."

22. For a history of excavations at Teotihuacán, see Rattray, *Teotihuacan*.

23. Lomnitz, *Deep Mexico, Silent Mexico*.

24. After considering the different ways in which Gamio attempts to establish an indigenous identity, Luis Villoro favors a mostly economic perspective: "We can call Indian all social groups subjected to work under pre-capitalist relations of production." Villoro, *Los grandes momentos*, 206.

25. Gamio, *La población*, vii.

26. Britton, "Moisés Sáenz," 78.

27. Dawson, *Indian and Nation*, 22.

28. Ibid., 28.

29. There was an intense dialogue between Mexican and Bolivian pedagogues regarding this type of indigenous *internados*. See the extensive and informative essay by Laura Giraudo, "De la ciudad 'mestiza.'"

30. Loyo, "La empresa redentora," 101. With colonization, language became the main marker of ethnographic belonging in Mexico. For an evolution of the study of indigenous languages up to the first decades of the twentieth century, see the opening chapter of Francisco Rojas González's *Ensayos indigenistas*.

31. Sáenz, *Carapan*, 189.

32. Villoro, *Los grandes momentos*, 240.

33. Conference pronounced on El Colegio Nacional in May 1956, reproduced in Serra Puche, *Alfonso Caso*, 141.

34. I am referring here to John Beverley's classic 1993 book, *Against Literature*, in which, incidentally, the image of the transcultural indigenous plays an essential role in signaling the limits of literature as a device for the rationalization of the world.

35. Carlo Antonio Castro, who published *Los hombres verdaderos* in 1959, was a linguist and ethnographer. Francisco Rojas González, author of the volume *El diosero* (1952) was an ethnographer and sociologist who participated in different scientific missions to indigenous areas. In the foreword to his novelized biography of a Tzotzil Indian (*Juan Pérez Jolote*, 1952), the ethnographer Ricardo Pozas presents his work as "a brief monograph on Chamula culture" (7).

36. Castellanos, *Oficio de tinieblas*, 29.

37. Conn, *Politics of Philology*, 15.

38. See Monsiváis, "México y la toma de partido."

39. Faber, "Don Alfonso o la fuerza del sino."

40. Reyes's intervention appears that same year (1936) in *Sur* under the title "Notas sobre la inteligencia americana"; reprinted in *Ultima tule y otros ensayos*.

41. Reyes's susceptibility to the ethical interpellation of his time is exemplified in his characterization of the Indian as "an elevated duty" (*altivo deber*) in "Notas sobre la inteligencia americana," 19. For Monsiváis's reading of Reyes as state thinker, see "México y la toma de partido."

42. Clifford, *Predicament of Culture*, 96.

43. Henríquez Ureña, *Estudios mexicanos*, 29.

44. Section 4 of "La crítica en la Edad Ateniense," begins with the question, "But what is criticism?" After asking the question, Reyes goes through a rapid overview of what criticism is not without actually finding an appropriate fulfillment for the concept. *Obras completas*, 13: 17.

45. Ibid., 1: 97.

46. Esther Gabara observes that "the genre of the essay in Spanish contains a fascinating if contradictory history of literature's relationship to critique." Gabara, *Errant Modernism*, 147.

47. Nancy and Lacoue-Labarthe, *The Literary Absolute*.

48. Reyes, *Obras completas*, 13: 15.

49. Reyes's notion of criticism comes quite close to the one espoused by Walter Benjamin in his doctoral dissertation, entitled, precisely, "The Concept of Criticism in German Romanticism." In Benjamin's words, insofar as criticism partakes of the ontology of the work of art, it seeks "the intensification of the consciousness of the work" (152). Any reader of "Visión de Anáhuac" knows how indebted Reyes's prose is to the process of reawakening of past consciousness.

50. Reyes also wrote a brief book on Mallarmé, *Culto a Mallarmé*, included in volume 25 of his *Obras completas*.

51. Reyes, *Obras completas*, 1: 95, 101 (first quote), 103 (second quote).

52. Ibid., 1: 94

53. Ibid., 2: 18.

54. Ibid., 1: 22.

55. Ibid., 2: 28.

56. Ibid., 2: 15.

57. Mauricio Magdaleno is one of the few readers of the text that has perceived this transcendental quality and has linked it to the question of the political constitution of the postrevolutionary state. See Magdaleno, "Presencia de Alfonso Reyes."

58. Reyes, *Obras completas*, 2: 16.

59. Ibid., 13: 546.

60. Ibid., 2: 15.

61. Ibid.

62. Ibid.

63. The quote belongs to Ignacio Sánchez Prado's *Naciones intelectuales* (78). See his enlightened, although perhaps too condensed, discussion of Reyes's "La sonrisa," and "Visión de Anáhuac" as a counterpoint between a Hegelian notion of the subject and the practice of historical writing.

64. Reyes sent the manuscript of "Visión de Anáhuac" to his Costa Rican friend Joaquín García Monge for publication at the press El Convivio. The manuscript is titled "Mil quinientos diecinueve," but Reyes alerts García Monge that he also considers "Visión de Anahuác (1519)" as a more descriptive and serious title. See Alicia Reyes, *Genio y figura de Alfonso Reyes*, 59.

65. See chapter 2 in this volume.

66. Paz, "El jinete del aire."

67. My reading of Reyes has some obvious points of contact with the one produced by Gareth Williams in the fourth chapter of *The Mexican Exception*. Like Williams, I read Reyes as advancing a subtle, structural, and, in my view, unapologetic rationale for state sovereignty. Unlike Williams, I have chosen here to emphasize two aspects of sovereignty: first, its historicity, exemplified by its incarnation and codification in the materiality of culture; and second, its ambiguous—rather than exclusionary—relationship to the notions of democracy and hegemony.

68. Derrida, *Specters of Marx*, 54.

69. Acevedo, "La arquitectura colonial en México," in *Disertaciones de un arquitecto*, 86.

70. Two of the best sources for the study of the period are Fernando González Gortázar's, *La arquitectura en México en el siglo 20*, and Enrique de Anda's, *La arquitectura de la Revolución mexicana.*

71. As do all oppositions, this one, established as it is, has something artificial about it. Jesús Acevedo, who was the most lucid proponent of the colonial style, argued in favor of the use of new materials such as iron and glass at his conferences in the Ateneo.

72. For an overview of architecture in the early revolutionary period, see Patrice Elizabeth Olsen, *Artifacts of Revolution.* On the question of architecture and revolution, see also Israel Katzman, *La arquitectura contemporánea mexicana*, 80–83.

73. Acevedo, *Disertaciones de un arquitecto*, 11.

74. The conference of 1908 at the Ateneo is reproduced with the title "Apariencias arquitectónicas" in the first edition of Acevedo's *Disertaciones*, published in Mexico in 1920. Acevedo discusses the difficulties of reviving a mostly unknown indigenous architectonic principle (63–64).

75. For an excellent study of both monuments see chapter 5 of Luis Carranza's *Architecture as Revolution.*

76. Ibid., 34.

77. On the national stadium, see Rubén Gallo's enlightening discussion in *Mexican Modernity.*

78. The California neocolonial style was, according to the lively prose of Carlos Obregón Santacilia, "the most hybrid and disgraceful style ever seen in Mexico; it originates in popular Mexican architecture, from where it was taken to the South of the United States first, and to California later. There, it got mixed with Italian and Spanish styles . . . and then shipped back to Mexico where the Latinos devoted themselves to copying it . . . reading about its virtues in magazines when they could just make a trip to the pueblos in the countryside and behold the real thing." Obregón Santacilia, *Cinquenta años de arquitectura mexicana*, 76.

79. This building stands near Chapultepec Forest, surrounded by a deteriorated and improvised bus terminal that makes it difficult to see from the outside.

80. Olsen, *Artifacts of Revolution*, 17.

81. For an informed and detailed account of the building and architecture of the SEP, see Luis Carranza, *Architecture as Revolution*, 34–55.

82. Vasconcelos commissioned four allegorical reliefs for the first courtyard: a reproduction of the Spanish vessel *Las Casas*; the Mexican Quetzalcoatl; an Indian Buddha; and a representation of the Greek philosopher Plato.

83. Quoted in Katzman, *La arquitectura contemporánea mexicana*, 18.

84. Le Corbusier never visited Mexico. He completed only two projects in the whole Americas: the Carpenter Center in Boston and the house Curuchet in La Plata, Argentina.

85. In 1924 O'Gorman used for the construction of twenty-four schools and the

repair of another twenty-nine the same amount of money that Obregón Santacilia has demanded for the construction of the school center Benito Juárez.

86. For the Porfirist reworking of downtown Mexico in the process of modernization, see chapter 2.

87. Pani shared the direction of the project with three other architects.

88. This emphasis was not lost on Carlos Lazo, general director of the construction project, who declared (as he was setting the foundational stone for the construction of the Ciudad Universitaria), "Mexico has been made by the intersection of diverse forces and cultures. . . . The Ciudad Universitaria is but one more instance of this tradition. In this same place where the Nahuas and Olmecas met in the valley of Mexico . . . where the most ancient culture of the continent appeared from the contemplation of this land and this sky, we are building a university . . . integrating the thought, the hope, and the labor of everyone, through culture." See Lazo, *Pensamiento y destino de la Ciudad Universitaria*, 6.

CHAPTER 4. LIFE

1. Bakhtin, *Speech Genres*, 71.

2. Hegel, *Aesthetics*, 220.

3. Quoted in Monsiváis, "La aparición del subsuelo," 12.

4. Ibid., 16.

5. Ibid.

6. Vaughan, *Cultural Politics in Revolution*, 39. See also vom Hau, "Unpacking the School."

7. Kelley, *Yaqui Women*.

8. On this point see Doris Sommer's comments in chapter 6, "Hot Pursuits and Cold Rewards of Mexicaness," in *Proceed with Caution*, 138-159.

9. Lefebvre, *Production of Space*, 54.

10. Barthes, *Pleasure of the Text*, 7.

11. See Enrique Krauze's discussion of Carranza in *Mexico: Biography of Power*, 334–372.

12. Edmundo Valadés, a witness contemporary to the events, observed that characters like Villa are so fascinating because they are "a symbol of that time of extreme fatalism in which everything ran astray and life was just a spectacle, [a] mixture of tragedy and epic." Valadés, *La Revolución y las letras*, 57–58.

13. Max Parra's discussion of Rafael Muñoz's *¡Vámonos con Pancho Villa!* often underlines references to the tragic and the heroic. See Parra, *Writing Pancho Villa's Revolution*, 23–46.

14. Bakhtin, "Epic and Novel," in *The Dialogic Imagination*, 3–40.

15. This presence of the sensual exists in a variety of registers. I have analyzed how, in *Eagle and the Serpent*, Guzmán perceives Villa's imposing presence purely as a bodily phenomenon. See Legrás, "Martín Luis Guzmán."

16. Lacan, *Seminar I*, 28–33.

17. López Velarde, *Novedad de la patria*, 8.

18. The photo is reproduced in *Daybooks of Edward Weston*, 37.

19. Herrera, *Frida Kahlo*, 9.

20. The photo that Álvarez Bravo takes of Kahlo in which the painter is standing in front of a mirror is revealing in this context. Kahlo's own pose—her own production and staging of the scene—rivals the framing produced by the photographer. The photo is reproduced in Carlos Monsiváis's essay "Soy porque me parezco," included in Enrique Florescano, *Espejo mexicano*.

21. On this point see Olga Cárdenas Trueba, "Amelia Robles," at www.bibliotecas.tv/zapata/zapatistas/amelia_robles.html.

22. Cano, "Unconcealable Realities of Desire," 40.

23. Ibid., 37.

24. They are Antonio Castro Leal (editor of the ultracanonical *The Novel of the Mexican Revolution*), Vicente Lombardo Toledano (key figure in the political formation of the Mexican working class), Alfonso Caso (brother of Antonio Caso and one of the most important archaeologists and experts on ancient Mesoamerican civilization), Manuel Gómez Morín (an economist, with whom most of this section is concerned), Teófila Olea y Leyva, Alberto Vásquez del Mercado, and Jesús Moreno Baca.

25. Quoted in Krauze, *Caudillos culturales*, 14; Octavio Paz, *Labyrinth of Solitude*, 140–141.

26. Gómez Morín, "1915," 23–24. The previous government had identified itself as "scientific," so for decades "scientific" was synonymous with "upper-class."

27. Ibid., 25.

28. Ibid., 26.

29. Gómez Morin was already interested in the Russian Revolution in the years 1918–1919. "No other member of his generation," Enrique Krauze comments, "had the same consciousness of the comparative value that the Russian events had for the development of the Mexican Revolution." Krauze, *Caudillos culturales*, 68.

30. Robles, *Entre el poder y las letras*, 69.

31. Fell, "Introducción del coordinador," xxxv–xxxvi.

32. Pitol, "Liminar," xxvi. Commenting on Vasconcelos's political platform for the 1929 election, Arnaldo Córdova notes, "A few years later, all these ideas will appear as a manifestation of a crude Bolchevism to Vasconcelos, but in 1929 he was still an archetypical Mexican revolutionary." Córdova, *La Revolución en crisis*, 81.

33. Marentes, *José Vasconcelos*, 16.

34. Vasconcelos, *La tormenta*, in *Obras completas*, 1: 732.

35. Vasconcelos, *Ulises criollo*, in *Obras completas*, 1: 345, 378.

36. Ibid., 387.

37. Vasconcelos, *La tormenta*, in *Obras completas*, 1: 899.

38. Zum Felde categorically rejects the notion of Vasconcelos as an original contributor to Latin American culture: "The little that there is of serious meditation in his work is not original . . . and whatever is original is not serious." Quoted by Claude Fell in the 2000 Archivos critical edition of *Ulises criollo*, 570. In "Liminar," his con-

tribution to the Archivos edition, Sergio Pitol registers a change in tone elicited in Mexico by the mention of Vasconcelos. During Pitol's childhood Vasconcelos was revered as a "maestro" or was sometimes attacked for his immorality, but by the time Pitol entered the university, "He was no longer called 'maestro,' unless the word was used to convey 'irony and scorn.'" "Liminar," in *Ulises criollo*, xxxii.

39. Vasconcelos, *Ulises criollo*, in *Obras completas*, 1: 651.

40. Vasconcelos, *El desastre*, in *Obras completas*, 1: 1391.

41. Ibid., 1456.

42. According to Vasconcelos, the collective reading of Kant's first Critique tested the resolve of the Ateneístas. Although the group never seems to have undertaken the reading of Kant's *Critique of Practical Reason* or his work on aesthetics, its members had second-hand knowledge of the Kantian doctrine through Schopenhauer. Antonio Caso was another intellectual who held a reading group on Kant's philosophy in which Vasconcelos was included. See Antonio Caso, "Kant en Argentina y en México," *El Universal*, 17 February 1939.

43. Vasconcelos had clashed with Carranza over Vasconcelos's refusal to publicly condemn Zapata and his army. Although Vasconcelos claimed to have no connections with Zapatismo, Alberto Pani mentions in his memoir a note signed by Zapata and sent to Vasconcelos a few hours into de la Huerta's coup d'état against Madero. See Pani, *Apuntes autobiográficos*, 170.

44. Vasconcelos, *Ulises criollo*, in *Obras completas*, 1: 415.

45. In this light the mission to London seems like a repetition of the mission to Washington, DC, with which Francisco Madero trusted Vasconcelos in 1910. Vasconcelos was supposed to serve as a liaison between the Maderista revolution and the American press, but Vasconcelos would only receive American reporters in the evening, after spending most of the day at the Library of Congress.

46. Vasconelos, *La tormenta*, in *Obras completas*, 1: 746.

47. Ibid.

48. Ibid., 747. Lord Elgin reached an agreement with the Ottoman Empire to remove these statues from the Parthenon in the early years of the nineteenth century. At the time there was already considerable opposition to what was perceived by many as an act of plundering.

49. Vasconcelos, *Ulises criollo*, in *Obras completas*, 1: 336.

50. In *The Cosmic Race* (1925)—written ten years after the visit to the British Museum and ten years before the publication of *Ulises criollo*—the cosmic race is the spiritual or aesthetic race possessed by an aesthetic instinct able to guide humanity in the convoluted, modern world.

51. In 1921 Jaime Torres Bodet became editor of *La Falange*, a journal sponsored by Vasconcelos's SEP. Beyond the vaguely fascist title that evokes a French journal admired by Torres Bodet, *La Falange* championed a decisively Arielist ideology. In the first issue and under the heading of *propósitos*, Torres Bodet announces, "In the discouragement that prevails among the Latin masses we can feel the hand of the autumnal civilization of our Anglo-Saxon rivals" (1).

52. The book, whose publication started as a serial in Spain and Cuba, was origi-

nally titled *Odiseo en Aztlán*. It was only in 1934 that Vasconcelos decided to change the title of the memoir. See Fell, "Nota filológica," in Ulises criollo, lxxii.

53. Vasconcelos, *La tormenta*, in *Obras completas*, 1: 748. Vasconcelos's reference is to the "Invincible Armada" that King Phillip II of Spain sent to conquer England in 1588. This war effort, which almost exhausted Spain's military might, ended in resounding failure and marked the beginning of England's ascendance as a European power.

54. Vasconcelos, *Ulises criollo*, in *Obras completas*, 1: 454.

55. In *The Mexican Revolution*, Alan Knight writes, "The transaction which ended the Diaz regime represented not the logical culmination of a narrow, controlled, political revolution, but rather the alarmed reaction—on the part of elites on both sides—to a mounting social upheaval" (204).

56. The text is included in *La tormenta* under the title "La convención de Aguascalientes." Vasconcelos, *Obras completas*, 1: 859–866.

57. Plan de San Luis de Potosí, in Castañeda Batres, *Revolución mexicana y constitución de 1917*, 183.

58. Vasconcelos, *La tormenta*, in *Obras completas*, 1: 678.

59. See Hegel, *Elements of the Philosophy of Right*, §14.

60. Vasconcelos, *El desastre*, in *Obras completas*, 1: 1266.

61. Sergio Pitol notes the importance of the will (*la voluntad*) in Vasconcelos's narrative: "Vasconcelos knew . . . that the will is that which opposes any reality, no matter how closed and strong that reality presumes to be." Pitol, "Liminar," in *Ulises criollo*, xxvii.

62. Magdaleno, *Las palabras perdidas*, 51.

63. I am not arguing that Vasconcelos's utopia was impractical or impossible to realize. Many developed societies rest on strong communal organizations that are quite similar to the one envisioned by Vasconcelos. However, the dynamics of capitalist modernization in the periphery is greatly at odds with this ideal.

64. The family followed Vasconcelos senior in his itinerant job as an employee of the Mexican customs office. Vasconcelos spent his infancy in five different states: Oaxaca, Chiapas, Campeche, Sonora, and Coahuila. None of these places have any important figuration in the memoirs.

65. Vasconcelos, *Ulises criollo*, in *Obras completas*, 1: 322.

66. Ibid., 333.

67. A significant passage in the 1936 preface to *La tormenta* reads, "Any full life is a vast experience, not unlike those majestic cathedrals that are a summa of the faith. There, despite their sacred character, we tolerate a corner containing some obscene images, images that are only shown to the initiate but are kept out of sight of the inexperienced visitor. Without these images, the building would lose its faithful sense of totality" (5).

68. Vasconcelos, *Ulises criollo*, in *Obras completas*, 1: 333.

69. Ibid., 335.

70. Ibid.

71. Ibid., 334.

72. For more on the *casas del pueblo,* see the section on *indigenismo* in chapter 3.

73. Vasconcelos, *Ulises criollo,* in *Obras completas,* 1: 335.

74. Ibid., 353.

75. Ibid., 358.

76. Vasconcelos, *Ulises criollo,* in *Obras completas,* 1: 359.

77. Ibid.

78. The idea that the provincial festivals had not been co-opted by the state was not a fantasy of Vasconcelos's. Commenting on celebrations of national independence, David Beezley states, "The capital city celebration . . . expressed the liberal ideas of a secular, civilian society, and the provincial one represented actual society." Beezley, *Mexican National Identity,* 74.

79. Article 39 of the liberal 1857 constitution states that sovereignty lies "originally and essentially in the people."

80. The aspiration was not to build an academy in the countryside, but to produce self-sustaining farmers and laborers. The minister is clear about the goals of education: "Let us take the farmer under our care and teach him to increase his yield one-hundredfold through better tools and better methods. This will be more important than training him in the conjugation of verbs, since, perforce, culture is a natural consequence of economic development." Quoted in Folgarait, *Mural Painting,* 17.

81. Vasconcelos, *Ulises criollo,* in *Obras completas,* 1: 333.

82. The original appearance of the Virgin of Guadalupe happened in 1531. Vasconcelos's reference to "four hundred years" is only approximate, since it would place the action in 1931: that is, at the moment he was drafting those pages.

83. The original banner with the Virgin's image that Miguel Hidalgo used as a war insignia at the onset of the revolution of independence was ordered to be transferred to the national armory in Mexico City for the celebrations surrounding the crowning of the Virgin. A day before Hidalgo's banner was to make the trip to Mexico City, it disappeared. It was found at the residence of the Archbishop of Guanajuato and from there remitted to the capital.

84. Beezley, *Mexican National Identity,* 89.

85. Ibid., 90.

86. O'Gorman, *Destierro de sombras.*

87. Meyer, *La Cristiada,* 68.

88. Villegas, *Autognosis,* 52.

89. Ibid., 63.

90. One of the few studies of this election is *José Vasconcelos y la cruzada de 1929,* by John Skirius, who documents the many fraudulent practices that affected the election. What is not conclusive, however, is if this fraud was the determining factor in the outcome of the election. Although he does not doubt the existence of widespread fraud, Mexican historian Javier Garciadiego speaks of a myth overblown by Vasconcelos's proverbial capacity for resentment. See Garciadiego, "Vasconcelos y el mito del fraude."

91. The most exhaustive study on the historical constitution of the PNR-PRI is Miguel González Compeán and Leonardo Lomeli, *El partido de la Revolución.*

92. Vasconcelos, *El proconsulado*, in *Obras completas*, 2: 1362.

93. Quoted in Villegas, *Autognosis*, 54.

94. After learning of his electoral defeat Vasconcelos fled to the United States. From there he declared himself the true president of Mexico and called for a general uprising. Despite the vehement tone of Vasconcelos's declarations to the American press, there are good reasons to doubt that he actually expected popular support for his cause.

95. Vasconelos, *El desastre*, in *Obras completas*, 1: 1365.

96. Ibid., 1366.

97. Ibid., 1367.

98. Guzmán, *Eagle and the Serpent*, 87.

99. Badiou, *The Century*, 185.

100. Krauze, "Introducción" to the 2000 Trillas edition of *La Tormenta*, 7.

101. Elena Arizmendi answered the picture that Vasconcelos painted of her in *Ulises criollo* with her book *Vida incompleta*; and later, in reference to *La tormenta*, she disputed his version of her in a letter directed to the editor of the printing house Botas. As argued by Gabriela Cano, the picture of Elena Arizmendi as a femme fatale implies an enormous simplification of Arizmendi's character. She was, among other things, the main force behind the League of Iberian and Hispano-American Women and the editor of *Feminismo Internacional*. See Cano, "Elena Arizmendi."

102. More concretely, for Badiou politics and love (along with art and the sciences) are domains where "truth procedures" appear.

103. Vasconcelos, *La tormenta*, in *Obras completas*, 1: 1012.

104. Ibid., 997.

105. See the revelatory reading of Vasconcelos's memoirs by Sylvia Molloy in *At Face Value*.

CHAPTER 5. FANTASY

1. Laplanche and Pontalis, *Vocabulaire de la psychanalyse*, 54.

2. Žižek, *Looking Awry*, 6.

3. Rancière, *Le partage du sensible*, 23–27

4. Guzmán, *Eagle and the Serpent*, 38.

5. In Guzmán the fantasy of the will shares the stage with another fantasy that is, in some sense, its exact opposite, one that presents the subject as completely offered to fate.

6. According to Isidro Fabela, Mexico pioneered the use of military airplanes. See Fabela, *Mis memorias de la revolución*, 261.

7. This translation is taken from Katz, *Life and Times of Pancho Villa*, 615. As with most *corridos*, there are several versions, as well as different *corridos* that share the same title.

8. See Klahn, "La frontera imaginada."

9. Quoted in Charlot, *Mexican Mural Renaissance*, 76.

10. In *Dream of a Sunday Afternoon in the Alameda*, Rivera depicts the skeleton of an upper-class woman flanked by Posada on the right and Rivera himself on the left. In "Revolution and the Visual Arts," Ronald Paulson observes that Rivera paints himself "as he looked at the time of Posada's innovation" to underline Posada's role in awakening Rivera's revolutionary consciousness (250).

11. There are conflicting accounts regarding Guadalupe Posada's political stances. While some people picture him as a staunch anti-Porfirist, others depict him as an admirer of President Díaz.

12. All through the twenties, Siqueiros privileged union activism over artistic engagement. He was the secretary-general of Mexico's Revolutionary Painters, Sculptors, and Engravers Union and in 1926 he even became secretary-general of the Miners Union of Jalisco. In 1931 he was sent into internal exile in the city of Taxco, where Alma Reed and Sergei Eisenstein, among others, helped organize an exhibit of his work that traveled later to Mexico City. In 1934, as the left-oriented Lázaro Cárdenas became president of Mexico, he was allowed to return from his exile. It was a short return, as Siqueiros enlisted himself as a volunteer in the international forces that fought against Francisco Franco in the Spanish Civil War. He stayed in Spain until the defeat of Republican forces in 1939.

13. Rodríguez, *History of Mexican Mural Painting*, 36.

14. Rivera painted *Creation* in encaustic, a complex and arduous technique. The muralists could not, at the beginning, master the fresco technique. Frescos existed in Mexico as decorations for *pulquerías* and other commercial establishments. But this tradition seemed lost. The technical secrets of the Italian frescos appeared even more remote and unfathomable. The muralists owned an old copy of a manual for fresco production written by Cennino Cennini, but they were never able to figure out the exact formula or even find the mentioned components in Mexico. In the end, it was the intervention of Xavier Guerrero (who, in a story permeated with national mysticism, is said to have retrieved an ancient Toltec technique of fresco painting) combined with Rivera's dexterity that allowed the muralists to create a reliable fresco technique. This struggle with the technical means of production further cemented the muralists' conviction that they were breaking down the barriers between craftsmanship and art, manual and intellectual labor. The problem that remained, however, was how to put this dexterity to an expedient political use.

15. Rodríguez, *History of Mexican Mural Painting*, 182.

16. Ibid., 186.

17. Rochfort, *Mexican Muralists*, 62.

18. The murals were commissioned by U.S. ambassador Dwight Morrow; while Calles credited him with normalizing relationships between the United States and Mexico, Vasconcelos accused him of ruining his presidential bid in 1928. The Palace of Cortés is the oldest standing civil building in the Americas. Built on top of a destroyed tribute palace of the Tlahuica culture, the surrounding area is an important archaeological site.

19. Folgarait, *Mural Painting and Social Revolution*, 101.

20. Ibid., 102.

21. In his 1997 book *Diego Rivera as Epic Modernist,* David Craven also underlines the way in which ideological options command Rivera's complex rendering of his subjects. In *Art and Revolution in Latin America,* Craven returns to his discussion of Rivera's murals in terms of a nuanced and complex construction of historical temporality.

22. Discovered in 1926 during excavations near the National Palace, the *Teocalli* is a monolith of complex symbolism that includes the iconic eagle devouring the serpent. Since the sixteenth century, when Cortés tried to legitimize his power over New Spain, the symbol has been synonymous with the city of Mexico and has appeared in several paintings and coats of arms.

23. Betty Ann Brown, "The Past Idealized," 144.

24. Eder, "Las imágenes de lo prehispánico," 81.

25. Catlin, "Political Iconography," 198.

26. Paz, *Los privilegios de la vista,* 231.

27. Goldwater, *Primitivism in Modern Art,* 1–14. The lack of psychological connection among characters is also a pervasive feature of Rivera's murals.

28. Goldwater, *Primitivism in Modern Art,* 89.

29. This is especially true of Rivera's murals at Cuernavaca. See Stanton Catlin's excellent study "Political Iconography in the Rivera Frescoes at Cuernavaca."

30. See for instance my analysis (in chapter 4) of Vasconcelos's rabid reaction to the British Museum, an episode narrated in *La tormenta.*

31. Quoted in Rodrígez, *History of Mexican Mural Painting,* 39.

32. Rubin, "Modernist Primitivism," 3–4.

33. Things appear slightly different in the case of the influence of children's painting on Mexican artists. Although Orozco scorned Alfredo Ramos Martínez's "open-air schools" in his autobiography, these popular centers of artistic formation seem to have had a considerable impact on the renovation of the Mexican artistic scene of the 1920s. Catalogs of children's paintings curated by important intellectuals—among them Paul Strand—circulated amply throughout Mexico and were sent to Europe as representative of new directions for educational development in Mexico.

34. In *Dis-agreement,* Rancière writes, "Any subjectification is a disidentification" (36).

35. Lloyd, *Irish Times,* 12.

36. Rodríguez, *History of Mexican Mural Painting,* 189.

CHAPTER 6. SYNCHRONICITY

1. "Soy porque me parezco," 182. Of course, the portrait was the dominant form of photographic activity in the nineteenth century. According to Pierre Sorlin, close to 90 percent of all the photos produced in Europe in the nineteenth century were

portraits. See Sorlin, *Les fils de Nadar.* However, the absence of a more mundane photographic register in Mexico is notorious when compared to other Latin American countries such as Brazil, Argentina, or Chile.

2. Vanderwood and Samponaro, *Border Fury*, 9. On the international journalistic coverage of the revolution, see Gautreau, "La Revolución mexicana."

3. Casasola (1874–1938) only published the first volume of the *Album histórico-gráfico.* The work as we know it today was compiled by his son Gustavo (1901–1980). All of Casasola's six children were involved in the photographic business set up by their father.

4. Manuel Ramos photographed dead bodies and horses near the Zocalo. A reproduction can be found in Berumen and Canales, *México: Fotografía y revolución*, 34–35.

5. Casasola was in the habit of erasing the names of the photographers from the negatives he bought and replacing them with his own. In *Photographing the Mexican Revolution*, John Mraz notes that Casasola seems not to have been the most active photographer in the revolutionary period and that recent research on the archive has detected photos authored by more than 350 different photographers (48). On this point, see Gautreau, "La ilustración semanal."

6. The absence of state censorship—when the subject was not of the state itself—greatly facilitated the task of photographers. As John Mraz comments, unlike the First World War, where commanders restricted photographers' access to the front, in Mexico, "All the *caudillos* understood the importance of projecting themselves and their movements visually." *Photographing the Mexican Revolution*, 13.

7. Debroise, *Mexican Suite*, 177.

8. In "Nuestras artes populares," Salvador Novo comments on the strange economy by which the recently acquired icons of Mexican race and nationality are perceived as pinnacles of artistic expression by illustrious visitors.

9. Weston, *Daybooks*, 57.

10. Mraz, *Photographing the Mexican Revolution*, 13.

11. Tellingly, this apparently secondary scene provides the still for the film's poster and the cover of all subsequent reproductions.

12. Leduc coalesces in one shot what, according to Reed, was a long photographic session that included Urbina's wife and mother as well as one of his sons, who was holding the banner. See Reed, *Insurgent Mexico*, 39.

13. This ontological function of photography has nothing to do with André Bazin's argument that photography is a modern equivalent of the memento mori (see "The Ontology of the Photographic Image") or with Susan Sontag's association of photography and death in *On Photography.* The object of the ontological function is not so much lost as inexistent. Carlos Monsiváis comments on this aspect of Mexican photography in "Notas sobre la historia de la fotografía": "Even the most avant-garde Mexican photographers are possessed by an expressive anguish that we can call 'ontological'" (21).

14. Canales, "La densa materia de la historia," 56.

15. Ibid., 57.

16. *La Ilustración Semanal* published over one thousand photos of the revolutionary war between 1913 and 1915.

17. In the history of photography, this tension between subject and context gave origin to two different schools in relationship to the portrait: one called for the isolation of the subject from all surrounding elements; the other deemed it impossible to define a subject except for the mundane attributes that belonged intrinsically to him or her. Richard Avedon is a representative of the first position, while Arnold Newman, who coined the expression "environmental portrait," is a representative of the second.

18. In Barthes's theorization—which is heavily influenced by Lacanian psychoanalysis—these areas of failed subjectivization are also and paradoxically where the possibility of a subject figures intensely. See Barthes, *Camera Lucida*.

19. In *Seeing Mexico Photographed,* Leonard Folgarait provides an extensive analysis of one photo by Agustín Casasola in which people from different conditions and social classes informally pose against the background of a train.

20. My reference is to §§15–18 of Heidegger, *Being and Time*.

21. Sorlin, *Les fils de Nadar,* 36.

22. Weston, *Daybooks,* 135. See also Monsiváis, *Maravillas que son*.

23. Monsiváis, *Maravillas que son,* 5.

24. The photo in question, widely reproduced, shows Zapata in dark clothes holding a rifle in his right hand while his left rest on a sword's hilt. Inv. # 6364, Fondo Casasola, SINAFO-Fototeca Nacional del INAH.

25. Mariana Figarella makes the case for Brehme as a pictorialist in *Edward Weston y Tina Modotti en México*: see pages 59–60. Aurelio de los Reyes objects to this view in the foreword to the book.

26. Of the thirty million pictures taken in the United States between 1840 and 1860, 95 percent were portraits. See Heine, *Photography,* 23.

27. To remain closer to the letter of Rancière's text, we should say that while photography always aims to picture a distribution of the sensible as a naturalized and shared form of perception, the demand to photograph a revolution turns this simple distribution into a redistribution.

28. The almost iconic nature of Modotti's life explains why so many critical analyses are, to an important extent, mixed with or completely tilted to the biographical. Christiane Barckhausen won the Premio Literario Casa de las Américas with an exhaustive biography in 1988 (*Verdad y leyenda de Tina Modotti*). Equally biographical are Elena Poniatowska's text *Tinísima* and Margaret Hooks's *Tina Modotti*. The 1982 exhibition of Modotti's photos at the Whitechapel Art Gallery in London was the occasion for a short piece composed by Laura Mulvey and Peter Wollen and contained in the catalog *Frida Kahlo and Tina Modotti,* of which a video version also exists.

29. Figarella, *Edward Weston y Tina Modotti,* 184.

30. Quoted in Nieto Sotelo and Lozano Álvarez, *Tina Modotti,* 29, 61.

31. Folgarait, *Seeing Mexico Photographed,* 5–7.

32. Mora, *Mexican Cinema,* 40.

33. The unrealistic unity of many films of this period reflects the heterogeneous nature of the film-going public. For an overview of the study of audiences in Mexican film, see Patricia Martín, "La recepción del cine mexicano." A more historically circumscribed study can be found in María Luisa Amador, "La exhibición en México." For the internationalization of Mexican film, see Robert McKee Irwin and Maricruz Castro Ricalde, *Global Mexican Cinema*. Also of interest is the already classic collection of essays *A través del espejo*, edited by Carlos Monsiváis and Carlos Bonfil.

34. De los Reyes writes, "From the moment cinema arrived in Mexico, intellectuals linked it to the illustrated press and, following the positivist spirit of the era, to science." De los Reyes, "Silent Cinema," 65.

35. De los Reyes notices that while under Porfirism filmmakers "avoided . . . disagreeable aspects of reality," the triumph of the Maderista revolution elicited a tide of "workers strikes" movies that became a sensation in Mexico City. See de los Reyes, *Cine y sociedad en México*, 118.

36. "Cinema documented real events and informed the public." De los Reyes, "Silent Cinema," 69.

37. Ibid.

38. By 1911 the Alva brothers had premiered *Insurrección en México*, a chronicle of Madero's ascension to power.

39. Juan Bustillo Oro's debut *Dos monjes* (1934) plays with German expressionism and includes camera distortions to reflect the slow decline in the rational power of one of its protagonists. Carlos Mérida has left a scene-by-scene account of three films by Emilio Amero, *Desolación* (based on a text by Federico García Lorca); *3-3-3* (made with Gilberto Owen); and *Río sin tacto*. (The exact dates of these films remain uncertain.) The Filmoteca at UNAM is now restoring several recently discovered short experimental films. See Rangel and López Ibañez, "La influencia de expresionismo alemán."

40. Mora, *Mexican Cinema*, 31.

41. Eisenstein's unfinished movie has attracted considerable critical attention over the years. However, few of these texts add to the extensive research undertaken in the late 1960s by Harry Geduld and Ronald Gottesman, who coauthored *Sergei Eisenstein and Upton Sinclair*. More recently, Masha Salazkina's *In Excess* extensively documents the different stages in the production of the film. Zuzana Pick offers an up-to-date discussion of the movie and puts it in dialogue with the Mexican culture of the 1930s in chapter 4 of *Constructing the Image of the Mexican Revolution*. An excellent video from CONACULTA—*Eisenstein en México* (1996), directed by Alejandro Islas—is one of the most insightful commentaries on the meaning of Eisenstein's trip to Mexico for the filmmaker and for the future of Mexican cinema. Also historical in nature is Aurelio de los Reyes's fine book *El nacimiento de ¡Que viva México!*

42. See Berg, "Cinematic Invention of Mexico."

43. Best Maugard, *La mancha de sangre* (1937). For a long time, only a few scenes were in public circulation, but the film was recently rescued by the Mexican Cineteca and is now available online.

44. The prologue was to be dedicated to Siqueiros; "Sandunga" to Jean Charlot; "Maguey" to Diego Rivera; "Soldadera" to José Clemente Orozco; and the epilogue to José Guadalupe Posada. Eisenstein, however, often found more affinities with other artists one degree removed from the center of revolutionary politics such as Manuel Álvarez Bravo and the Guatemalan painter Carlos Mérida.

45. In this sense the opening of the film, which shows the profiles of Mexicans with indigenous features superimposed against ancient pyramids, can be slightly misleading. A variety of authors have noticed a certain exoticism in chapters like "Sandunga." (See, for instance, Laura Podalsky's treatment of the movie in "Patterns of the Primitive.") While Eisenstein's views on indigenous people do reveal some points of contact with the scientific *indigenismo* of the time, the overall movement of his symphonic film points to an increasing coevalness of the popular with the historical moment of its (intended) reception.

46. The Mexican blockbuster of 1933, *Juárez y Maximiliano,* directed by Miguel Contreras and Rafael Sevilla, featured an exalted vision of Carlota and Maximilian.

47. "The *hacendado* Mendoza, in his cynical manipulation of both sides, represents the newly emerging postrevolutionary bourgeoisie that replaced the Porfirian aristocracy, but which in its principles differed little from the deposed elite." Mora, *Mexican Cinema,* 40.

48. Mraz, *Looking for Mexico,* 235.

49. Noble, *Mexican National Cinema,* 55.

50. While Andrea Noble correctly points out that the trilogy is made up of personal dilemmas, she closes off the topic prematurely by reducing the tension of these lives to a metaphor of the revolution at large.

51. It is not obvious, however, why presenting the action of the film twice removed from reality could placate in any way the alleged discomfort of the army with the movie.

52. As the credits appear at the start of the movie, de Fuentes masterfully introduces each of the main characters through a shot that reveals the inner truth of their subjective condition in the movie: ambivalence in Mendoza, fright in Dolores, naive idiocy in Nieto.

53. The institutional history of *Vámonos* also complicates the reading of the film as oppositional to the government. The government subsidized the film through the financial assistance offered to the CLASA studios—equipped with state-of-the-art technology that included the latest in sound synchronization and rear projection—and even rescued CLASA with one million pesos after de Fuentes's costly movie bankrupted the studio.

54. The intellectual silence around Francisco Villa began to be pierced by Nellie Campobello with the publications of *Cartucho* (1931) and *Las manos de mamá* (1937).

55. The report by A. Margo for the Latin American News Association, dated 1916, is partially reproduced by Miguel Berumen in *Pancho Villa,* 48.

56. See Pick, *Constructing the Image,* 88–92.

57. For a comprehensive study of the construction of feminine roles in early Mexican cinema, see Tuñón, *Mujeres de luz y sombra.*

58. No doubt the most emblematic character here is that of the "mute" in *El compadre Mendoza*. The *muda* is the classic melodramatic domestic maid who observes all and weighs everything. She knows of the plot to kill Nieto (she has read the lips of Mendoza and Bernáldez as they finalize the details of the assassination) and silently confronts Mendoza with his guilt.

59. Mora, *Mexican Cinema*, 47.

60. Interview in *El Universal*, 8 April 1934.

61. James Krippner's *Paul Strand in Mexico* included a copy of *Redes*.

62. Most of what is known about *Redes* comes from Krippner's meticulously documented "The Making of *Redes*," included in *Paul Strand in Mexico*, 69–95.

63. De los Reyes, *Manuel Gamio y el cine*. Gamio's ethnographic films were very short productions. Gamio himself was responsible for a narrative film, *Rebelión*, that he referred to as ethnographic although it was, by all accounts, a fictional film. See Florescano, *El patrimonio cultural de Mexico*, 276.

64. In 1935 Carlos Navarro released *Janitzio*, which contains a thematic—and even filmic—treatment quite close to that of Strand and Zinnemann's movie.

65. Krippner, *Paul Strand in Mexico*, 70.

66. Quoted in Krippner, *Paul Strand in Mexico*, 76.

67. Morales, "Spanish for Your Mexican Visit," 254.

Works Cited

GENERAL WORKS

Acevedo, Jesús. *Disertaciones de un arquitecto*. Mexico City: Instituto Nacional de Bellas Artes, 1967.

Agamben, Giorgio. *Homo Sacer: Sovereign Power and Bare Life*. Translated by Daniel Heller-Roazen. Stanford, CA: Stanford University Press, 1998.

Aguilar Camín, Héctor. *La frontera nómada: Sonora y la Revolución mexicana*. Mexico City: Cal y Arena, 1997.

———, and Lorenzo Meyer. *In the Shadow of the Mexican Revolution: Contemporary Mexican History, 1910–1989*. Translated by Luis Alberto Fierro. Austin: University of Texas Press, 1993.

Aguilar Mora, Jorge. *Una muerte justa, sencilla, eternal: Cultura y guerra durante la Revolución mexicana*. Mexico City: Ediciones Era, 1990.

Aguirre Beltrán, Gonzalo. *Formas de gobierno indígena*. Mexico City: Universidad Nacional Autónoma de México, 1953.

Amador, María Luisa. "La exhibición en México, 1930–1970." *Alteridades* 22, no. 44: 35–48.

Arendt, Hannah. *Lectures on Kant's Political Philosophy*. Chicago: University of Chicago Press, 1982.

Arizmendi, Elena. *Vida incompleta: Ligeros apuntes sobre mujeres en la vida real*. New York: Danon, 1927.

Atl, Dr. *Gentes profanas en el convento*. Mexico City: Ediciones Botas, 1950.

———. *Las artes populares en México*. Mexico City: Cultura, 1921.

Azuela, Mariano. *The Underdogs: A Story of the Mexican Revolution*. Translated by Enrique Munguía. London: Signet Classics, 2008.

Azuela de la Cueva, Alicia. *Arte y poder: Renacimiento artístico y revolución social México, 1910–1945*. Mexico City: El Colegio de Michoacan-FCE, 2005.

Baca Barajas, Gandhi. "Prensa, quehacer cultural y lo mexicano durante el primer año de gobierno de Alvaro Obregón." PhD diss., Universidad Nacional Autónoma de México, 2002.

Badiou, Alain. *The Century*. Translated by Alberto Toscano. Cambridge, MA: Polity Press, 2007.

Bailey, David C. "Revisionism and the Recent Historiography of the Mexican Revolution." *Hispanic American Review* 58, no. 1: 62–79.

Bakhtin, Mikhail. *The Dialogic Imagination: Four Essays*. Translated by Michael Holquist and Caryl Emerson. Austin: University of Texas Press, 1981.

———. *Speech Genres and Other Late Essays*. Translated by Vern W. McGee. Austin: University of Texas Press, 1986.

Bantjes, Adrian. "Burning Saints, Molding Minds: Iconoclasm, Civic Ritual, and the Failed Cultural Revolution." In *Rituals of Rule, Rituals of Resistance: Public Celebrations and Popular Culture in Mexico*, edited by William Beezley, Cheryl English Martin, and William E. French, 261–294. Wilimington, DE: Scholarly Resources, 1994.

Barckhausen, Christiane. *Verdad y leyenda de Tina Modotti*. Havana: Casa de las Américas, 1989.

Barthes, Roland. *Camera Lucida: Reflections on Photography*. New York: Hill and Wang, 1981.

———. *Image, Music, Text*. Translated by Stephen Heath. New York: Hill and Wang, 1977.

———. *Mythologies*. Translated by A. Lavers. New York: Simon and Schuster, 1972.

———. *The Pleasure of the Text*. Translated by R. Howard. New York: Hill and Wang, 1975.

Bazant, Mílada. "Lecturas del Porfiriato." In *Historia de la lectura en México: Seminario de historia de la educación en México*, 205–242. Mexico City: Ediciones del Ermitaño, 1988.

Bazin, André. "The Ontology of the Photographic Image." *Film Quarterly* 13, no. 4 (Summer 1960): 4–9.

Beezley, William H. *Mexican National Identity: Memory, Innuendo, and Popular Culture*. Tucson: University of Arizona Press, 2008.

———, Cheryl English Martin, and William E. French, eds. *Rituals of Rule, Rituals of Resistance: Public Celebrations and Popular Culture in Mexico*. Wilmington, DE: Scholarly Resources, 1994.

———, and David E. Lorey, eds. *Viva Mexico! Viva la Independencia! Celebrations of September 16*. Wilmington, DE: Scholarly Resources, 2001.

Bendersky, Joseph. *Carl Schmitt: Theorist for the Reich*. Princeton, NJ: Princeton University Press, 1983.

Benjamin, Thomas. *La Revolución: Mexico's Great Revolution as Memory, Myth, and History*. Austin: University of Texas Press, 1999.

Benjamin, Walter. *Illuminations*. Translated by H. Zohn. New York: Schocken Books, 1968.

Berg, Charles Ramírez. "The Cinematic Invention of Mexico: The Poetics and Politics of the Fernández-Figueroa Style." In *The Mexican Cinema Project*, edited by

Chon A. Noriega and Steven Ricci, 13–24. Los Angeles: UCLA Film and Television Archive, 1994.
Berumen, Miguel Angel. *Pancho Villa: La construcción del mito*. Mexico City: Océano, 2006.
———, ed. *México: Fotografía y revolución*. Mexico City: Lundwer-Televisa, 2010.
Beverley, John. *Against Literature*. Minneapolis: University of Minnesota Press, 1993.
Boas, Franz. *The Mind of Primitive Man*. New York: McMillan, 1917.
Bonfil Batalla, Guillermo. *El país de las tandas: Teatro de Revistas, 1900–1940*. Mexico City: Secretaría de Educación Pública, 1984.
———, ed. *Mi pueblo durante la revolución: Un ejercicio de memoria popular*. 3 vols. Mexico City: Instituto Nacional de Antropología e Historia, 1985.
Borch-Jacobsen, Mikkel. *Lacan: The Absolute Master*. Translated by D. Brick. Stanford, CA: Stanford University Press, 1991.
Brading, David. "Manuel Gamio and Official Indigenismo in Mexico." *Bulletin of Latin American Research* 7, no. 1: 75–89.
———. *Mito y profecía en la historia de México*. Mexico City: Fondo de Cultura Económica, 1997.
———. *Octavio Paz y la poética de la historia mexicana*. Mexico City: Fondo de Cultura Económica, 2002.
Bradú, Fabrienne. *Antonieta*. Mexico City: Fondo de Cultura Económica, 2000.
Brenner, Anita. *Idols behind Altars*. New York: Payson and Clarke, 1929.
Britton, John. "Moisés Sáenz: Nacionalista mexicano." *Historia Mexicana* 22, no. 1: 77–97.
Brizuela, Natalia. *Fotografia e império: Paisagens por um Brasil moderno*. São Paulo: Companhia das Letras, 2012.
Brown, Betty Ann. "The Past Idealized: Diego Rivera's Use of Pre-Columbian Imagery." In *Diego Rivera: A Retrospective*, edited by C. N. Helms, 139–155. New York: Norton, 1985.
Brown, Wendy. *Walled States, Waning Sovereignty*. New York: Zone Books, 2010.
Bryan, Susan E. "Teatro popular y sociedad durante el porfiriato." In *Cultura, ideas y mentalidades: Lecturas de historia mexicana*, edited by A. Solange. Mexico City: Colegio de México, 1992.
Burke, Edmund. *Reflections on the Revolution in France*. Edited by Connor Cruise O'Brien. New York: Penguin, 1983.
Cabrera, Luis. "La revolución es (la) revolución." In *Luis Cabrera: Teórico y crítico de la revolución*, edited by Eugenia Mayer. Mexico City: Secretaría de Educación Pública, 1927.
———. *Obras completas*. 2 vols. Mexico City: Oasis, 1975.
Campobello, Nellie. *Cartucho: Relatos de la lucha en el norte de México*. Mexico City: Ediciones Era, 2000 [1931].
Canales, Claudia. "La densa materia de la historia." In *México: Fotografía y revolución*, edited by Miguel Ángel Berumen, 51–118. Mexico City: CONACULTA, 2010.
Cañizares-Esguerra, Jorge. *How to Write the History of the New World: Histories, Epis-*

temologies, and Identities in the Eighteenth-Century Atlantic World. Stanford, CA: Stanford University Press, 2001.

Cano, Gabriela. "Elena Arizmendi: Una habitación propia en Nueva York, 1916–1938." *Arenal* 18, no. 1: 85–114.

———. "Unconcealable Realities of Desire: Amelio Robles's (Transgender) Masculinity in the Mexican Revolution." In *Sex in Revolution: Gender, Politics, and Power in Modern Mexico*, edited by Jocelyn Olcott and Mary K. Vaughan, 35–56. Durham, NC: Duke University Press, 2006.

Carbo, Teresa. *Los indígenas debatidos y legislados: La educación indígena en la cámara de diputados, 1920–1969*. Mexico City: Centro de Investigaciones y Estudios Superiores en Antropología Social, 1982.

Carr, Barry. *El movimiento obrero y la política en México, 1910–1929*. Mexico City: Secretaría de Educación Pública, 1976.

Carranza, Luis E. *Architecture as Revolution: Episodes in the History of Modern Mexico*. Austin: University of Texas Press, 2010.

Casasola, Gustavo. *Historia gráfica de la Revolución mexicana*. Mexico City: Trillas, 1960.

Caso, Alfonso, ed. *Métodos y resultados de la política indigenista*. Mexico City: Memorias del Instituto Nacional Indigenista, 1954.

Castañeda Batres, Oscar. *Revolución mexicana y constitución de 1917*. Mexico City: Porrúa, 1989.

Castellanos, Rosario. *La novela mexicana contemporánea y su valor testimonial*. Mexico City: Instituto Nacional de la Juventud Mexicana, 1965.

———. *Oficio de tinieblas*. New York: Penguin, 1982.

Castro, Carlo Antonio. *Los hombres verdaderos*. Xalapa: Universidad Veracruzana, 1959.

Castro Leal, Antonio. *La novela de la Revolución mexicana*. Mexico City: Aguilar, 1971.

Catlin, Stanton L. "Political Iconography in the Diego Rivera Frescoes at Cuernavaca." In *Art and Architecture in the Service of Politics*, edited by Henry A. Millon and Linda Nochlin, 194–215. Cambridge: Cambridge University Press, 1978.

Charlot, Jean. *The Mexican Mural Renaissance, 1920–1925*. New York: Hacker Art Books, 1980.

Chatterjee, Partha. "Sovereign Violence and the Domain of the Political." In *Sovereign Bodies: Citizens, Migrants, and States in the Postcolonial World*, edited by Thomas Hanson and Finn Stepputat, 82–100. Princeton, NJ: Princeton University Press, 2005.

Chytry, Joseph. *The Aesthetic State: A Quest in Modern German Thought*. Berkeley: University of California Press, 1989.

Clifford, James. *The Predicament of Culture: Twentieth-Century Ethnography, Literature, and Art*. Cambridge, MA: Harvard University Press, 1988.

Conn, Robert. *The Politics of Philology: Alfonso Reyes and the Invention of the Latin American Literary Tradition*. Lewisburg, PA: Bucknell University Press, 2002.

Connolly, William. *Democracy, Pluralism, and Political Theory*. London and New York: Routledge, 2008.

Contreras Vaccaro, Roberto. "Identidad urbana y folklore." *Urbano* 4, no. 4: 8–11.

Córdova, Arnaldo. *La ideología de la Revolución mexicana: La formación del nuevo régimen*. Mexico City: Instituto de Investigaciones Sociales/Universidad Nacional Autónoma de México, 1985.

———. *La revolución en crisis: La aventura del maximato*. Mexico City: Cal y Arena, 1995.

Cosío Villegas, Daniel. *Memorias*. Mexico City: Joaquín Moritz, 1976.

Craven, David. *Art and Revolution in Latin America, 1910–1990*. New Haven, CT: Yale University Press, 2002.

———. *Diego Rivera as Epic Modernist*. New York: G. K. Hall, 1997.

Dallal, Alberto. "El nacionalismo prolongado: El movimiento mexicano de danza moderna, 1940–1955." *Estudios de Arte y Estética* 25: 297–345.

Davis, Diane. "El rumbo de la esfera pública: Influencias locales, nacionales e internacionales en la urbanización del centro de la ciudad de México, 1910–1950." In *Actores, espacios y debates en la historia de la esfera pública en la ciudad de México*, edited by Cristina Sacristán and Pablo Picatto, 233–271. México: Instituto Mora, 2005.

———. *Urban Leviathan: Mexico City in the Twentieth Century*. Philadelphia: Temple University Press, 1994.

Dawson, Alexander. *Indian and Nation in Revolutionary Mexico*. Tucson: University of Arizona Press, 2004.

De Anda Alanis, Enrique. *La arquitectura de la Revolución mexicana: Corrientes y estilos en la decada de los 20*. Mexico City: Universidad Nacional Autónoma de México, 1988.

Debroise, Olivier. *Mexican Suite: A History of Photography in Mexico*. Austin: University of Texas Press, 2001.

De Carolis, Massimo. "Toward a Phenomenology of Opportunism." In *Radical Thought in Italy: A Potential Politics*, edited by Paolo Virno and Michael Hardt, 37–52. Minneapolis: University of Minnesota Press, 1996.

de la Vega Alfaro, Eduardo. "Alvarez Bravo, stillman o la génesis de una estética." In *Gabriel Figueroa: Travesías de una Mirada*, by Gabriel Figueroa et al., 31–52. Mexico City: CONACULTA, 2008.

Deleuze, Gilles, and Félix Guattari. *What Is Philosophy?* Translated by Hugh Tomlinson and Graham Burchel. New York: Columbia University Press, 1994.

De María y Campos, Armando. *El teatro de género chico en la Revolución mexicana*. Mexico City: Biblioteca del Instituto Nacional de Estudios Históricos de la Revolución Mexicana, 1956.

Derrida, Jacques. *Acts of Literature*. Translated by Dereck Attridge. New York: Routledge, 1992.

———. *On the Name*. Edited by Thomas Dutoit and translated by David Wood, John P. Leavy Jr., and Ian McLeod. Stanford, CA: Stanford University Press, 1995.

———. *Politics of Friendship*. Translated by George Collins. London: Verso, 2005.

———. *Rogues: Two Essays on Reason*. Translated by Pascale-Anne Brault and Michael Naas. Stanford, CA: Stanford University Press, 2005.

———. *Specters of Marx: The State of the Debt, the Work of Mourning, and the New International*. Translated by P. Kamuf. New York: Routledge, 2012.

Díaz y de Ovando, Clementina. "Las fiestas del 'Año del Centenario': 1921." In *México: Independencia y soberanía*, 103–187. Mexico City: Archivo General de la Nación, 1996.

Eder, Rita. "Las imágenes de lo prehispánico y su significación en el debate del nacionalismo cultural." In *El nacionalismo y el arte mexicano*. Mexico City: Universidad Nacional Autónoma de México, 1986.

Escobar, Ticio. *El mito del arte y el mito del pueblo: Cuestiones sobre arte popular*. Asunción, Paraguay: Peroni/Museo del Barro, 1986.

Espinosa Medrano, Juan. *Apologético*. Caracas: Biblioteca Ayacucho, 1982.

Fabela, Isidro. *Mis memorias de la Revolución*. Mexico City: Editorial Jus, 1977.

Faber, Sebastiaan. "Don Alfonso o la fuerza del sino: Reyes, la cultura latinoamericana y la defensa de la distinción." In *Alfonso Reyes y los estudios literarios latinoamericanos*, edited by Adelan Pineda and Ignacio Sánchez Prado, 15–49. Pittsburgh: Iberoamericana, 2004.

Fabian, Johannes. *Time and the Other: How Anthropology Makes Its Object*. New York: Columbia University Press, 1983.

Fell, Claude. "Introducción del coordinador" and "Nota filológica preliminar." In *Ulises criollo*, edited by Claude Fell, xxxv–lxv, lxvii–lxxxiv. San José: Archivos/Universidad de Costa Rica, 2000.

———. *José Vasconcelos: Los años del águila, 1920–1925: Educación, cultura e iberoamericanismo en el México postrevolucionario*. Mexico City: Universidad Nacional Autónoma de México, 1989.

———. "Théâtre et société dans le Mexique post-révolutionnaire." *Etudes et Documents: Université de Rennes-Klinskied* 2: 47–68.

Figarella, Mariana. *Edward Weston y Tina Modotti en México*. Mexico City: Universidad Nacional Autónoma de México, 2002.

Florescano, Enrique. *El nuevo pasado mexicano*. Mexico City: Cal y Arena, 2009.

———, ed. *El patrimonio cultural de Mexico*. Mexico City: Fondo de Cultura Económica, 2010.

———. *Espejo mexicano*. Mexico City: Biblioteca Mexicana de la Fundación Miguel Alemán, 2002.

———. *Etnia, estado y nación: Ensayo sobre las identidades colectivas en México*. Mexico City: Aguilar, 1997.

———. *Memoria mexicana*. Mexico City: Fondo de Culura Económica, 2006.

Folgarait, Leonard. *Mural Painting and Social Revolution in Mexico, 1920–1940: Art of the New Order*. New York: Cambridge University Press, 1998.

———. *Seeing Mexico Photographed: The Work of Horne, Casasola, Modotti, and Álvarez Bravo*. New Haven, CT: Yale University Press, 2008.

Furet, François. *Interpreting the French Revolution*. Translated by E. Forster. Cambridge: Cambridge University Press, 1981.

Gabara, Esther. *Errant Modernism: The Ethos of Photography in Mexico and Brazil*. Durham, NC: Duke University Press, 2008.

Gallo, Rubén. *Mexican Modernity: The Avant-Garde and the Technological Revolution*. Cambridge, MA: MIT University Press, 2005.

Gamboa, Federico. *Diario*. Mexico City: Ediciones Botas, 1932.

Gamio, Manuel. *Forjando patria*. Mexico City: Editorial Porrúa, 1960.

Garciadiego, Javier. "Vasconcelos y el mito del fraude en la campaña electoral de 1929." *Memorias de las revoluciones en México* 10: 8–31.

Garro, Elena. *Recollections of Things to Come*. Translated by Ruth L. C. Simms. University of Texas Press, 1969.

Gautreau, Marion. "La ilustración semanal y el Archivo Casasola: Una aproximación a la desmitificación de la fotografía de la Revolución mexicana." *Cuicuilco* 14, no. 41: 113–142.

———. "La Revolución mexicana a los ojos del mundo: Diferentes perspectivas en la prensa ilustrada." In *México: Fotografía y revolución*, edited by Miguel Ángel Berumen, 119–178. Mexico City: CONACULTA, 2010.

Geduld, Harry, and Ronald Gottesman. *Sergei Eisenstein and Upton Sinclair: The Making and Unmaking of ¡Que viva Mexico!* Bloomington: Indiana University Press, 1970.

Giraudo, Laura. "De la ciudad 'mestiza' al campo 'indígena': Internados indígenas en el México posrevolucionario y en Bolivia." *Anuario de Estudios Americanos* 67, no. 2: 519–547.

Goldwater, Robert John. *Primitivism in Modern Art*. New York: Vintage Books, 1966.

Gómez Morín, Manuel. *1915 y otros ensayos*. Mexico City: Editorial Jus, 1973.

González Casanova, Pablo. *La democracia en México*. Avena, Mexico: Ediciones Era, 1965.

González Compeán, Miguel, and Leonardo Lomeli, eds. *El partido de la Revolución: Institución y conflict, 1928–1999*. Mexico City: Fondo de Cultura Económica, 2003.

González Gamio, Ángeles. *Manuel Gamio: Una lucha sin final*. Mexico City: Universidad Nacional Autónoma de México, 2003.

Gonzalez Gortázar, Fernando, ed. *La arquitectura en México en el siglo 20*. Mexico City: CONACULTA, 2004.

Graue, Federico E. *La noche mexicana en los lagos del bosque de Chapultepec: Septiembre 26 de 1921*. Mexico City: Comité Ejecutivo de las Fiestas del Centenario, 1921.

Gruening, Ernest. *Mexico and Its Heritage*. New York: Century, 1928.

Guedea, Virginia. *Asedios a los centenarios, 1910–1921*. Mexico City: Fondo de Cultura Económica, 2009.

Guha, Ranajit. *Elementary Aspects of Peasant Insurgency in Colonial India*. Durham, NC: Duke University Press, 1999.

———. "The Prose of Counter-Insurgency." In *Selected Subaltern Studies*, edited by Ranajit Guha and Gayatri Chakravorty Spivak, 45–87. New York: Oxford University Press, 1988.

Guzmán, Martín Luis. *The Eagle and the Serpent*. Translated by Harriet de Onís. Garden City, NY: Dolphin Books, 1965.

Hegel, George Wilhelm Friedrich. *Aesthetics: Lectures on Fine Arts*. Translated by Malcom Knox. Oxford: Oxford University Press, 1977.

———. *Elements of the Philosophy of Right*. Translated by H. B. Nisbet. Cambridge: Cambridge University Press, 1965.

Heidegger, Martin. *Being and Time*. New York: Harper, 1962.

Heine, Florian. *Photography: The Groundbreaking Moments*. Munich: Prestel, 1990.

Henríquez Ureña, Pedro. *Estudios mexicanos*. México City: Fondo de Cultura Económica, 2004.

———. "La cultura de las humanidades." In *Conferencias del Ateneo de juventud*. Mexico City: Universidad Nacional Autónoma de México, 1962.

———. *La utopía de América*. Caracas: Biblioteca Ayacucho, 1978.

Herrera, Hayden. *Frida: A Biography of Frida Kahlo*. New York: Harper and Row, 1983.

———. *Frida Kahlo: The Paintings*. New York: HarperCollins, 1991.

Hobsbawm, Eric. *The Age of Revolution, 1789–1848*. New York: Vintage, 1996.

———. "Revolution." In *Revolution in History*, edited by Roy Porter and M. Teich, 5–39. Cambridge: Cambridge University Press, 1986.

Hooks, Margaret. *Tina Modotti: Photographer and Revolutionary*. London: Pandora, 1993.

Hu-DeHart, Evelyn. "Sonora: Indians and Immigrants on a Developing Frontier." In *Other Mexicos: Essays on Regional Mexican History, 1876–1911*, edited by Thomas Benjamin and William McNellie, 87–99. Albuquerque: University of New Mexico Press, 1984.

Iduarte, Andrés. *Un niño en la Revolución mexicana*. Second edition. Mexico City: Obregón, 1954.

Irwin, Robert McKee, and Maricruz Castro Ricalde. *Global Mexican Cinema: Its Golden Age*. London: Palgrave Macmillan, 2013.

Islas, Alejandra. *Eisenstein en México: El círculo eterno*. Mexico City: CONACULTA, 1997.

Joseph, Gilbert M. *Revolution from Without: Yucatán, Mexico, and the United States, 1880–1924*. Durham, NC: Duke University Press, 1988.

———, and Daniel Nugent, eds. *Everyday Forms of State Formation: Revolution and the Negotiation of Rule in Modern Mexico*. Durham, NC: Duke University Press, 1994.

Kant, Immanuel. *Critique of Judgment*. Translated by W. S. Pluhar. Indianapolis and Cambridge: Hackett, 1987.

Kantorowicz, Ernst. *The King's Two Bodies: A Study in Medieval Political Theology*. Princeton, NJ: Princeton University Press, 1957.

Katz, Friedrich. *The Life and Times of Pancho Villa*. Stanford, CA: Stanford University Press, 1998.

Katzman, Israel. *La arquitectura contemporánea mexicana*. Mexico City: Instituto Nacional de Antropología e Historia, 1964.

Kelley, Jane Holden. *Yaqui Women: Contemporary Life Histories*. Lincoln: University of Nebraska Press, 1991.

Klahn, Norma. "La frontera imaginada, inventada o de la geopolítica de la literatura a la nada." In *Mitos en las relaciones México–Estados Unidos*, edited by Ma. Esther Schumacher, 460–480. Mexico City: Fondo de Cultura Económica/Secretaría de Relaciones Exteriors, 1994.

Knight, Alan. "Frank Tannenbaum and the Mexican Revolution." *International Labor and Working-Class History* 77, no. 1: 134–153.

———. *Interpreting the Mexican Revolution*. Austin: Institute for Latin American Studies, University of Texas, 1988.

———. *The Mexican Revolution*. Lincoln: University of Nebraska Press, 1990.

———. "Weapons and Arches in the Mexican Revolutionary Landscape." In *Everyday Forms of State Formation*, edited by Gilbert M. Joseph and Daniel Nugent, 24–67. Durham, NC: Duke University Press, 1994.

Krauze, Enrique. *Caudillos culturales en la Revolución mexicana*. Mexico City: Siglo XXI, 1976.

———. "Introducción." In *La tormenta*, by José Vasconcelos. Mexico City: Trillas, 1998.

———. *Mexico: Biography of Power: A History of Modern Mexico, 1810–1996*. Translated by Hank Heifetz. New York: HarperCollins, 1997.

Krippner, James. *Paul Strand in Mexico*. Mexico City: Fundación Televisa, 2010.

Lacan, Jacques. *Seminar I: Freud's Papers on Technique*. Translated by J. Forrester and edited by Jacques Alain Miller. New York: Norton, 1979.

Lacy, Elaine. "The 1921 Centennial Celebration of Mexico's Independence: State Building and Popular Negotiation." In *Viva Mexico! Viva la Independencia! Celebrations of September 16*, edited by William H. Beezley and David E. Lorey, 199–232. Wilmington, DE: Scholarly Resources, 2001.

Laplanche, Jean, and J-B Pontalis. *Vocabulaire de la psychanalyse*. Paris: Presses Universitaires de la France, 2007.

Lazo, Carlos. *Pensamiento y destino de la Ciudad Universitaria*. Mexico City: Editorial Porrúa, 1952.

Lefebvre, Henri. *The Production of Space*. Cambridge, MA: Blackwell, 1991.

Legrás, Horacio. *Literature and Subjection: The Economy of Writing and Marginality in Latin America*. Pittsburgh: University of Pittsburgh Press, 2008.

———. "Martín Luis Guzmán: El viaje de la Revolución." *Modern Language Notes* 118, no. 2: 427–454.

Lempérière, Annick. "Los dos centenarios de la independencia mexicana: 1910–1921." *Historia Mexicana* (October–December 1995): 321–337.

Lloyd, David. *Irish Times: Temporalities of Modernity*. Dublin: Field Day, 2008.

———. "Nationalism against the State." In *The Politics of Culture in the Shadow of Capital*, edited by Lisa Lowe and David Lloyd, 173–196. Durham, NC: Duke University Press, 1997.

Lomnitz, Claudio. *Death and the Idea of Mexico*. New York: Zone Books, 2008.

———. *Deep Mexico, Silent Mexico: An Anthropology of Nationalism*. Minneapolis: University of Minnesota Press, 2001.

———. *Exits from the Labyrinth: Culture and Ideology in the Mexican National Space*. Berkeley: University of California Press, 1992.

———. "Final Reflections." In *The Eagle and the Virgin: Nation and Cultural Revolution in Mexico, 1920–1940*, edited by Mary K. Vaughan and Steven E. Lewis, 335–350. Durham, NC: Duke University Press, 2006.

López, Rick Anthony. *Crafting Mexico: Intellectuals, Artisans, and the State after the Revolution*. Durham, NC: Duke University Press, 2010.

———. "Lo más mexicano de México: Popular Arts, Indians, and Urban Intellectuals in the Ethnicization of Postrevolutionary National Culture, 1920–1972." Phd diss., Yale University, 2001.

López Bárcenas, Francisco. *Autonomía y derechos indígenas en México*. Mexico City: Universidad Nacional Autónoma de México, 2005.

López Velarde, Ramón. *Novedad de la patria y otras prosas*. Mexico City: Asociación Nacional de Libreros, 1987.

Loyo, Engracia. "La empresa redentora: La casa del estudiante indígena" *Historia Mexicana* 46, no. 1: 99–131.

———. "La lectura en México, 1920–1940." In *Historia de la lectura en México: Seminario de historia de la educación en México*, 243–294. Mexico City: Ediciones del Ermitaño, 1988.

Magdaleno, Mauricio. *Las palabras perdidas*. Mexico City: Fondo de Cultura Económica, 2006.

———. "Presencia de Alfonso Reyes." *Letras de México* 25: 1–2.

———. *Retórica de la Revolución*. Mexico City: Instituto Nacional de Estudios Históricos de la Revolución Mexicana, 1978.

Maples Arce, Manuel. *Urbe*. Mexico City: Ediciones Botas, 1924.

Marentes, Luis A. *José Vasconcelos and the Writing of the Mexican Revolution*. New York: Twayne Publishers, 2000.

Mayer, Eugenia. *Luis Cabrera: Teórico y crítico de la Revolución*. Mexico City: SepSetentas, 1972.

Médiz Bolio, Antonio. *La tierra del faisán y del venado*. Mexico City: Ediciones Botas, 1965.

Memoria de los trabajos emprendidos y llevados a cabo por la Comisión nacional del centenario de la independencia, designada por el presidente de la república el 1 de abril de 1907. Mexico City: Imprenta del Gobierno Federal, 1910.

Meyer, Jean. *La Cristiada: The Mexican People's War for Religious Liberty*. Translated by L. Villares. New York: Square One, 2013 [1968].

Miller, Nicola. *In the Shadow of the State*. London: Verso, 1999.

Mistral, Gabriela. "Pasión agraria." In *El recado social en Gabriela Mistral*, edited by Hugo Marcos Cid Jiménez, 38–42. Santiago, Chile: Primicias, 1990.

Molina Enríquez, Andrés. *Los grandes problemas nacionales*. Mexico: A. Carranza, 1909.

Molloy, Sylvia. *At Face Value: Autobiographical Writing in Latin America*. New York: Cambridge University Press, 1991.

Monsiváis, Carlos. "La aparición del subsuelo: Sobre la cultura de la Revolución mexicana." *Historias* 8–9 (Jan.–June): 159–177.

———. "México y la toma de partido de Alfonso Reyes." In *Escribir, por ejemplo: De los inventores de la tradición*, by Carlos Monsiváis, 79–124. Mexico City: Fondo de Cultura Económica, 2008.

———. "Notas sobre la historia de la fotografía en México." In *Maravillas que son, sombras que fueron: La fotografía en México*, by Carlos Monsiváis, 5–28. Mexico City: Ediciones Era, 2012.

———. "Prólogo: El mundo soslayado (donde se mezclan la confesión y la proclama)." In *La estatua de sal*, by Salvador Novo, 11–41. Mexico City: Fondo de Cultura Económica, 2008.

———. "Soy porque me parezco: El retrato en el México del siglo XX." In *Espejo mexicano*, edited by Enrique Florescano, 178–221. Mexico City: Biblioteca Mexicana de la Fundación Miguel Alemán, 2002.

Monsiváis, Carlos, and Carlos Bonfil, eds. *A través del espejo: El cine mexicano y su publico*. Mexico City: Instituto Mexicano de Cinematografía, 1994.

Mora, Carl J. *Mexican Cinema: Reflections of a Society, 1896–1980*. Berkeley: University of California Press, 1982.

Morales, Alfonso. *El país de las tandas: Teatro de revistas, 1900–1940*. Mexico City: Secretaría de Educación Pública, 1984.

———. "Spanish for Your Mexican Visit: Paul Strand South of All Borders." In *Paul Strand in Mexico*, edited by Alfonso Morales and James Krippner, 239–264. Mexico City: Fundación Televisa, 2010.

Mraz, John. *Looking for Mexico: Modern Visual Culture and National Identity*. Durham, NC: Duke University Press, 2009.

———. *Photographing the Mexican Revolution: Commitments, Testimonies, Icons*. Austin: University of Texas Press, 2012.

Nancy, Jean-Luc, and Philippe Lacoue-Labarthe. *The Literary Absolute: The Theory of Literature in German Romanticism*. Translated by Philip Barnard and Cheryl Lester. Albany: State University of New York Press, 1988.

Nieto Sotelo, Jesús, and Elisa Lozano Álvarez. *Tina Modotti: Una nueva mirada*. Mexico City: Centro de la Imagen, 2000.

Noble, Andrea. *Mexican National Cinema*. London: Routledge, 2005.

Novo, Salvador. *La estatua de sal*. Mexico City: Fondo de Cultura Económica, 2008.

———. "Nuestras artes populares." *Nuestro México* 1, no. 5 (July 1932): 54–56, 74.

Obregón Santacilia, Carlos. *Cinquenta años de arquitectura mexicana, 1900–1950*. Mexico City: Patria, 1952.

O'Gorman, Edmundo. *Destierro de sombras: Luz en el origen de la imagen y culto de Nuestra Señora de Guadalupe del Tepeyac.* Mexico City: Universidad Nacional Autónoma de México, 1991.

———. *Reflexiones sobre la distribución urbana colonial de la ciudad de México.* Mexico City: Fondo de Cultura Económica, 1938.

Oikión Solano, Verónica. "De la Revolución mexicana a la revolución mundial: Actores políticos michoacanos y la internacional comunista en México." *Signos Históricos* 21: 60–103.

Olcott, Jocelyn, Mary Kay Vaughan, and Gabriela Cano, eds. *Sex in Revolution: Gender, Politics, and Power in Modern Mexico.* Durham, NC: Duke University Press, 2006.

Olguín, David, ed. *Un siglo de teatro en México.* Mexico City: CONACULTA, 2011.

Olivé Negrete, Julio César. *Antropología mexicana.* Mexico City: Colegio Mexicano de Antropólogos, 1981.

Olsen, Patrice Elizabeth. *Artifacts of Revolution: Architecture, Society, and Politics in Mexico, 1920–1940.* Lanham, MA: Rowman and Littlefield, 2008.

———. "Revolution in the City Streets: Changing Nomenclature, Changing Form, and the Revision of Public Memory." In *The Eagle and the Virgin,* edited by Mary Kay Vaughan and Stephen Lewis, 119–135. Durham, NC: Duke University Press, 2006.

O'Malley, Ilene. *The Myth of Revolution: Hero Cults and the Institutionalization of the Mexican State, 1920–1940.* New York: Praeger, 1986.

Orellana, Margarita. *La mirada circular: El cine norteamericano de la Revolución mexicana, 1911–1917.* Mexico City: Artes de Mexico City, 1999.

Orozco, José Clemente. *Autobiografía.* Mexico City: Ediciones Era, 1981.

Ortiz Bullé Goyri, Alejandro. *Cultura y política en el drama mexicano posrevolucionario, 1920–1940.* Alicante, Spain: Universidad de Alicante, 2007.

———. "Orígenes y desarrollo del teatro de revistas en México, 1869–1953." In *Un siglo de teatro en México,* edited by David Olguin, 165–182. Mexico City: Fondo de Cultura Económica, 2011.

———. *Teatro y vanguardia en el México posrevolucionario, 1920–1940.* Mexico City: UAM-A, 2005.

Pani, Alberto J. *Apuntes autobiográficos.* Second edition. Mexico City: Porrúa, 1950.

Paranaguá, Paulo Antonio. *Mexican Cinema.* Austin: University of Texas Press, 1995.

Parra, Max. *Writing Pancho Villa's Revolution: Rebels in the Literary Imagination of Mexico.* Austin: University of Texas Press, 2005.

Paulson, Ronald. "Revolution and the Visual Arts." In *Revolution in History,* edited by Roy Porter and Mikulas Teich, 240–260. Cambridge: Cambridge University Press, 1986.

Paz, Octavio. "El jinete del aire: Alfonso Reyes." *Cuadernos* 41 (1960): 4–8.

———. *El laberinto de la soledad.* Mexico City: Fondo de Cultura Económica, 1969. [English edition published as *The Labyrinth of Solitude.* New York: Grove Press, 1985.]

———. *Los privilegios de la vista*. Mexico City: Fondo de Cultura Económica, 1987.

Pereira, Armando. *Las palabras perdidas*. México City: Ediciones Era, 1999.

Pérez Montfort, Ricardo. *Bajo el cielo de México, 1920–1921*. Mexico City: Universidad Nacional Autónoma de México, 1993.

———. *Estampas de nacionalismo popular mexicano: Ensayos sobre cultura popular y nacionalismo*. Mexico City: Centro de Investigación y Estudios Superiores en Antropología Social, 1994.

———. "Las invenciones del México indio: Nacionalismo y cultura en México, 1920–1940." http://indigenas.bioetica.org/not/nota43.htm.

Pick, Zuzana. *Constructing the Image of the Mexican Revolution: Cinema and the Archive*. Austin: University of Texas Press, 2010.

Pitol, Sergio. "Liminar." In *Ulises criollo*, by José Vasconcelos, edited by Claude Fell, xix–xxxiii. San José: Archivos/Universidad de Costa Rica, 2000.

Podalsky, Laura. "Patterns of the Primitive: Sergei Eisenstein's *¡Qué viva México!*." In *Mediating Two Worlds: Cinematic Encounters in the Americas*, edited by John King, Ana M. Lopez, and Manuel Alvarado, 18–28. London: British Film Institution, 1993.

Poniatowska, Elena. *Hasta no verte Jesús mío*. Mexico City: Ediciones Era, 2007.

———. *Tinísima*. New York: Farrar, Straus, and Giroux, 1966.

Pozas, Ricardo. *Juan Pérez Jolote: Biografía de un Tzotzil*. Mexico City: Fondo de Cultura Económica, 1952.

Programa oficial de las fiestas del centenario de la consumación de la independencia de México. Mexico City: La Helvetia, 1921.

Quiroga, José. *Understanding Octavio Paz*. Columbia: University of South Carolina Press, 1999.

Ramírez Plancarte, Francisco. *La ciudad de México durante la revolución constitucionalista*. Mexico City: Impresores Unidos, 1941.

Ramos Pedrueza, Rafael. *La lucha de clases a través de la historia de México*. Mexico City: Talleres Gráficos de la Nación, 1936.

Rancière, Jacques. *Dis-agreement: Politics and Philosophy*. Translated by J. Rose. Minneapolis: University of Minnesota Press, 1999.

———. *Dissensus: On Politics and Aesthetics*. Translated by S. Corcoran. London: Continuum, 2010.

———. *Hatred of Democracy*. Translated by S. Corcoran. London: Verso, 2006.

———. *Le partage du sensible: Esthétique et politique*. Paris: La Fabrique, 2000.

———. *Staging the People: The Proletarian and His Double*. Translated by D. Fernbach. London: Verso, 2011.

Rangel Illoldi, Magdalena, and Elmira López Ibáñez. *La influencia de expresionismo alemán en Juan Bustillo Oro, cineaste mexicano*. PhD diss., Universidad Intercontinental, Mexico City, 1995.

Rattray, Evelyn Childs. *Teotihuacan: Cerámica, cronología y tendencias culturales/Ceramics, Chronology, and Cultural Trends*. Mexico City and Pittsburgh: Instituto Nacional de Antropología e Historia/University of Pittsburgh, 2001.

Reed, John. *Insurgent Mexico*. Westport: Greenwood Press, 1969.

Revueltas, José. *Obras completas*. Vol. 19, *Ensayos sobre México*. Mexico City: Ediciones Era, 1978.

Reyes, Alfonso. "Notas sobre la inteligencia americana." In *Ultima tule y otros ensayos*, by Alfonso Reyes. Caracas, Venezuela: Biblioteca Ayacucho, 1991.

———. *Obras completas*. 26 vols. Mexico City: Fondo de Cultura Económica, 1955.

Reyes, Alicia. *Genio y figura de Alfonso Reyes*. Buenos Aires: Editorial Universitaria, 1976.

Reyes, Aurelio de los. *Cine y sociedad en México, 1896–1930*. Mexico City: Universidad Nacional Autónoma de México, 1983.

———. *El nacimiento de ¡Que viva México!* Mexico City: Universidad Nacional Autónoma de México, 2006.

———, coord. *Historia de la vida cotidiana en México*. Vol. 5, *Campo y ciudad/La imagen, espejo de la vida?*. Mexico City: Fondo de Cultura Económica, 2005.

———. "La cultura en los años '20," *Diálogos* 18, nos. 2–3: 29–37.

———. *Manuel Gamio y el cine*. Mexico City: Universidad Nacional Autónoma de México, 1991.

———. "The Silent Cinema." In *Mexican Cinema*, edited by Antonio Paranaguá, 63–78. London: British Film Institute, 1996.

Rivas Mercado, Antonieta. *Cartas a Manuel Rodríguez Lozano*. Mexico City: Ediciones Era, 1975.

Robb, James. *El estilo de Alfonso Reyes: Imagen y estructura*. Mexico City: Fondo de Cultura Económica, 1965.

Robles, Martha. *Entre el poder y las letras: Vasconcelos en sus memorias*. Mexico City: Fondo de Cultura Económica, 1989.

Rochfort, Desmond. *Mexican Muralists: Orozco, Rivera, Siqueiros*. London: Chronicle Books, 1998.

Rodríguez, Antonio. *A History of Mexican Mural Painting*. New York: Thames and Hudson, 1969.

Rodríguez, María de las Nieves. "La 'noche mexicana' como parte de los festejos de celebración de la independencia de 1921." *Estudio* 105, no. 11: 57–71.

Rojas González, Francisco. *El diosero*. Mexico City: Fondo de Cultura Económica, 1952.

———. *Ensayos indigenistas*. Mexico City: Colegio de Jalisco, 1998.

Romero de Terreros, Manuel. *Historia sintética del arte colonial de México, 1521–1821*. Mexico City: Porrúa, 1922.

Ross, S. R. *Is the Mexican Revolution Dead?* Philadelphia: Temple University Press, 1975.

Rousseau, Jean-Jacques. *On the Social Contract*. Translated by D. A. Cress. Indianapolis: Hackett, 1983.

Rubin, William. "Modernist Primitivism: An Introduction." In *Primitivism in Twentieth-Century Art: Affinity of the Tribal and the Modern*, edited by William Rubin, 3–27. New York: Museum of Modern Art, 1984.

Ruiz, Ramón Eduardo. *The Great Rebellion: Mexico, 1905–1924*. New York: Norton, 1980.

Sáenz, Moisés. *Carapan: Bosquejo de una experiencia*. Lima, Peru: Librería e Imprenta Gil, 1936.

Salazkina, Masha. *In Excess: Sergei Eisenstein's Mexico*. Chicago: University of Chicago Press, 2009.

Samano Rentería, Miguel Ángel. "El indigenismo institucionalizado en México, 1936–2000." In *La construcción del estado nacional: Democracia, justicia, paz y estado de derecho*, edited by J. E. Ordoñez, 141–158. Mexico City: Universidad Nacional Autónoma de México, 2004.

Sánchez Prado, Ignacio. *Intermitencias americanistas: Estudios y ensayos escogidos, 2004–2010*. Mexico City: Universidad Nacional Autónoma de México, 2012.

———. *Naciones intelectuales: Las fundaciones de la modernidad literaria Mexicana, 1917–1959*. West Lafayette, IN: Purdue University Press, 2009.

Schmidt, Henry. *The Roots of lo Mexicano: Self and Society in Mexican Thought, 1900–1934*. College Station: Texas A&M University Press, 1978.

Schwab, George. *The Challenge of Exception: An Introduction to the Political Ideas of Carl Schmitt between 1921 and 1936*. New York: Westport, 1989.

Scott, James. "Foreword." In *Everyday Forms of State Formation: Revolution and the Negotiation of Rule in Modern Mexico*, edited by G. M. Joseph and Daniel Nugent, vii–xii. Durham, NC: Duke University Press, 1994.

———. *Seeing Like a State: How Certain Schemes to Improve the Human Condition Have Failed*. New Haven, CT: Yale University Press, 1998.

Serra Puche, Marí Carmen, ed. *Alfonso Caso: De la arqueología a la antropología*. Mexico City: Universidad Nacional Autónoma de México, 1998.

Siqueiros, David Alfaro. "A New Direction for the New Generation of American Painters and Sculptors." *Vida Americana* no. 1 (1921).

———. *Art and Revolution*. London: Larence and Wishart, 1975.

Skirius, John. *José Vasconcelos y la cruzada de 1929*. Mexico City: Siglo XXI, 1978.

Skocpol, Theda. *Social Revolutions in the Modern World*. Cambridge: Cambridge University Press, 1994.

———. *States and Social Revolutions*. Cambridge: Cambridge University Press, 2013.

Sluis, Ageeth. "City of Spectacles: Gender Performance, Revolutionary Reform, and the Creation of Public Space in Mexico City, 1915–1939." Phd diss., University of Arizona, 2006.

Sommer, Doris. *Proceed with Caution, When Engaged by Minority Writing in the Americas*. Cambridge, MA: Harvard University Press, 1999.

Sommers, Joseph. *After the Storm: Landmarks in the Modern Mexican Novel*. Albuquerque: University of New Mexico Press, 1968.

———. "El ciclo de Chiapas: Nueva corriente literaria." *ICACH* 14 (1965): 7–22.

Sorlin, Pierre. *Les fils de Nadar: Le "siecle" de l'image analogique*. Paris: Nathan, 1997.

Spenser, Daniela. *Stumbling Its Way through Mexico: The Early Years of the Communist International*. Translated by P. Geller. Tuscaloosa: University of Alabama Press, 2011.

Spivak, Gayatri Chakravorty. "Subaltern Studies: Deconstructing Historiography."

In *Selected Subaltern Studies*, edited by Ranajit Guha and Gayatri Chakravorty Spivak, 3–33. New York: Oxford University Press, 1988.

Stavenhagen, Rodolfo. *Derecho indígena y derechos humanos en América Latina*. Mexico City: Instituto Interamericano de Derechos Humanos/Colegio de México, 1990.

Tablada, José Juan. *La feria de la vida*. Mexico City: Ediciones Botas, 1937.

Tannenbaum, Frank. *The Mexican Agrarian Revolution*. Hamden, CT: Archon Books, 1968.

Taracena, Alfonso. *La verdadera Revolución mexicana*. Mexico City: Porrúa, 1992.

Teja Zabre, Alfonso. *Panorama histórico de la Revolución mexicana*. Mexico City: Ediciones Botas, 1939.

Tejada, Roberto. *National Camera: Photography and Mexico's Image Environment*. Minneapolis: University of Minnesota Press, 2009.

Tenenbaum, B. A. "Streetwise History: The Paseo de la Reforma and the Porfirian State, 1876–1910." In *Rituals of Rule, Rituals of Resistance: Public Celebrations and Popular Culture in Mexico*, edited by William H. Beezley, Cheryl English Martin, and William E. French, 127–150. Wilmington, DE: Scholarly Resources, 1994.

Tenorio Trillo, Mauricio. "1910 Mexico City: Space and Nation in the City of the Centenario." *Journal of Latin American Studies* 28, no. 1: 75–104.

Torres Bodet, Jaime. "Propósitos." *La Falange* 1 (1922): 1–4.

Torres San Martín, Patricia. "La recepción del cine mexicano y las construcciones de género." *La Ventana: Revista de Estudios de Género* 3, no. 27: 59–103.

Tuñón, Julia. *Mujeres de luz y sombra en el cine mexicano: La construcción de una imagen, 1939–1952*. Mexico City: Instituto Mexicano de Cinematografía, 1998.

Urías Horcasitas, Beatriz. *Historias secretas del racismo en México, 1920–1950*. Mexico City: Tusquets, 2007.

Usigli, Rodolfo. *Mexico en el teatro*. Mexico City: Imprenta Mundial, 1932.

Valadés, Edmundo, and Luis Leal. *La Revolución y las letras: Dos estudios sobre la novela y el cuento de la Revolución mexicana*. Mexico City: Dirección General de Publicaciones, 1990.

Vanderwood, Paul J., and Frank N. Samponaro. *Border Fury: A Picture Postcard Record of Mexico's Revolution and U.S. War Preparedness, 1910–1917*. Albuquerque: University of New Mexico Press, 1988.

Vasconcelos, José. "A Mexican's Point of View." In *American Policies Abroad*, edited by J. Fred Rippy and Guy Stevens, 101–143. Chicago: University of Chicago Press, 1928.

———, and Manuel Gamio. *Aspects of Mexican Civilization*. Chicago: University of Chicago Press, 1927.

———. *The Cosmic Race*. Translated by D. T. Jaén. Baltimore: Johns Hopkins University Press, 1997 [1925].

———. *El desastre: Tercera parte de Ulises criollo y continuación de La tormenta*. Mexico City: Acción Moderna Mercantil, 1938.

———. *El proconsulado: Cuarta parte de Ulises Criollo*. Mexico City: Ediciones Botas, 1939.

———. *La flama: Los de arriba en la revolución, historia y tragedia*. Mexico City: Continental, 1960.

———. *La tormenta*. México: Trillas, 1998 [1936].

———. *Obras completas*. 4 vols. Mexico City: Libreros Mexicanos Unidos, 1959.

———. *Ulises criollo: Edición crítica*. Edited by Claude Fell. San José: Archivos/Universidad de Costa Rica, 2000 [1935].

Vásquez Mellado, Alfonso. *La ciudad de los palacios: Imágenes de cinco siglos*. Mexico City: Diana, 1987.

Vaughan, Mary K. *Cultural Politics in Revolution: Teachers, Peasants, and Schools in Mexico, 1930–1940*. Tucson: University of Arizona Press, 1997.

———, and Stephen Lewis. *The Eagle and the Virgin: Nation and Cultural Revolution in Mexico, 1920–1940*. Durham, NC: Duke University Press, 2006.

———, Jocelyn Olcott, and Gabriela Cano, eds. *Sex in Revolution: Gender, Politics and Power in Modern Mexico*. Durham, NC: Duke University Press, 2006.

Vela, Arqueles. *La señorita etcétera*. Mexico City: La Novela Semanal/Universal Ilustrado, 1922.

Velázquez Andrade, Manuel. *Fermín*. Mexico City: Textos Modernos, 1931.

Villaurrutia, Xavier. "Una galería de arte moderno en México." *Revista de Revistas* (Oct. 1926): 3.

Villegas, Abelardo. *Autognosis: El pensamiento mexicano en el siglo 20*. Mexico City: Instituto de Geografía e Historia, 1968.

Villoro, Luis. *Los grandes momentos del indigenismo en México*. Mexico City: Colegio de México, 1996 [1950].

Virno, Paolo. "Virtuosity and Revolution: The Political Theory of Exodus." In *Radical Thought in Italy: A Potential Politics*, edited by Paolo Virno and Michael Hardt, 189–212. Minneapolis: University of Minnesota Press, 1996.

vom Hau, Matthias. "Unpacking the School: Textbooks, Teachers, and the Construction of Nationhood in Mexico City, Argentina, and Peru." *Latin American Research Review* 44, no. 3: 127–154.

Warman, Arturo, ed. *De eso que llaman antropología mexicana*. Mexico City: Nuestro Tiempo, 1970.

Weston, Edward. *The Daybooks of Edward Weston*. New York: Aperture, 1981.

Williams, Gareth. *The Mexican Exception: Sovereignty, Police, and Democracy*. New York: Palgrave, 2011.

———. "Sovereign (In)hospitality: Politics and the Staging of Equality in Revolutionary Mexico." *Discourse* 27, nos. 2–3: 95–123.

Womack, John. *Zapata and the Mexican Revolution*. New York: Knopf, 1971.

Wright de Kleinhans, Laureana. *Biografía de mujeres notables mexicanas de la época prehispánica, la colonia y el siglo 19*. Mexico City: Secretaría de Educación Pública y Bellas Artes, 1910.

Yúdice, George. *The Expediency of Culture: Uses of Culture in the Global Era*. Durham, NC: Duke University Press, 2004.

Zavala, Eleazar, ed. *Mi pueblo durante la Revolución*. 3 vols. Mexico City: Instituto Nacional de Antropología e Historia, 1985.

Zerilli, Linda M. G. *Feminism and the Abyss of Freedom*. Chicago: University of Chicago Press, 2005.

Žižek, Slavoj. *Looking Awry: An Introduction to Jacques Lacan through Popular Culture*. Boston: MIT Press, 1992.

———. *Organs without Bodies: Deleuze and Consequences*. London and New York: Routledge, 2004.

———. *The Plague of Fantasies*. London: Verso, 1997.

FILMOGRAPHY

3-3-3 (n.d.), Emilio Amero, dir.

Ahí está el detalle (1940), Juan Bustillo Oro, dir.

Allá en el Rancho Grande (1936), Fernando de Fuentes, dir.

Desolación (n.d.), Emilio Amero, dir.

Don Juan Tenorio (1889), Salvador Toscano, dir.

Dos monjes (1934), Juan Bustillo Oro, dir.

El compadre Mendoza (1934), Fernando de Fuentes, dir.

El prisionero 13 (1933), Fernando de Fuentes, dir.

Fiestas patrias en Morelia en el año 1908, Alva brothers, dir.

Frida Kahlo and Tina Modotti (1984), Laura Mulvey and Peter Wollen, dirs.

Historia completa de la Revolución mexicana (1927), Salvador Toscano, dir.

Insurrección en México (1911), Alva brothers, dir.

Janitzio (1935), Carlos Navarro, dir.

Juárez y Maximiliano (1933), Miguel Contreras and Rafael Sevilla, dirs.

La mancha de sangre (1937), Adolfo Best Maugard, dir.

La mujer del puerto (1933), Arcady Boytler, dir.

La población del valle de Teotihuacán (1922), Manuel Gamio, dir.

Memorias del subdesarrollo (1968), Tomás Gutiérrez Alea, dir.

Memorias de un mexicano (1950), Salvador Toscano, dir.

¡Que viva México! (1978), Sergei Eisenstein, dir.

Rebelión (n.d.), Manuel Gamio, dir.

Redes (1936), Emilio Gómez Muriel and Fred Zinnemman, dirs.

Reed: México insurgente (1973), Paul Leduc, dir.

Río sin tacto (n.d.), Emilio Amero, dir.

Tepeyac (1917), José Manuel Ramos, Carlos Gonzáles, and Fernando Sáyago, dirs.

Un espectador impertinente (1932), Arcady Boytler, dir.

¡Vámonos con Pancho Villa! (1936), Fernando de Fuentes, dir., Rafael Felipe Muñoz, writer

Viaje del señor Madero a los estados del sur (1911), Alva brothers, dir.

Index